WHAT READER

"*On Shattered Wings* helped me to better understand the grief of others. I wish I had read this a long time ago." —Anne, Basel, Switzerland

"Every parent should stop what they're doing and get this book into the hands of their teenagers." — Joel, Austin, Texas

"This story gripped me. I couldn't stop reading it." —Leisa, West Des Moines, Iowa

"I started reading and couldn't stop. I just had to know what happened to this family." — Tina, Topeka, Kansas

"This book showed me that moving on is a decision, sometimes taken over and over again, and in little steps at a time, with the help of God and His grace. Toward the end, I felt an almost physical sensation of a burden being lifted, like the sun coming out." — Betsy, Dallas, Texas

"As someone who has experienced unexpected and immeasurable loss, this book impacted me deeply. It has powerful insights on those dealing with profound grief." — Sally, Fort Collins, Colorado

"After reading what this family went through, I sat down and had a chat with my kids...and myself...about the dangers of drinking and driving." — Thomas, Jacksonville, Florida

"Immensely powerful in a direct, head-on manner. It is moving, gut-wrenching, and haunting. It takes the reader through a very personal journey." — Clare, Fort Collins, Colorado

"I cried many times throughout the story. And yet, the remarkable thing about this book is that even as I was crying, it was a story I wanted to hear. I wanted to know how each person survived such a devastating life event. I wanted to see goodness overcome such despair. It is impossible to comprehend the loss of a daughter without living it. But this story brings the reader into their lives and their minds. It teaches us how much a life can truly be worth." — Natalie, Salt Lake City, Utah

When I look at old pictures of us all, before Jennifer died, I feel sorry for the people in the photos...even those of me...because I know what's coming.

I know, but they don't. God help them.

—Lori Dultmeier, Jennifer's Mom

I went to bed that night trying to forget the words I'd said to Jennifer before she left that evening. I hadn't meant them, at least not as they sounded. I don't know why I even said them. I was irritated and trying to get through to my headstrong teenage daughter. I would apologize later. But later never came.

Instead, the phone rang. It was 2:20 a.m. Our lives would never be the same.

—Jim Dultmeier, Jennifer's Dad

On Shattered Wings

A Family's Journey from Grief to Hope

Jim & Lori Dultmeier
with
Nancy Sprowell Geise

Fred & Bonnie ~
This is a first run
copy of this heartbreaking
but powerful story. I hope
it will save lives!
With hope & joy,
Nancy Geise
Jan. 2021

On Shattered Wings: A Family's Journey from Grief to Hope
Published by Life Changing Stories, LLC
Topeka, Kansas

Publisher's Cataloging-in-Publication data

Names: Geise, Nancy Sprowell, author. Dultmeier, Jim, author. Dultmeier, Lori, author.
Title: On shattered wings : a family's journey from grief to hope / by Nancy Sprowell Geise, Jim Dultmeier, and Lori Dultmeier.
Description: First hardcover original edition. | Topeka [Kansas] : Life Changing Stories, LLC, 2021. | Also published as paperback. | Also being published as an ebook. | Index included.
Identifiers: ISBN 978-1-7359591-1-5
Subjects: LCSH: Bereavement. | Premature death. | Death—Christianity.
BISAC: BIOGRAPHY & AUTOBIOGRAPHY / Personal Memoirs. | RELIGION / Christian Living / Death, Grief, Bereavement. | FAMILY & RELATIONSHIPS / Death, Grief, Bereavement.
Classification: LCC BF575.G7 | DDC 248.866 GEISE–dc22

Cover design by Nick Zellinger, NZ Graphics
Interior layout design by Victoria Wolf, Wolf Design and Marketing
Professional photos of Jennifer Dultmeier on the front and back covers, and dedication page:
Nathan Ham, © 2002 Nathan Ham Photography

Bible Excerpts: World English Bible (WEB)

Hold on to your faith. 1-16-2021

FOR JENNIFER RENEE DULTMEIER

SEPTEMBER 23, 1983 – OCTOBER 26, 2002

"I know who I am, and I respect myself."
—Jennifer Dultmeier, October 2, 2002
Written twenty-four days before she was killed at the age of nineteen

Contents

About the Foreword

Throughout the two and a half years I worked with the Dultmeier family in bringing *On Shattered Wings* to life, I sought the input and insight from my beloved and extraordinarily talented former high school English teacher, John Forssman.

Mr. Forssman taught English and Literature for over forty-three years; many of those were in my hometown of Ames, Iowa. Mr. Forssman's ability to grasp what is behind the words is a gift unlike any I've ever known. He was critically important to the development of my first two books: *Auschwitz #34207—The Joe Rubinstein Story*, and *The Eighth Sea*.

I was fortunate to have tremendous teachers throughout my life. I am especially grateful for the insight, wisdom, and life-long mentoring of Mr. Forssman. Every student should be so blessed.

Nancy Sprowell Geise
Ames High School
Class of 1979

Foreword

The Freedom To Choose

As hard as it is to say it in light of the monumental pain and suffering in this book, one of the greatest blessings that God gives us is freedom. That each person who grieved Jennifer had the freedom to choose their own way through their unfathomable sorrow made all the difference for them, for those they loved, for Jennifer's memory, and for everyone who will read their story. That they had the freedom to find God on their individual paths took us into a world of mystifying grace that was personal and theirs alone. How could they experience such suffering and pain and yet, over time, find new life? If there was ever a gospel that speaks to the human condition with such raw energy, life-changing insight, and soulful penetration, this is it.

This is a book that should be read by every human being. There are so many insights woven throughout that if a teacher were teaching this book, they'd never get through it. What a lasting impact this book has had on me!

What was also powerfully true is how Jim, Lori, Justin, and David have wonderful language skills commensurate with their pain to the point that they are able to express it in memorable ways, at times artfully. The use of metaphorical language is so effectively done it makes what they are saying visually impactful and enduringly universal. I cannot imagine anyone reading this powerful testament and then drinking and driving. In so many important ways, this book reveals our shattered society and our shattering human nature so filled with contradictions.

Jim and Lori reform and recompose themselves out of the power of composing itself, from keeping a journal of pain, honesty, and essential pleadings with God and with their fellow human beings. Few people have journeyed into such an abyss and survived to live again so fully. Few have gone that deeply into such darkness and articulated it with such memorable power, divine wisdom, and authenticity as this family has done. Here is an Easter message composed out of shattered wings and the freedom to choose. Here is a profound witness that says in living truth: *a heart can heal enough to live again but not enough to forget.*

—John Forssman, English and Literary Teacher, Retired, Ames, Iowa

Note from Author Nancy Sprowell Geise

I write stories of people whose lives exemplify the power of the human spirit—overcoming the unimaginable—stories with life lessons for us all.

When I called contractor Jim Dultmeier to bid a roof replacement for our house, I never dreamed that it would result in this book. But when Jim and his wife, Lori, shared with me the journals they kept following the death of their beloved daughter, I knew this was a story that needed to be told. In both journals, I was moved by the raw emotions and powerful insights into life and death.

Jim and Lori, and their sons, Justin and David, are some of the strongest and most forthright people I've ever known. Telling this story was very painful for them and, at times, embarrassing. Yet they have done so in the hope of saving lives, helping others deal with grief, and as a tribute and legacy to Jennifer's beautiful life. Sharing their stories was a sacrifice of love.

Before their world was turned upside down, Lori and Jim were a typical middle-class family of two boys and a girl. They were church-going, fun-loving, and hardworking. They had little drama in their lives. Lori devoted her life to staying at home and raising her children. Jim worked hard to build a wonderful future for his family.

This book is written from the perspective of Jim and Lori, gathered not only from their individual diaries, but through many hours of interviews with them, bringing together their feelings from notes, letters, and experiences. Through conversations I had with their family and friends, Jim and Lori were reminded of events that they had either forgotten due to the passage of time, or the stress they were under when the events occurred. Such recollections were woven back into the story. To not disrupt the flow of the diary narrative, these were shared through the voices of Jim and Lori.

Neither Jim nor Lori wrote their journals for publication. Rather, they were streams of consciousness. There were times in reading Lori's journal I found myself shaking with emotion. Jim's words left me awestruck with their simple truths. Since the journals focus on their feelings, understandably, there were many gaps that left the reader unaware of what was happening in their lives outside the pages. For those details, Jim and Lori patiently shared with me what was happening beyond the confines of their journals. Those events were then added to the story. I've taken the liberty of combining entries and inserting, removing, and changing dates. While not always their exact words, the sentiments are derived from their feelings and experiences.

The entries in this story of the first hours and days following the accident were derived from interviews of Jim, Lori, their family and friends, and from later journal writings of Jim and Lori. Lori's actual journal began nine days after Jennifer died. Jim's began a few days earlier. Lori did not write about the details of the accident and the first few days following it for over two years. Thus, those thoughts were moved to an earlier time for the purpose of this book.

I was often struck by how differently Jim and Lori handled their grief, and yet, interwoven in each of their journeys was love, faith, and commitment. Like each of us, the people in this story are not perfect. But their stories face head-on the impact on all facets of life when a parent loses a child: stressors on a marriage; the devastation to siblings; the strains on relationships when grandparents lose not only a grandchild but also the happiness and well-being of their daughter or son; the insignificance of regrets; the power of debilitating grief; and the shattering impact on so many lives after the call that changed everything.

Jennifer's brothers, Justin and David, graciously allowed some of the most private and painful parts of their lives to be revealed so that others may learn from them and know that there is hope even in the darkest experiences. Everyone involved in this story provided powerful lessons, not only in how to deal with grief, but how to live beyond it.

The driver, Carolyn, could have been any one of us. I cannot begin to imagine what she has had to endure since the night Jennifer died. It breaks my heart to think of it. She can't do anything to undo what happened. All she can do is move forward and live the most productive life she can. She knows that is what Jennifer would have wanted. Everyone I spoke with who knew Jennifer agreed and wished Carolyn well. In one way or another, everyone told a variation of the same sentiment: "It could have been me."

The people in this story are amazingly strong, everyone, in their own unique way. It's been a privilege to be brought into the most private parts of their lives and share their powerful story of love, loss, faith, hope, and redemption. It is a story not of death— but of life.

My best friend is Carolyn. We met on our bus and our relationship went on from there. Carolyn and I do a lot of things together. I feel safe telling Carolyn my deepest darkest secrets because I know she will not tell anyone. Carolyn and I do a lot of things together. It's kind of like having the sister I never had. —Jennifer Dultmeier (Sixth Grade)

My Future

I plan to go to college as soon as I get out of high school.
I will go to college for four years.
While I'm in college I hope to play girls basketball.
I want to get a teaching degree.

I want to start teaching at 22 years old and teach 1st grade.
While I am teaching I want to look for the right husband.
When I retire I want to travel the world
just like my Grandma and Grandpa

—Jennifer Dultmeier (Sixth Grade)

Angels

In 2001, the year before she died, eighteen-year-old Jennifer Dultmeier made a ceramic wind chime for her family. On the front was a painting of an angel holding a child in her arms as she flew toward Heaven. On the back of the chime, Jennifer wrote an excerpt from the popular song "Angel" by Sarah McLachlan.

Jennifer's life was interwoven with angels. Over the years, family and friends frequently gave her gifts adorned with angels.

Each year for Christmas, Jim gave his daughter a different porcelain angel from the Seraphim Angels collection. Jennifer loved to read, so one figurine was of an angel holding a book. Jim and Jennifer enjoyed being outdoors together, so several of the porcelain angels depicted nature: an angel cradling a dove, another was of an angel walking beside a deer. The angel Jim most looked forward to giving Jennifer was that of an angel holding a baby. Jim planned to give this special angel to his daughter on the first Christmas after she had a child of her own.

After she died, Jennifer's costume for an upcoming Halloween party was found in her room. It was enormous, life-sized wings of black feathers that she had borrowed from her friend Carolyn. They were wings Jennifer would never have a chance to wear. Instead, she would soar to Heaven on a different kind of wings.

Jennifer Dultmeier was a girl, not an angel. But she was nearly as pretty as one. She had a quiet beauty about her and an angelic face. Her hands were so delicate, so perfectly formed, they looked, as her Aunt Melissa described, "Like they were sculpted from fine porcelain."

Jennifer had a compassionate and tender heart, with an occasional fiery temper to match. She was tenacious when she believed in something, quick to forgive others, and was not one to hold on to grudges.

If the measure of one's heart is, as stated in the book *The Wonderful Wizard of Oz*, judged not by how much we love, but by how much we are loved by others, then Jennifer Dultmeier's life was a triumph. For above all else, she was loved.

And for everyone who loved her, Jennifer will forever be their precious angel.

Note from the Driver

She was my best friend since we were kids. I first met Jennifer on the school bus when we were in the second grade. I told her I liked her Tweety Bird shirt. After that, we sat next to each other every day. Soon, we were inseparable.

I thought of her as my other half. We understood each other in ways that only best friends who are as close as sisters can.

The first time I spent the night at her house, we stayed up all night talking about anything, everything, and nothing. I could always make her laugh. Since her twin brother was also our age, I grew up with him too. I loved her whole family like they were mine. I sometimes even traveled with their family on vacations. Jennifer's dad taught me to waterski. He used to pull us around Lake Shawnee with his boat as we rode on a tube shaped like a giant banana. Jennifer and I would scream with laughter as we bounced around, hanging on for dear life.

A big part of me died the night Jennifer died. It was the death of my teenage innocence—the death of what had once been wonderful childhood memories with my best friend. Now, each memory with her is forever tainted with the pain of knowing what is to come.

Jennifer's death was the death of the best friend I will ever have, and my future without her in it—and with it, all our childhood dreams.

There isn't a day, an hour, or a second that has passed since that night that I haven't wished it had been me that had died instead of Jennifer. The problem with guilt is that there is nowhere for it to go—no one else who can carry its terrible burden.

No matter how I wish it were otherwise, there is one truth I cannot escape: I cannot change what happened. All I can do is try to be the very best person I can be, which I've tried to do. I hope somehow, someway, it's enough for Jennifer.

Knowing her as I did, I do not believe that she would have wanted what happened to destroy me or define the rest of my life.

To this day, I've talked very little about the accident. Every time I try, I start to shake violently.

The Before

October 26, 2002 Past Midnight

The night was chilly. A light mist hung in the air.

Five months after they graduated high school, the two girls, eighteen-year-old Carolyn and nineteen-year-old Jennifer, decided to go out for the evening. Best friends from the time they were young, the girls, with their blonde hair and wisplike physiques, looked so much alike they could have been twins.

Carolyn picked Jennifer up at her house.

It was well past midnight when the girls left the party where they had both been drinking. Carolyn was driving her red Grand Am with a sporty sunroof. Both girls fastened their seat belts. They had the music turned up.

On the east side of the capital city of Topeka, Kansas, California Avenue is a straight, two-lane road running North/South, transitioning the city to the country. Rural homes on small acreages dotted the landscape. An occasional driveway interrupted long stretches of grass-lined ditches. It was easy for a vehicle to pick up speed quickly.

Jennifer said she wanted a different CD. Carolyn told her it was on the back seat.

Jennifer unbuckled her seat belt.

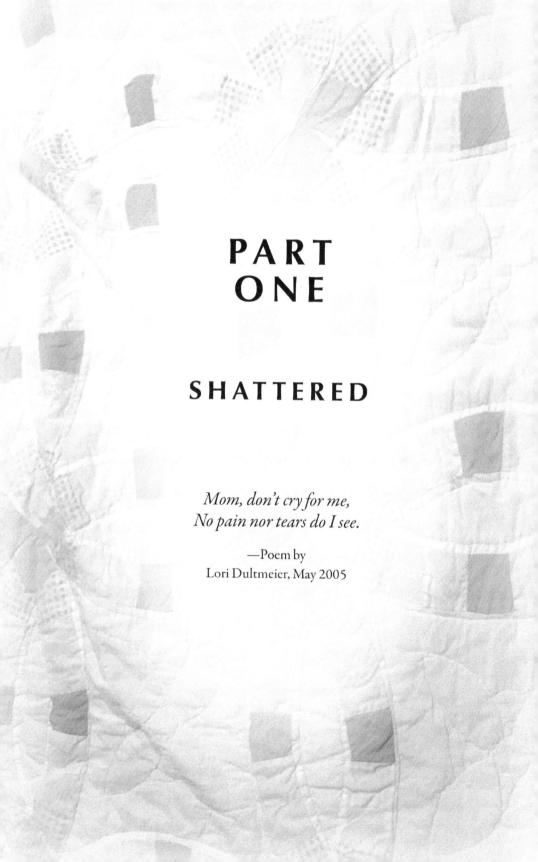

PART ONE

SHATTERED

Mom, don't cry for me,
No pain nor tears do I see.

—Poem by
Lori Dultmeier, May 2005

Jennifer's Fifth Grade Class Journal

(In her words and spelling)

8/28/94: Don't count your chickens intill there hacted.

8/29/94: On Rainy day I like to read. Because I like hearing the rain. It takes me places.

8/31/94: I got band with my new instrument the calernet.

9/16/94: I think Friday is spacial because we do fun things.

9/19/94: On Saturday I had a baskit ball game. We lost by one point 12 to 13. On Sunday we went and got my Dad Birthday present.

9/21/94: Todays Wednesday and 2 more day then it is my birthday. I will be 11. Wednesday are my best days because it is the middle of the week.

9/22/94: My worst subject is spelling. I was not really good at spelling. But the last few test have been easy.

9/26/94: Friday I went to the mall for my birthday. My cousin Brooke came to. After that we went home and had cake and ice cream and open presents. I got a neckless and earring from Brooke.

I wish that my Friends that are being mean to me will be nice to me. I found a friend who is funny, understanding to me. We both gone though the same thing.

Tonight I am going to basketball practice. I don't want to go. But sometimes I do.

Sometime I wish that my hole class whould have Duck tape on theier mouth. Then they whould all be quite. Then we whould all not loss a ticket.

Jim

Jim Dultmeier's recollections of the hours of October 26, 2002

I'd been in the *crash room* before. That's the name I call the room in the hospital where it's too late for healing. It's the place no one ever wants to go—especially any parent.

I was in that room when my eldest son, Justin, lost his best friend in an auto accident a few years earlier. Justin and I had gone to the hospital as soon as we heard about the wreck. Just as we got there, the young man's parents were leaving the crash room.

I knew by their faces that their son had died. I didn't know what to say, so I said nothing. We stood in the hallway for a long time. When it was Justin's turn to say a final goodbye to his buddy, I went with him. I'll never forget the cold in that room, and it wasn't just from temperature. Everything about it was cold, sterile, and terrible.

The young man's body was lying flat, covered with a white sheet. I hated that white veil of death, covering what had been a person full of life less than an hour earlier.

I prayed I'd never see that room again.

Now, I was being led into it to face the unimaginable.

TWO HOURS EARLIER

It's what I dread most in the middle of the night: a phone ringing. As soon as I heard ours, I knew something was wrong. A surge of adrenaline made me feel weaker, not stronger. I looked at the clock next to the bed. 2:20 a.m. Whatever this was, it wasn't good. I hoped it was a wrong number or even a prank call. Lori grabbed the phone.

The woman's voice was loud enough for me to hear. "I need to speak to Jennifer Dultmeier's father."

"I'm her mother. What is it?"

She hesitated. Something in her pause scared me. "I'm a nurse in the ER. Jennifer has been in a car accident. You need to come to the hospital—immediately."

My body felt odd, like it wasn't connected to my brain. I could hear Lori running down the stairs toward our son's room in the basement. She was screaming, "Justin, Justin! Jennifer's been in an accident."

She was downstairs. I wasn't out of bed.

How was I supposed to go to the hospital when my body wouldn't move?

When I finally opened the door to the driver's side of our Jeep, Lori and Justin were waiting inside. The engine was running.

I'd driven that highway every day for years, but as I pulled out of our muddy driveway onto the pavement, it felt like the first time. Everything seemed too close, like I was driving through a tunnel. I stared straight ahead, concentrating only on the white, reflective ribbon of paint just ahead, on both sides. I gripped the steering wheel, taking my hands off only long enough to wipe the sweat on them against my jeans. Lori was on the phone. I think with her sister. Justin was silent in the back seat.

We emerged from the darkness and into town. Finally, a big, red Emergency Room sign blazed through the misty night. The words hung in the air, as if suspended by some unseen force, as if they were the only words that ever mattered.

How could this be happening?

I pulled the Jeep into the first spot next to the door. We ran through emergency room doors. "We're here to see our daughter, Jennifer Dultmeier!" I was breathless.

"I'm sorry. She's in surgery," said the woman behind the desk. "You'll need to wait for the doctor."

I felt like I'd been punched in the gut. I looked around for anyone who could help. A policeman walked over, holding Jennifer's purse. He showed us her ID. He wanted us to confirm it was hers. "The vehicle your daughter was riding in rolled. Your daughter was ejected. The paramedics were able to resuscitate her twice before she arrived at the hospital."

"Wait! What? Jennifer was ejected from a car? She stopped breathing?" I couldn't have heard him right.

Lori gasped. I started to ask him another question when my mom and dad rushed through the doors. "How is she?" The officer moved away. I told them what we knew. Mom was pale. Her eyes had a strange look as if she might faint. "Mom, you should sit." She did. Dad waited with her until he knew she was okay, then began walking with Lori and me, up and down the halls. Lori had called them on the way to the hospital.

Dad said when they hung up, he told Mom that Jennifer probably had broken her arm. Mom said she didn't think so. She'd heard something in Lori's voice, "I don't know what we're facing, but it isn't a broken arm."

Oh God, how I wished it was just a broken arm!

A nurse came and took us to a private waiting room. Neither Lori nor I could sit. We paced the small room, praying.

More family and friends started arriving. Every time I turned around, someone else was there.

How could there be so many people? How long had it been since we got the call?

Everyone kept asking about Jennifer. I didn't want to answer questions. I wandered into the hall and found the police officer. He said a fire crew had been a couple of blocks away from the accident when they got the call.

"The first responders were there within minutes. They were unable to find Jennifer's pulse. They worked on her and were finally able to revive her. In the ambulance, they had to do it again. The driver of the car is injured but alive. They had a hard time getting her out of the vehicle. She's been transported to the hospital.

"Is her name Carolyn? How badly is she hurt?"

The office shrugged. "That's all I know. When I learn more, I'll let you know."

I didn't know what to do. I walked back into the waiting room.

More family and friends were there, along with our pastor. He asked Lori if it was okay if we all prayed. She nodded. We gathered in a circle, holding hands. One by one, people began praying aloud—for the doctor's steady hand, for wise decisions, for strength for our family, and for Jennifer to be healed. Everyone prayed for Jennifer to be okay.

"No!"

It was Lori. I opened my eyes. "No. We need to pray for God's will to be done."

I looked at her to see if she was serious. Others were looking too. Some heads began nodding in agreement. I'm sure they were thinking, "Yes, that's what we as good Christians should be praying for."

I fought the urge to shout, "Wait! I don't want God's will! I want my daughter to be okay! I want my will, not God's!"

And that was the truth. I didn't trust God's will over mine. Not with this. Not with Jennifer's life.

How could I? How could Lori?

The wait was killing me.

How long could a surgery take?

I wanted answers! I wanted to see Jennifer and know that she was okay.

When the doors finally opened and a man in hospital scrubs walked in, I wanted him to go away. I didn't want to be there! I didn't want any of us to be there!

It was obvious he was the surgeon. He looked wiped out. I didn't like the way he turned his head to watch the door close behind him, like he wanted to be on the other side of it rather than with us.

The doctor introduced himself. Then he looked me straight in the eyes and said the words that I knew would echo in my head for the rest of my life, "We did everything we could for your daughter."

My body was still in the hospital, but my mind wasn't. My breath wasn't. My body felt like a collection of separate parts—parts that just ceased functioning. Everything was still and silent. It was as if the earth stopped moving.

I heard my brain ask my heart, "Why have you quit beating?"

I grabbed Lori's arm and cried, "Lori! Hang on to your faith!" I knew in that instant that if Lori lost her faith, there was no hope for any of us surviving.

I left the room. My body was pacing the halls. I heard myself praying, but I have no idea what I was praying for. I was scared in a way I'd never known—a deep, to the bone, primeval kind of scared.

I grabbed the hallway railing, and I felt myself slipping, not to the ground, but to a place much scarier—a place of nothingness.

An hour later, I found Lori still in the waiting room. She was sitting on the floor, her back against the wall. Her friend Lisa was next to her on one side, her sister Melissa was on the other. Lori's face was white and dry. She hadn't been crying.

"Lori. We need to go see Jennifer."

"Okay." She sounded like a robot.

I reached for her hand.

Lori, Melissa, and I followed a nurse through a maze of halls.

We were being led to the crash room.

"No!" I wanted to scream. "Please don't make me go in there! I can't face that cold, white sheet again! I don't want Lori seeing it!"

I wanted to grab Lori, pull her against my chest, and tell her we didn't need to go in there.

Instead, I took her hand, and we walked through the door.

I was expecting a stark, bright room. It wasn't. The lights were dim and soft. A nurse was standing in the back of the room. She didn't speak.

Jennifer was lying partially elevated. Instead of the dreaded white sheet, she was cradled in a pale purple and white quilt. Purple was Jennifer's favorite color.

There was a large bump on her head, the only sign anything was wrong.

How could she be dead?

Lori and I stood there staring at her for a long time. Melissa stood behind Lori.

"She doesn't even look hurt." Lori's voice was barely a whisper. "She must be hurt on the inside."

I blinked hard.

Lori pulled back the soft quilt and began stroking Jennifer's arms, then her cheek. She rubbed a lock of Jennifer's gold hair through her fingers. Then she began to sob. "Oh, Jennifer, my precious baby girl."

Lori's cries were the most heartbreaking sounds I've ever heard. I felt my heart folding in on itself.

"Oh, baby girl," Lori could barely get out the words, "Why...why didn't you have your seat belt on?"

I reached out and touched my daughter's forehead. Her skin was cold.

"Jennifer's not here." Lori's voice was a whisper. "She's in the arms of an angel."

I closed my eyes, wanting to open them in my bed. Jennifer would be asleep down the hall. I would go to her in the morning and apologize for what I had said before she left last night for the evening. She would smile and say, "It's okay, Dad."

Instead, when I opened them, the still body of my daughter was all I could see.

How could she be lifeless when only a few hours ago we had an argument? Jennifer had been animated—angry—alive!

I looked at her, trying to shut out my hurtful words.

Did I really say them? OH GOD, NO!

I wanted to shake her and tell her to wake up! I wanted to tell her how much I loved her—how beautiful she was! How beautiful she had always been, from the moment the nurse placed her in my arms just after she was born.

All I could do now was stare at her.

She was already out of reach. I lifted her hand. Her fingers were lifeless. I squeezed them harder. I tried to imagine her in the arms of Jesus.

Lori was right. Jennifer was no longer in that body, and we all knew it.

There was no need to stay.

I needed to get my wife home. I let go of Jennifer's hand and softly kissed her forehead.

As we walked toward the door, the nurse said softly, "I can feel the love you have for your daughter. I think Jennifer can too." I opened my mouth to speak but couldn't.

We walked down the hall and stepped into an elevator. When it bumped to a stop at the lobby, the doors opened. Standing right in front of us were Carolyn's parents.

I knew they were on their way to see their daughter.

We were going home to a future without ours.

Lori
Lori Dultmeier's recollections of the hours of October 26, 2002

When the doctor said, "We did everything we could for your daughter," everything went dark—like someone had turned off a light switch.

I didn't even cry. My mind left my body.

No one said a word. Everything was silent.

Jim grabbed my arm and told me to keep my faith. Then he left.

I slid against the wall to the floor and stared at the ceiling. I wanted to go up and through it.

Please, God, take me with her!

I have no idea how long I stayed there. Jim came with a nurse and said we could see Jennifer.

Afterward, we left the hospital and went home. Jim drove.

When we turned into our driveway, cars were everywhere. We went in through the garage. People were crowded in the kitchen. Jim's family was there and some of mine. Friends and leaders from church were there. They all looked at us. I followed Jim up the stairs and heard the front door open behind me. More people were coming in. Our bedroom was dark. I looked outside. The sun was not even up, and our house was full of people.

"Why are they here?"

"To help," Jim said.

Help? How could anyone help?

I went into the bathroom. When I came out, Melissa was there. She had straightened up the bed and pulled the covers back. I crawled inside, and she pulled the blankets over me. "Melissa, I need Mom! Please, find her!"

10

"We're trying. Kurt's been calling all over trying to figure out where in Canada they are. When we talked a few days ago, Mom said they're supposed to be flying somewhere remote today to see polar bears. But we'll keep trying. I promise."

I rolled over. "I want to talk to Mom."

I must have fallen asleep. Melissa was shaking my shoulder. "Lori. We found them. The local sheriff went to their lodge." Melissa held the phone. "It's Dad. He wants to talk to you."

I sat up and tried to swallow. I couldn't. My mouth was too dry. My hands were shaking. I didn't know if I could hold the phone. "Lori?" Dad's voice was so weak. It didn't sound like him. "Lori, we're coming home. We'll get there as soon as we can."

"I...I..." I wanted to tell him to put Mom on the phone. I wanted to hear her voice. But I couldn't say anything. I shoved the phone to Melissa and rolled over in bed. I never wanted to leave it.

Time passed. My friend Chris came. Her eyes were red. Her face was swollen. "Did you drive all the way from Wichita?" I was surprised my words came out.

"Oh Lori." She came to the bed and grabbed me tight. She was shaking all over.

"Jennifer loved you so much, Chris. Thank you for loving her."

"I can't believe you're trying to make me feel better! But you are, aren't you, Lori?"

I leaned my head back into the pillow. I didn't have the strength to talk any more.

I was so tired. I couldn't stay awake. I didn't want to stay awake. When I was awake, I had to remember why everyone was there.

Melissa, Chris, and Lisa stayed with me. Sometimes they'd lie on the bed and sometimes they'd sit next to me. Mostly they kept their arms wrapped around me.

I woke to Chris, whispering, "Do you hear that? I don't like the sound of her breathing. My grandmother made that sound right before she died. It's called the death rattle."

I didn't know I was making any noise, but it didn't surprise me if it was the sound of death. I was sure I was dying.

Shock is an odd thing. I knew I was in it, but I couldn't do anything about it.

Everything seemed louder, magnified. Time was a blur.

My head was pounding.

I didn't know where Jim was.

Our pastor came in and read to me a scripture about our bodies being a shell.

People kept bringing me food. I couldn't stand the smell of it. I told them to take it away.

Our house was full of people. I could see the outline of them outside my bedroom in the hall, but I couldn't focus long enough to know who they were. Everyone looked like shadows.

I was worried about Justin. He had been in and out of my bedroom ever since we'd come home, but he wasn't talking.

Finally, he came and stood in the doorway. He looked like he didn't know where he was. He sat down next to me on the bed. His shoulders were shaking. I took his hand.

"How can she be dead, Mom? I just went out to lunch with her yesterday. Yesterday!"

"I know." It was all I could say.

Melissa and her husband walked into the room. Justin left. Melissa said that she and Kurt were leaving to go to the Kansas City airport to pick up David, who was flying in from Houston. I sank back against the bed.

"We'll bring him right here." Melissa pressed the back of her hand against my cheek.

David! He didn't even know yet that his twin sister was dead. He knew she had been in a bad accident. He didn't know how bad it was.

I was lightheaded and sick.

David and Jennifer were not only twin siblings; they were buddies, playmates, and friends—and had been since before they were born.

My ears were ringing.

I didn't want David finding out she's gone! I didn't want her gone!

I grabbed Melissa's arm. I wanted to say, "I should be there! I should be there when he's told, but I can't go!"

She waited for me to speak. All I could do was shake my head.

"It's okay, Lori. We'll be with him. He'll be okay."

They left, and I buried my face into my pillow and sobbed.

My temples were pounding.

What would David do when he heard his twin was gone?

When Justin and David went to bed last night, they had a sister! How were they supposed to go on? How were any of us?

Jim walked into the bedroom and sat next to me. "Melissa's on her way back from the airport. They've got David."

More time passed. Jim was at our bedroom window. "Melissa and Kurt just pulled into the driveway." Jim held out his hand. I took it. It was hot. We walked downstairs and out the front door. Justin was standing outside on the porch. David opened the van door and got out. His hand was wrapped in gauze. His eyes were wide and his face red. He ran to me. Justin and Jim did too. We squeezed into each other's arms—a bundled mass, shaking and crying. "I love you. I love you too. So much." We were all saying it. We all felt it.

Back in the house, Justin went downstairs to his room. I told Jim and David that I had to lie down. They followed me into the bedroom. David looked so broken, as if half of him was gone. It was. "David, you should get some sleep."

"I will, Mom, but I want to be with you." He sat down next to me as I crawled under the covers.

I knew he wanted to talk.

Jim was too anxious to sit. He just kept moving around the room.

"She just called me last night! Just a few hours ago. I wasn't home. I'd cut my hand, and I was at the ER getting stitches. When I got home, my message machine said I'd missed her call, but she didn't leave a message. I was going to call her back, but it was late. My hand hurt. I wasn't in a very good mood, so I thought, 'I'll call her in the morning.' Oh, Mom, do you know why she called me?"

I shook my head. David looked at Jim. "I have no idea, Son."

David sank deeper into the bed, defeated. "So, I went to bed. Uncle Kurt called and woke me up about four this morning. He said that Jennifer had been in an accident. I asked him if she was okay. He said, 'Yeah, we think so, but we want you to come home. Melissa booked you a seat on a flight out. It's leaving in a couple of hours.'

He asked if I could get myself to the airport. I told him I could. I didn't ask him anything else. I didn't even ask to speak to you guys. So, I just said, 'Okay,' then I hung up."

David was barely able to get his words out between sobs. "I knew it wasn't true. I knew he didn't think she was going to be okay, not when they had already booked me a flight. I was numb. I couldn't stay in the apartment, so I went out to the parking lot. It was pitch black. I stood there for a long time, crying. Mom, I didn't want to come home to this."

In David's voice, I heard an echo of the sweet, little boy I used to hold in my arms when he was hurting and crying out for his mom. Now, he wanted something I would never be able to give him. I could not protect him. Not from this. We both knew it,

14

and it broke my heart. That realization was a creeping envelope of darkness, threatening to overcome me.

It was several minutes before he could continue. "When I got on the plane, I had the row to myself. The whole time I was flying, I had this feeling that Jennifer was sitting next to me in the empty seat. It was so real I actually reached out to see if I could touch her. I couldn't feel anything physically, but she was there. I know it. I didn't want to think about what that meant, but I knew the whole time on the flight that she was with me.

"When I walked out of the terminal, Aunt Melissa and Uncle Kurt were standing next to their van at the curb. They both hugged me but didn't say anything as I got in. When Aunt Melissa crawled into the back to sit with me, that's when I knew for sure. She didn't say a word, but I knew." David broke down completely.

Every part of me ached for him.

When he finally spoke, he was hoarse. "And now Jennifer's dead. And I'll never even know why she called me. Why didn't I call her back? Why?"

I couldn't look at him. I couldn't stand it.

He would never know why she had called. None of us would.

I was terrified for him, terrified for Justin, terrified for all of us.

David realized it. "Mom and Dad, I want you to know something important—really important. You don't have to worry about me hurting myself. I would never do that to you. Never!" His look was so forceful it surprised me.

I dissolved into sobs of hot tears of relief. He was wise beyond his years to know our greatest fear was that despair might cause one of our boys to do something rash. Our sorrow for Jennifer was all we had the strength to deal with. We couldn't handle worrying about anyone else's life right now, especially our sons'.

"Thank you, David," said Jim. "We needed to hear that."

I wanted to tell him that he'd just given us the greatest of gifts, but I couldn't. My throat was in a knot. I just nodded. David left. I pulled the covers over my head.

Hours had passed, or was it days? I wasn't sure. More friends and family had come to sit with me. I told them, "I lost my girl."

I was asleep. When I opened my eyes, Mom and Dad were looking at me. They looked so tired and sad. Mom had been crying. "OH, MOM!"

She sank to the bed next to me and pulled me into her arms. I melted against her. I couldn't tell my trembling body from hers.

Neither one of us could talk. Not for a long time. Then softly, Mom began whispering, "Sweet Jesus, help us." Over and over.

Later, Mom held my hand as we sat on the bed, my head resting against her shoulder. "Last night in the hotel, I had this terrible feeling something bad was going to happen to your family. I wanted to call you, but it was late, and I didn't want to wake you. And even if I did, I didn't know what I would say. What good would it do to upset you for some vague feeling I had? Oh, Lori, I wish I had called! It wouldn't have changed anything, but I still wish I had."

Dad came and said he was taking Mom home to get some sleep.

After she left, I couldn't leave the bed. There wasn't enough left of me to go anywhere or do anything.

Jim
Jim's recollections of Saturday—nine hours after the call

I was suffocating. I had to get out of the house. People were everywhere, crying and weeping.

I got in my truck and found myself driving, knowing where I was going but not wanting to admit it. As I turned on to a two-lane highway running on the far eastern edge of town, I began to shake, hard.

I was headed in the same direction that Jennifer had traveled only hours before.

I came to a four-way stop on California Avenue, then drove a mile or so past homes on small acreages with long driveways. If I hadn't been looking for it, I would have driven right by the accident site. I pulled into the driveway at the address the officer at the hospital had given me. I opened my car door, but I couldn't bring myself to get out. It was early afternoon. It was the kind of fall day I love, a bluebird sky, and the air filled with the smell of burning leaves. But I could see no beauty in this day or this place. I was numb, completely numb, but somehow my body figured out how to get out of my truck.

The homeowner, a man who looked to be in his late fifties, opened his front door and walked right towards me before I was even out of my truck. He must have guessed why I was there. "My daughter died here." It was all I could say.

Neither of us talked as we walked down his drive toward the road. Our hands stayed tucked inside our coat pockets.

He pointed to the place where the car had landed upside down. There was little evidence it had been there. There was no shattered glass, no twisted metal. Every trace of the car and its contents was gone. The man said the police told him the car had rolled several times and landed several yards from where they had found Jennifer unconscious next to a tree.

What happened here? The question kept repeating over and over in my head like a record player needle stuck on a single note.

We walked across a low culvert of his driveway. The edge of it was crushed and rutted deeply where the car had hit. It was the only visible sign that I could see of the accident. The man said that if the car hadn't hit the culvert, he thinks it would likely have just slid along the ditch. Instead, when it struck, it began rolling. It rolled a long way.

A car was headed toward us but was a long way off, so we stepped out onto the pavement. There were sideways skid marks just before the culvert, on the opposite side of the road. It was clear the driver had veered out of her lane and crossed the centerline. At that point, something happened to cause her to swerve back hard the other way, resulting in the skid marks of all four tires showing. Then it looked like the vehicle came back across its lane and down into the ditch, hitting the culvert.

I asked the man, "What do you think happened to make the car swerve in the first place, then back again so dramatically?"

"I have no idea," he said.

The car was coming closer, so we moved off the road, back into his driveway. As we were standing there, he exclaimed, "Look!" A large buck, with a big rack, casually came walking across the road.

Then it hit me. *Rutting season.* This buck was likely searching for a mate. Rutting season is the only time I know that a buck would not flinch at the sight of two big men standing so near. He didn't even glance at us or run across the road. Instead, he slowly took his time crossing the highway.

The man and I both had the same thought. If the driver had swerved, maybe it was because there was a deer in her lane. Perhaps she moved to the other lane to avoid hitting it. Because deer often travel in pairs, maybe a second deer moved in that lane. This would have caused her to turn the wheel violently to avoid it.

I had no way of knowing for sure, but it was possible. Or, maybe she swerved to avoid hitting a deer for some other reason, then overcorrected in the opposite direction.

No matter the cause, Jennifer was gone.

The man pointed to a nearby house. "There was a group of teenagers over there last night, having a bonfire. They told me that they heard the sound of a car coming fast, skidding tires, and then the impact of the crash. One of them called 911, while the others ran over here. They found the car upside down. They could see the driver, still buckled in her seatbelt, hanging upside down, with the roof caved in. They didn't know how to get her out. They thought she had been alone in the car until they heard moaning. They searched until they found your daughter several yards away, unconscious, her back resting against the trunk of a large tree. They tried to talk to her, but she didn't respond. They said they had just reached her when a fire truck arrived."

I remembered that the police officer at the hospital told me the fire truck happened to be less than two blocks away, its crew just having finished up with another call.

The man wanted me to know how sorry he was. Then, he turned and walked toward his house, shaking his head. I think he knew I needed time alone.

If Jennifer hit the tree, there was no evidence of it—no missing bark, no fragments of her clothing, no blood or hair—nothing. The only thing I found was a short, brass stake. I pulled it out of the ground, turning it over in my hand. There was a number etched on it. This wasn't something the homeowner would have in his yard, as he would hit it when he mowed. Then it hit me. I knew what that was. It was the pin marking the spot where they found Jennifer. The air left my lungs. I dropped to my knees on the last place Jennifer was alive and breathing on her own.

I closed my eyes against the waves of dizziness and nausea. *How could Jennifer be gone?*

When I opened my eyes, everything looked so peaceful and uninterrupted.

How could Jennifer's life have ended here?

Oh, Jennifer, what were you thinking alone in the dark and cold? Were you aware of anything? Were you struggling to live? Oh God! Were you calling for me? For Lori?

It was a long time before I was able to stand. My body felt as heavy as if I was wearing full-length fishing waders that had leaked and filled with icy water.

I struggled my way back to the truck. I started the engine and closed my eyes again. I didn't have the strength to drive. I didn't want to go home.

My God! What just happened to our lives?

Lori
Lori's recollections beginning Sunday morning—thirty-one hours after the call

"Your dad called." Jim said. "He's coming to take us to church."

"Okay." It was all I could say. I was a zombie. I didn't even know it was Sunday. I didn't care what I did or how I did it. If Jim said, "Let's walk off this cliff," I would have said "okay" and gone with him.

I was in no condition to talk to anyone. We walked into the sanctuary just after the service started and sat in our usual spot in shock and silence. When the pastor announced Jennifer's death, there was a gasp around the room. I don't remember much after that, other than we left before the service ended so we wouldn't have to face anyone.

Friday night, Jennifer had left our house for the evening. Sunday afternoon, we walked into a funeral home to pick out her casket.

I didn't want to make any decisions, but I had no choice. I just had to get through the funeral. Nothing else mattered, none of it. Nothing seemed real. The decisions we had to make seemed like we were planning a wedding.

Jim picked out a dove for the theme of the service. I selected a silver coffin with black handles. It was classic, simple, and elegant—just like Jennifer.

Jim and his dad selected the tomb. Melissa made arrangements for the flowers, program, and music.

Everyone was making decisions, and I couldn't stop thinking of what happened when I had gone to Kansas City the week before. All that day, I kept looking behind me. When I got home that night, I had called my mom.

"I have this nagging feeling something's gonna happen to me."

"What sort of thing?"

"I don't know, but I keep feeling like something is going to hit me from behind."

"From behind? That's weird."

"I know. I think I'm going to be in a car accident, but I won't be able to stop it because I won't see it coming."

It never occurred to me that the danger was to any of our kids. I thought my physical being was in danger, not theirs!

Oh, God! Something did blindside me—all of us! How was it possible that something so monumental was about to happen to my daughter, and I was so clueless? As her mom, I should have known!

Sunday night, Justin pulled a chair next to my bed. I was relieved he wanted to talk. "Ever since I moved back home, whenever I'd come home late, if Jennifer's bedroom light was on, I'd toss pebbles at her window to let her know to come down. She always did. Sometimes we'd stay up most of the night talking."

I knew it was true. Last weekend I got up to go to the bathroom. It was late. I looked out the window and saw Jennifer and Justin sitting on the open tailgate of his truck. I was glad he didn't let their three-year age gap prevent him from confiding in his younger sister. Justin was big and strong, and Jennifer was so dainty and petite. I know he thought of himself as her protector.

"Now," he cried, "her light will never be on again. What am I going to do without her?"

I was scared for Justin. He'd had trouble with drugs and alcohol in the past, but he'd been doing so much better for the last few weeks. He'd even recently moved back home to get away from a bad situation. I'd finally started sleeping better when I thought about his future. Now, his sister, and closest confidant, was gone.

Oh God! Please help him stay strong!

Monday, we went to the funeral home to see Jennifer's body.

I was dead inside.

Melissa and her daughter Brooke had fixed Jennifer's hair and makeup. Melissa had painted Jennifer's nails a soft pearl pink. I had selected Jennifer's clothes: a black sweater and a beautiful black and cream skirt that she had sewn herself. The skirt was made of an intricate toile fabric, its scene was that of an old village. It was not a fabric that a typical girl her age would have selected, but then, there was not a lot typical about Jennifer.

Jennifer loved to sew, and she was good at it. Not long before she died, she asked Melissa to teach her to quilt. Jennifer had just started college yet wanted to learn to make something that she could easily buy. I think that said a lot about the woman she would have become.

I couldn't bear the thought of having to greet anyone at the viewing, let alone the many I knew would come. I asked my mother if I could sit on the front pew and do nothing. She said that would be fine. We ended up standing right next to Jennifer's body, greeting and hugging hundreds and hundreds of people for nearly seven hours. The line snaked down the corridors of the funeral home, out the front doors, and down the sidewalk. I didn't think it would ever end. God held us up. I could feel it. That was the only way any of us could have stood there that long. A man from the funeral home told me it was the most people they'd ever had for a viewing.

When we got home, Jim and I were too exhausted even to speak. We both took a pill for anxiety and collapsed into bed.

Friday night, Jennifer had fixed her hair for a night out of fun with friends. On Tuesday, I fixed my hair, styling it for her wedding. That's how I kept thinking of her funeral. The only wedding she would ever know.

Jim
Jim's recollections—Days three and four following the call

I couldn't believe the number of people coming to pay their respects at the viewing. Everyone was crying, in shock, or both. We had been there for nearly an hour when Justin whispered over my shoulder, "Dad, Carolyn is here."

I swear my heart stopped. I turned to see her being pushed in a wheelchair by her dad. I knew she had been injured, but I didn't know the severity. I was sad to see she needed a wheelchair. Her dad stopped in front of Jennifer's casket.

Melissa asked Lori if she wanted to take a break. Lori nodded. Melissa took Lori's arm, and they left.

Carolyn sat in front of the coffin for a long time before struggling to stand. Her dad and mom helped her to her feet. She looked so fragile and pale. I watched long enough to see her lean against the coffin. When she reached out a trembling hand toward Jennifer, I had to turn away. I could not stand to watch.

How could this have happened? I remember those two girls when they were young. On many weekends I took them out on my boat and pulled them around on a tube as they laughed and squealed, signaling for me to make the boat go faster. Now, those echoes of laughter in my head were replaced by sobs. Carolyn's anguished cries sounded like they were coming from somewhere deep and dark. Her wails continued as she was pushed away from the casket. "Two girls died the night of the crash," I thought, "one is in Heaven, and the other is in a living Hell."

I closed my eyes and prayed for Carolyn to find a way to move forward in peace and someday, even joy. From the sound of her torment, I didn't know how that was possible, but I know Jennifer would have been heartbroken to see her like this. Jennifer would not have wanted Carolyn to suffer.

When Carolyn was taken from the room, David, and my uncle, a Catholic priest from Missouri, followed them. David said afterward they accompanied Carolyn and her family into a private room. David was still in shock and later didn't remember much of what was said, except that he recalled putting his hand on Carolyn's shoulders and saying, "It's okay. It's not your fault she's dead."

I asked him if he knew that the police said alcohol was involved in the wreck. "I know, but I don't know what else happened in that accident. No one does. I had to say something, Dad. I couldn't stand to see her that way."

David said when he had turned to leave the room, my uncle patted him on the back and said, "David, that was very kind of you."

The next morning, before we got out of bed, Lori whispered, "I wasn't trying to avoid Carolyn. I just didn't have the energy to watch her see Jennifer. I just didn't."

"I know. It's okay," I knew it was more emotion than Lori had to spare.

The next day, just before the funeral began, I glimpsed Carolyn's wheelchair out of the corner of my eye. Her dad wheeled her down a ramp near the front of the sanctuary, opposite of where we were. Carolyn's family was with her. I was glad she had come but had no idea how she would hold up, or how any of us would.

As I turned and looked at Jennifer's casket, I knew our future with her would now only be a collection of what had been. Her life story here on earth had stopped. There would be no twentieth birthday celebration with her twin; no college graduation; no more holidays. And Jennifer would never be married in this, or any other, church. She would never have children. We would never hold her babies in our arms.

The church was packed. I'd never seen it so crowded. As I looked around at the sad faces, I felt sick and cheated that I would never be able to walk my beautiful daughter down the aisle and give her away to the young man of her dreams. That thought alone hurt so badly I didn't know what to do.

Months before she died, Jennifer and her friend Kelly were talking. Jennifer made an off-handed remark that if something ever happened to her, she wanted the song "Only Time" by Enya played at her funeral. And so it was—along with others that were Jennifer's favorites. Lori had requested the song "I Hope You Dance" by Lee Ann Womack.

More music was sung, prayers were said, and family and friends shared memories of Jennifer. At one point, I looked over and saw Lori's mom, Doris, slumped over in her seat. She had fainted. The ceremony paused as she was cared for. Once revived, she didn't want to leave, so the funeral continued with Doris looking pale and shaken. *Oh, God! How are we going to get through this without it killing us all?*

Jennifer's cousins filed up to the casket, one by one, each setting a rose inside.

I had never before put myself in a situation where I had to stand before a group of people and speak. Just the thought of it always caused my knees to shake.

As I looked at her casket, I knew that despite my fears of being able to speak in front of anyone, I could not let the service end without sharing what was in my heart. I didn't care that I was standing in front of a room full of people. I owed it to Jennifer. I felt God's presence as I stood, walked to the front of the church, and cleared my throat. "Parents love your children because tomorrow is not promised. Children, sisters, brothers, friends—love each other."

There was a huge lump in my throat. I didn't know if I would be able to continue, but I did.

"I will never be able to give Jennifer away on her wedding day, so I have to do it now." I looked around the room at the distraught faces of my family and friends. "But who does a father give his daughter away to at a time like this?" I straightened my shoulders, took a deep breath, and said, "I'm giving Jennifer away to the only man I can trust, and that man is Jesus."

There was a collective loud sob throughout the room. Everyone was crying.

So I did. To Jesus, I gave Jennifer...to have and to hold, to love and to cherish forever.

I took a dozen red roses, placed them in the casket, and gently kissed Jennifer on the forehead.

And her casket was closed forever.

Lori
Lori's recollections—four days following the call

After the funeral, we went to the gravesite. Our family was led to a row of chairs. More words and prayers were spoken. We had no desire to stay or watch her body being lowered. We left. Jim, Justin, David, and I went home to deal with a future none of us wanted.

I'm afraid of the days and years to come when I'm going to have to face Jennifer's death. She's dead. Jennifer is dead. She's not coming home. She's not just at work.

How could God have allowed this at such a beautiful time in her life when she was just spreading her wings and starting to fly? Dear God, why?

Jim

OCTOBER 30, 2002
What are we supposed to do with all these flowers? They're everywhere! The delivery trucks started coming right after Jennifer died, and they haven't quit. First, we put flowers in the kitchen, then the dining room, then the living room, then the garage, and now they're even in my shed! And this is after the dozens we took to the church for the funeral. More keep coming! Lori says she can't stand the smell of them anymore. They remind her of the funeral home. And the food—we could feed an army!

OCTOBER 31, 2002
I talked Lori into going with me to deliver flowers and leftover food to the people who tried to save Jennifer. I thought it would do her good to get out of the house, but I didn't think she'd come. I was surprised when she said, "Okay."

When we walked into the fire station, several men were sitting around a table, finishing eating dinner. I recognized the first one who stood up. I had roofed his house. I knew he was a fireman, but I didn't know what station. I introduced him to Lori.

He put his hand on my shoulder. "I'm so sorry about your daughter. I only recently made the connection. We've all been shaken over that accident."

"Everyone, this is Jim and Lori Dultmeier. They're the parents of the young woman killed on California Avenue last weekend."

I told them we wanted to thank them for all they did for Jennifer.

The men sat there staring at us with their mouths wide open. No one seemed to know what to say.

"We've got lots of food and supplies that have been given to us if you want them. If so, we could use some help unloading the car."

I think the men were relieved to have something to do. They all got quickly to their feet and followed us outside. As we carried in boxes, the man I knew said, "I gotta tell you, Jim, we rarely hear from family members after any accident, even the ones with the happy endings. Sometimes we'll get a thank-you from someone either thanking us for saving their life or someone they love, but I can't think of any time when the family of someone we were unable to save ever came in to thank us. It means a lot that you guys did this. Especially so soon."

Our next stop was the hospital. We went to the surgical floor nurses' station carrying a huge wreath Melissa had made out of several of the bouquets. When we told the nurse at the desk who we were and why we were there, she had the same reaction as the firemen. She couldn't believe it. She introduced us to several other nurses on the floor, and every one of them said how grateful they were that we had come to thank them personally. Several had tears in their eyes when they said how sorry they were for our loss.

NOVEMBER 1, 2002
This afternoon, Lisa, a friend of Lori's, was in our kitchen, making lunch for us. Lisa told me that when the surgeon came into the waiting room and said to us that Jennifer had died, she literally saw the light go out of Lori's eyes. She said she was scared by it.

It scares me too. But I'm not surprised. Everything seems dark right now to me, too.

NOVEMBER 2, 2002
This morning I was in the kitchen eating cereal when I heard Lori screaming Jennifer's name—over and over and over.

I ran upstairs and found her in the shower. I tried to calm her, but it didn't do any good. She kept screaming. She was yelling for Jennifer and screaming, "Why Lord? Why us?" Her eyes were wild, and she was shaking all over. I turned the water off and wrapped my arms around her, but she kept screaming. I don't even think she knew I was there. I got her out of the shower, put a robe around her, and pulled her into bed. I grabbed the phone to call 911. I was afraid she was going to have a heart attack and die. Our house has been packed full of people since the funeral. Today, no one else was around.

Nothing I could do would make her stop screaming, so I called her parents.

Lori was still crying when they arrived. I was pacing the bedroom. They tried everything to get her to stop. Finally, her mom crawled in bed with her. I couldn't take it. I couldn't take her hoarse wails, so I left and went outside.

If I stayed in that room, I was pretty sure I would die too.

NOVEMBER 4, 2002

The foundation of my life has cracked wide open. I know in my heart that Jennifer is safe and warm in the arms of God. You'd think that would comfort me, but it doesn't. I can't think of anything else but her. I have to remind myself, again and again, "She's not coming home."

I'm so angry right now, at everything and everyone. I'm mad at Jennifer for doing this to us. I'm mad that I couldn't save her, mad I can't go back in time and stop her from leaving that night. I keep reliving it.

No one forced Jennifer to drink with her friend that night or get in the car. But she did. She knew better. She knew she could have called us. She gambled, and she lost. We all did.

I can just hear Jennifer telling us if she could, "I didn't mean to hurt anyone! I especially didn't mean to hurt my family! I was just trying to have fun with my friends, trying to fit in!"

I want the rage out of me, but there's nowhere for it to go.

My brother has a pond behind his house where I sometimes go to get away. I went there today, and while my body was there, my mind wasn't. *How long can I live with my body in one place and my mind in another?*

There is darkness everywhere. My emotions rage and seethe with anger. I can't get the image of Jennifer's lifeless body out of my mind. Everywhere I go, my fists are clenched, my knuckles white.

And yet it's odd because along with my anger are feelings that don't belong—images of all God has given me: Lori, the kids, and how thankful I am for each living person on this earth.

As I stood looking at the sunlight reflect across the water today, I kept thinking about the wonders of our bodies and the things they can do, and how our eyes bring everything around us into our souls, from the rising sun each morning to the red sunsets.

Maybe it's because I saw how lifeless Jennifer's body was in that hospital that I finally realize now just how miraculous our bodies are when we are alive.

Everywhere I look, I see the splendor of God's work and sense His presence.

How can all these emotions at the same time be possible? Am I seeing and sensing all these things so acutely, because Jennifer no longer can? Is that how God is helping me through my pain and fury, by reminding me of His goodness?

If that's His plan, it helps, but it isn't enough.

I don't know how I'm ever going to get rid of my anger. It's trapped in me, eating me alive.

Lori

NOVEMBER 4, 2002

I want time to stand still, so I don't forget any part of Jennifer and her life, but I know if I don't move forward, I'll die of a broken heart. I'm trapped. I can't stay here, but I can't move on.

What am I going to do?

NOVEMBER 5, 2002

I know Jennifer died at the crash site. Paramedics got her breathing again, but her soul was already gone. I know it. I think that's why I never felt her presence at the hospital.

After we went home, I never gave her body a second thought. I never even thought about her being cold or alone. *Was that wrong? How could I not have?*

I didn't because I knew she wasn't there. I knew it the moment I saw her lying on that bed. I think that's God's doing. He wanted us to know that she was no longer in that body. Otherwise, I never would have been able to leave her.

The body we left in the hospital was an empty shell. I know it, but now I wish I had stayed with her longer. A lot longer! *Why didn't I?*

I want to hold her in my arms!

Jim

I was sitting today with no place to go and no place to hide from my pain. I believe evil exists in the form of the devil, and he's sitting right next to me now. I imagine him pulling up a chair and eating popcorn, just waiting and grinning. He knows he can't touch Jennifer because she's gone where he'll never enter, the gates of Heaven. But I'm not that safe, and he's playing head games with me. It's like a scene from a movie where I have two choices: remember God's word and follow it; or turn the other way, toward Hell.

There's a strip club just down the road. I keep thinking of going there, having a few beers and forgetting.

What could it hurt?

Going there might make me feel something besides sorrow and anger! Maybe I might feel like a man again! *Isn't a man with any sort of feelings, even bad ones, better than this shell walking around now—this soulless, more dead than alive, man?*

The devil has no time limits. He's been waiting patiently for this moment for a long time, a moment of my greatest weakness. My foundation has begun to shake. I can feel it.

What would it do to Lori and my family if I were to go there? How can I even be thinking about this?

I closed my eyes and prayed for strength.

When I opened my eyes, I let out a long, slow breath. I knew I wouldn't go. I couldn't do it—not to Lori, my family, myself, and not to God. What we don't need right now is more pain.

I shiver at how easy it would have been to give in.

Thank you, God, for giving me the strength to listen to you! Thank you that Jennifer died with a foundation of faith! Thank you that she's somewhere now where no pain or evil will ever enter!

I'm just glad she no longer has to worry about the devil eating popcorn at her side!

Lori

I wrote Jim a letter yesterday. I told him that someday enough of me would be back for him to love. But it's going to take a long time.

The wife I had been, the one who fell asleep next to him the night of the accident, that wife no longer exists. If that Lori returns, it won't be for a long time. And a long time is a long time in a marriage for one person to be gone.

Jim is hurting badly. He needs comfort, and I don't have any to give him.

Sometime in the early morning hours after the accident, I remember grabbing Jim and begging him, "Please, wait for me! Wait for me to come back." Even numb and in shock, I was scared for our marriage. I still am.

But I know this is going to take a very long time. I'm afraid eventually he'll get tired of waiting for me.

What if he thinks Jennifer's death destroyed us to the point there is no hope for us?
What then?

Jim

NOVEMBER 9, 2002
Lori wrote me a letter asking me to wait for her. As soon as I read it, she took it back and burned it in our fireplace. Lori couldn't stand the thought of anyone else reading anything so personal. She's afraid for our marriage—afraid of what I might do and afraid that there isn't enough left of her for me to love. She said for me to be patient with her. That someday the Lori that I loved will be back.

I'm afraid for us too. I will never be the same. She will never be the same. We lost more than Jennifer. We've lost our lives. I've lost my life because my wife is my life. And that wife is gone. I know it. I'm afraid she's gone forever.

I keep thinking of the bright Emergency Room sign. The good old boy who walked into the hospital that night is gone forever. He died in the operating room with Jennifer.

NOVEMBER 10, 2002

My brain has no ability to deal with the death of my daughter. All my thoughts are a jumbled mess. I have no clue what to do or where to go.

I keep seeing Jennifer's face, flashes of what must have happened during the crash, and I don't want to see it. Every time I do, my brain starts to hurt. I can feel the blood surging through the vein in my neck, straight to my head.

I keep sensing God telling me to pray. In the past, there have been many times when I've felt too busy to pray. *Too busy! Seriously?*

Lori and I are praying a lot together now, too, begging God to help us. We don't know what else to do. People keep telling us that time will heal our pain. I don't see how.

I try to keep busy. I cringe every time I think about what would have happened if I'd given in and gone to the strip club. Jennifer had no idea she was going to die the night she did. *What if I had been at that club when God decided that my time on this earth was over?*

That's a lesson I hope never to forget. When my time comes, I pray I'm doing something that is honoring God, my family, and myself. I pray that I will never again be tempted to drown my sorrows with that kind of evil.

NOVEMBER 11, 2002

Lori's parents are worried sick about her. I feel so sorry for them. They lost Jennifer, and now I know they fear they're losing Lori.

I pulled my truck in front of their house today, the same one-story ranch home where Lori lived when I met her. Her mom answered the door. I could tell she was surprised to see me in the middle of the day. "There's something I need to tell you," I said.

We sat down in the living room, and my father-in-law joined his wife on the couch. Concern was carved on their faces. "I know you know it, but I need you to hear it from me. You're worried about Lori. I am too. I want you to know that I'm going to take care of her. I'm going to do everything I can to help her. I wish I had a way to make it all better. But I don't. All I can do is to try and make life easier for her."

Lori

NOVEMBER 11, 2002

Everything I felt before Jennifer died is amplified. Stupid things are more stupid, wrong things are more wrong, and insignificant things are more insignificant.

I have no choice but to accept this life sentence, God has forced upon me. *I hate that I have no choice!*

Oh, Jennifer! I'm not mad at you. I'm just so sad.

NOVEMBER 12, 2002

I was going to the grocery store, and Jennifer said she wanted to go with me. It was a Sunday afternoon. *Was it really less than a month ago?* I told her she could get anything she wanted, just not a lot of junk. She got some specialty crackers and Gouda cheese. She loved crackers and cheese, and so did I. When we got home, she helped bring in the groceries and put them away. I never had to ask her to help. She just did it.

NOVEMBER 13, 2002

I couldn't believe it when Jennifer wanted me to take a pottery class with her at Washburn. What college freshman does that? I told her she should be in an advanced class, not a beginning one with me. She didn't care. She said we only had this one year when we'd be in college at the same time.

She was right, but it wasn't supposed to be because she died!!!! It was supposed to be because I graduate soon.

I'm supposed to be a teacher.

How am I going to do that now? I don't want to be around kids. I can't stand the thought! How can I be around kids without thinking of Jennifer?

NOVEMBER 14, 2002

David hasn't returned to school in Houston. He likes to talk about Jennifer. Justin's just the opposite. I worried so much about him before Jennifer died. Now, it's much worse. I don't think he's coping well. He told me something today though, that I didn't know. It happened on the last day of her life.

"We had a fight over something so stupid that I can't even believe it was a fight. We planned to go to lunch, but I didn't think she would go after the fight. But she surprised me when she showed up at the front door, looked at me with that exasperated look she had, and said, 'Well, are you coming or not?'

"And that was the end of our argument. She never said another word about it. We went to eat at her favorite restaurant, Tortilla Jack's."

Justin was looking at his hands. They were trembling. "What would have happened, Mom, if I hadn't gone to lunch with her? What if I had stayed mad and told her no? What if I'd done that? I couldn't live with myself. I get sick every time I think about how I almost didn't go! Mom, I don't care whatever happens in my life, if someone ever asks me to do something with them, I'm going to do everything I can to do it. It may be the last thing I will ever do with them!"

I've been trying to find anything good to come from Jennifer's death. Maybe it'll be in the little things, like what Justin learned. Maybe it's those little things that are going to make this survivable.

Justin was so good to Jennifer. Just last month I complimented him after seeing him open her car door. I didn't know a lot of brothers who would do that! He said he wanted her to remember how a good man should treat a woman when thinking about who she should marry.

Please God,

Don't let anything happen to my boys. Give us strength, give us hope, give us faith. In Jesus' name, Amen.

Jim

NOVEMBER 14, 2002

I'm haunted by something that I'll never be able to fix or undo.

All my life, I've never hugged anyone much: not my parents and, stupidly, not even my kids. Not even my only daughter! I allowed my concern over what I believed "society" thought was proper to dictate what I did—or didn't do.

When Jennifer was about fifteen, I stopped hugging her altogether. I got the idea in my head that it wasn't appropriate for a dad to hug his teenage daughter. *What a crock! How stupid could I have been?* Because of that stupid notion, I never really hugged her in the last few years of her life. I get sick every time I think of it.

Ever since the kids were young, Lori told me that I should be hugging the kids more, but I was proud, hardheaded, and I didn't listen. Now, my heart is aching to throw my arms around Jennifer. *What I wouldn't give to be able to do that now! How could I have wasted all those chances?* I would give anything, anything now, to have just one more chance to hug her. It would be the embrace of a lifetime, one that would leave her with no doubt about how much this father loved and adored her, with every fiber of his being!

I get enraged every time I think of all the things I didn't do. But there is nowhere for my fury to go. I caused it! Now, I'm going to have to live with it.

Lori

NOVEMBER 15, 2002

Justin has started back at work, but Jim hasn't. He can't sit still. At all!

He handles his grief by staying busy around the house, but he needs to send out invoices for past jobs! We have bills to pay and need money coming in, but he can't seem to sit long enough to do that part of the business.

Everyone says that we'll learn to live with our grief, but right now, I find that impossible to believe. *How am I supposed to live with something I don't want any part of?*

NOVEMBER 16, 2002

This morning I went into Jennifer's room for the first time since the accident. I sat at her desk. Among a pile of papers, I found her diary. I knew she kept one, but when I saw it, I froze. She had a diary with a lock on it when she was a little girl. I have no idea where it is. The one I found today was a spiral notebook.

I held it for a long time wondering what Jennifer would want me to do.

I opened a random page. It was dated two years ago. She was angry with me over something I wouldn't let her do. Her words were harsh.

I closed the notebook. I couldn't read any more. Jennifer would not want me reading this. Not now! She had written in anger. She may have meant those words in her teenage, hormone infused years, but they were not representative of the love she had for me. I know that. She would be heartbroken knowing I had seen it.

Jennifer never intended for me to read those words. And she wouldn't want anyone else reading them either. They were for herself, to sort through her thoughts and her feelings. To read the diary now that she was gone, without her permission, felt like a betrayal and an invasion of her privacy.

Had she lived, months, or years from now, she might have looked back on how she felt when she wrote them and laughed about how differently she felt with a little time, maturity, and perspective. I knew if I read any more, I would not have that advantage. Her words—helpful or hurtful—would stay with me forever. I didn't want them inside my head. I didn't want them distorting my memories of her.

A fire was burning in our fireplace. I clutched the journal to my heart and cried hard. If I didn't protect her privacy, who would? With a searing pain inside me, nearly as hot as the flames, I tossed the notebook in the fire and watched as her words turned to ash. I knew it was the right thing to do, but it took everything I had not to reach in and grab it out.

NOVEMBER 17, 2002

I have to go on living. It sounds easy, but it's the most daunting thing I've ever faced. I don't know if I have the strength.

God, Grant me the strength to live in this world without Jennifer. Amen.

Jim

NOVEMBER 17, 2002

I've thought of Jennifer all day, and I hate to admit it, but I don't want to think about her. Not today! I feel like I'm being killed from the inside. I don't know how much more of this I can take. I'm teetering on the edge of a cliff. *Where does pain go without a way out?*

It's the little things that are killing me. Things I didn't do enough of when she was here. Things like the two of us going on walks through the woods. But there was always work to do and bills I needed to pay. And it's hard to get a teenager to stop when they're on the go as much as Jennifer was. There were so many times I could have been more persistent and said, "Jennifer, how about grabbing lunch today?" I think she'd have been glad I asked.

As much as it hurts to think of the things I didn't do, I'll go insane if that's all I do. I have to force myself to remember the good times, like the time we went fishing, not that long ago. We'd spent a couple of hours on the lake, but the fish weren't biting. I would have stayed a lot longer, but Jennifer was having none of it. "Dad! I've had enough. Let's go!" I would give anything to hear her say that now. Anything!

Lying in bed at night, I keep thinking of all the ways I didn't show Jennifer enough how much I loved her.

Shortly before Jennifer died, Lori told her that the way I showed my love for my children was not through hugs and kisses, but through the things I did for them—like working on their cars when they needed fixing. Lori was right. I loved helping Jennifer with her car. It was my way of trying to protect her.

There were other ways I tried to keep her safe. Some of them, the teenager in her didn't appreciate very much. She thought I made her life difficult when I told her to be home by midnight.

There were times when I was her friend, but mostly, I was her dad. I know Jennifer loved me, but I was strict. I think too often kids are given too much and then believe that somebody owes them things. I tried to do my best for all my kids and give them a strong home foundation where they could love each other and trust in God. At least, that is what I tried to do, but I was far from perfect.

But it's the things I didn't do that haunt me the most because I always thought that we'd have tomorrow.

Lori

NOVEMBER 17, 2002

The hospital chaplain called yesterday to see if she could come to the house. A nurse wanted to come with her. Jim asked me, and I said it was fine. I don't know what good it'll do. I don't really want to talk to them, but it's fine.

NOVEMBER 18, 2002

I can't believe it! The hospital nurse—the one in the room when we saw Jennifer—brought us the quilt. It was folded up in a basket. She said they normally wash and reuse it, but she said she felt compelled to bring it to us. She'd washed it but said it hadn't been used since it covered Jennifer.

I just stared at it, afraid to touch it.

The nurse and the chaplain stayed. We prayed together. I was glad Mom and Melissa were there. Jim said how afraid he'd been to have me see the white sheet and how comforted he'd been by the quilt. The nurse said she hoped we'd find more comfort in having it.

After they left, I pulled the quilt from the basket and buried my face in it.

NOVEMBER 19, 2002

Jim and I usually each take a sleeping pill, then fall asleep holding hands. Last night, I curled up inside the quilt and cried.

Life goes on. That hurts. I don't want it to go on without Jennifer!

The thing about death is that for the living, there are no rewards. Most of life's challenges, the ones that are the hardest, have a reward at the end: giving birth, training for a marathon, or running a business. But this hurt has no reward, no prizes, and no heartwarming homecomings like on TV.

The last three weeks seem like a terrible, terrible dream.

I'd die without Jim. He keeps me going. He moves, and I move. He's my motivation. If it weren't for him, I wouldn't get out of bed.

I still have to be a mom to Justin and David. But I'm so scrambled inside. *How do I put the pieces of our family back together when so much of me is missing?*

Jennifer was being ugly the day before she died, so I grabbed her and hugged her. I made her repeat, "You're a good mom. I love you, Mom. You're the best mom." She said, "I love you, Mom. You're the BEST mom." She was giggling by the time I let go of her.

Then, she grabbed me. She looked me straight in the eyes and said, "Repeat: I love you, Jennifer." I repeated it. "You're the BEST daughter," she said. I repeated it. We laughed and hugged each other again, even tighter.

That was the last time I held her, and I can't remember now what she felt like in my arms.

Jim

Sympathy cards keep coming in every day, many from people I've never met. No one seems to understand why anyone so young had to die. I don't either.

I keep looking at Jennifer's senior picture, and it just pulls my heart out.

The moon is bright tonight. Like nearly every other night since she died, I find myself standing outside, staring at the sky, searching for Heaven. I know it's there, but I can't see it or feel it. No matter how long I stare at it, no answers come. Heaven gives no hint of its location.

"Why, God, why her? She was so young!"

I think if Jennifer could speak to me, she would say, "Dad, you don't have to worry about anything. Where I am, there's no pain and no tears."

I pray that when I die, this will all make sense. But now, it doesn't—not at all.

This morning, before we got out of bed, Lori said that she doesn't cry for Jennifer, but she cries because Jennifer is not here. I had to stop and think about that one. My head knows what she means but convincing my heart is another matter.

Lori says she knows that Jennifer is in the arms of God, and, one day, His angels will come to take us home for good too.

Lori is a lot stronger than I am.

Lori

NOVEMBER 19, 2002

We got a letter that Jennifer was named *Employee of the Month* for October at her job at the record store. She had been selected before the accident. She died, never knowing.

Jennifer was always so responsible. Even when she was young, she'd come home from school and do her homework before doing anything else.

She would have finished college, probably majoring in something medical. She was good at math, but she was creative too.

She had plans! It's not fair! It's just not fair!

NOVEMBER 20, 2002

Yesterday, I waited for Jim to leave the house. It was the first time I'd been alone in a long time. I found myself moving like a zombie toward our CD player. I pushed play.

The CD was a recording of the music from Jennifer's funeral; many were her favorite songs. I wanted to cry and hurt. I wanted to feel. I held Jennifer's picture tight. I wanted to feel her, to touch her. I felt my own hair, just to get a sense of feeling hers. I stroked her picture and stroked the outline of her face and arms. From deep inside, I cried. Harder than I thought possible.

When the song "I Hope You Dance" filled the room. I nearly collapsed.

I first heard the song over a year ago, when I was driving with Jennifer. It was everything I wanted for her, and I told her so. I wanted her to enjoy music, laughter, and love. I wanted her to take chances. I wanted her to experience things I never had. I wanted her to dance! I wanted her to LIVE LIFE!

Hearing the words made me grieve from the deepest part of me. *How could I not have known how much Jennifer was a part of who I am?*

Listening to the music was like eating poison and nectar at the same time.

42

I fell to my knees in front of the couch. Warm sunbeams streamed in. I let them. I began whispering, then begging for God to do something, anything to stop my pain. Then I started to scream. From every part of my lungs, I screamed, begging God to help me because I didn't know what to do.

NOVEMBER 21, 2002

It's good we live in the country, otherwise, someone might have called the police yesterday when I was screaming. Once I started, I couldn't stop. I screamed until my throat was raw, and no sound came out.

I started with Kleenex. When the box was empty, the floor was covered with soaked tissues. I grabbed a kitchen rag.

I spent hours rocking back and forth on my knees, begging God to help me. To help us all! I had no idea what to do.

Hours later, I woke up, realizing that I had fallen into a deep sleep. I realized that I felt better. Maybe God had helped me after all by knocking me out cold.

Did Jennifer know how much we loved her? Did I tell her enough? Did she know? Did she feel that her home was her haven from the world? Did she know how much a part of me she was? Did she?

Did I do my best? Was I a good mom? What more could I have done? I wanted her to bury me!

Jim

NOVEMBER 21, 2002

At nineteen, I'm pretty sure Jennifer was not thinking about dying. She had a full tank of life in her, and yet, God came calling. I don't understand how God picks the ones that are going to die. All I know is that when our time is up, it is up, and we'd better be right with Him.

Jennifer was active in Sunday school when she was young, and youth group as a teenager. She knew God and loved Him. I'm grateful for that.

God made her, and He took her home—with no warning to her or us. We had nineteen years with her on this earth, but it wasn't enough, not by a long shot.

I don't know what it is, but, since Jennifer died, it seems like everywhere I turn, I hear someone talking about their "fun" weekend, how they drank too much, then drove home, and later couldn't remember getting there. The newspaper is filled with stories about the ones that didn't make it home.

I was a wild teenager and, at times, reckless. I could have killed myself or killed someone else. Why can some people flirt with disaster and walk away, and others like Jennifer, pay the price with their life?

Why am I alive when she isn't? Did God want her to die?

NOVEMBER 22, 2002

Does Jennifer know she's dead? What's she thinking about right now? Does she know that she's not coming back to this earth? Is she looking down on us and saying, "You all need to quit crying because I'm happy, and you're stuck in that sinful world!"

I wish Jennifer could come to me, and I could see how happy she is. I want to hear her say, "I'm all right, Dad. I love you. I'm keeping you all close to my heart. My love is with you."

That's what I want.

Lori

NOVEMBER 24, 2002

The right side of my body has started shaking. I don't know why. I wonder if it's my subconscious way of telling the world that I'm in pain. If I concentrate hard enough, I can stop it, but I can feel my anxiety rise when I force it to stop. I feel anxious right now. *Will I shake forever?*

I'm mad at the world. Jennifer is gone! *How can it just go on as if nothing happened?*

Everyone around me has perfect families, and ours is shattered!

I find myself staring for minutes on end. *Or is it hours?* I don't know, and I don't care. I'm numb and angry; beyond that, I feel nothing.

I've been following Jim around like a puppy. I don't know what else to do. He never stops, so neither do I. He's writing a lot in his journal. After Jennifer died, I told him I thought it would help him to write out how he's feeling. I think it's his way of letting people know he's hurting. I shake, and he lets people read his writings. Jim doesn't even know I'm keeping a journal. I'm not trying to hide it. It just doesn't seem important that he knows about it. I wait until he's out of the house to write.

People say they're worried about my shaking. Give me a break! They should worry when I'm standing on the Kansas Bridge and ready to jump. I've lost my daughter! They would be shaking too! I HATE people pitying me! But even more, I hate that I'm in a situation deserving of being pitied!

There's nothing I can do. I'm sorry I have to go on, but I have to—Jim needs me and the boys need me. I'm still a wife, mother, sister, and daughter to my parents. I don't want to stay where I am, but I don't want to go on either. I can't believe I'm here, facing this!

Jennifer's journey is finished, and I have to go on.

How is that possible when I have so little strength?

Jim

NOVEMBER 25, 2002

The holidays are coming, and all I want to do is crawl in a hole, hide until they're over, and save my pain for a better time. This morning I stood beneath one of our trees and had to talk myself out of slamming my head against it just to move the pain to some other part of my body.

Lori and I can't stand the thought of the empty place at our table without Jennifer, so we're leaving tomorrow for Texas to be with Lori's brother and his family.

At least the long drive will give us something else to look at.

NOVEMBER 26, 2002

When I was a kid, I used to play a game of trying to make my shadow go away. I'd run, duck, and crawl, but it was always there unless I moved to the shade. Now, my grief is my shadow, but there's no shade. It's always there.

NOVEMBER 28, 2002

Next to Christmas and Easter, Thanksgiving has always been my favorite day of the year. At the table with our bellies full, we'd all sit around telling jokes and stories. Jennifer's laughter was always contagious.

Today, Thanksgiving was just another painful hurdle. Lori's brother and his wife helped us as best they could. The food was really good, and everyone tried to talk about happy things, but in the end, the Thanksgiving table in Texas was just as empty as ours would have been in Kansas. Lori's brother said the blessing, thanking God for our lives, our children, and our country. That prayer had a very different feel this year.

Across the table, Lori was pale. Her hands trembled as she clenched at the cloth napkin. I knew she was struggling to keep it together long enough to eat. I thought of all the families like ours who had someone missing from their tables. Anyone who drinks and drives should be required to spend one holiday with a family that has lost their loved ones because of it. Somehow, I don't think they'd find the idea of driving home drunk much fun. Not fun at all.

Before we finished eating, Lori finally gave up and left the room. I watched her go thinking, "Lord, how are we ever going to get through Christmas?" I had no idea. I keep forcing myself to remember that we're not facing these hurdles alone. God is with us. I know He is. We're going to need Him. Otherwise, there's just no way.

Lori

DECEMBER 1, 2002

Jennifer loved clothes and was stylish in them. She wanted a black leather coat. I told her I'd get her one for Christmas. I never got the chance to buy it.

DECEMBER 2, 2002

You've lost a child. Jennifer is gone. You've lost a daughter. Jennifer is dead. I keep hearing these words over and over in my head.

I feel more dead than alive. I'm just doing what needs to be done, what's expected of me. The only thing that gives me any feeling at all is doing things for Jim and the boys. Everyone else has to care for themselves. I have nothing left to give.

I'm living in a fog, but I feel like I'm part of the fog, protected by it. I think it's God's way of sheltering me. I'm scared of it lifting when I will have to face what's before me. The worst is yet to come. I can feel it, and I'm scared.

God, Watch over my family. In Jesus' name, Amen.

DECEMBER 3, 2002

I dreamt last night that I was pleading with God to let me keep Jennifer.

When I woke, I was so sad that even in my sleep, this inner person inside me pleads with God not to let what happened happen.

It's like there's a separation of my emotional and intellectual self. My conscious, intellectual self can't resolve my grief, so my emotional self goes to sleep and pleads with God for something that I can't have because the terrible thing has already happened, and yet, I still keep pleading.

Jim

DECEMBER 3, 2002

My office is next to Jennifer's bedroom on the second floor of our house. Her door has been shut since the night she died. Today, the sunlight was streaming from under her door. A bad feeling came over me as I stared at that light. When she was alive, her room was full of life. From it, we'd hear her fighting with her brothers, talking on the phone with friends, whispering about boys, laughing at good things, and crying at the bad.

Now, hers is a cold, empty room. Her bed is covered with the clothes she carelessly tossed on it before she left for the night—a night she thought was like any other when she would come home and crawl back into her warm bed.

Her room is a place no one wants to enter…not family, not friends, not anymore. I don't think this room will ever be used again. *How could we stand it?*

Lori

DECEMBER 3, 2002
Another day. This is new territory. The feelings aren't new, but they're unrecognizable.

Is this still shock?

I'm numb, but I'm not a zombie. I function. I laugh, I cry, and I get angry. I'm trying to re-identify who I am. I am a mother of two boys—a family of four now, not five.

Jim says he's doing fine, but I don't think he realizes that he's ignoring all his work responsibilities. I think he's paralyzed by grief, but he's good at hiding it.

Justin is so distant. I keep putting myself in front of him. Not pushing but letting him know I'm there. I think he's forcing himself to be around us.

David is very receptive to talking. He just wants to be with Jim and me.

I tell everyone I'm doing fine. I get up every day. I get dressed, and I eat. But I would not be surviving this without my sister. Melissa deputized herself to help. Thank God! I'm so grateful because I could not function without her.

DECEMBER 4, 2002
I've gone back to school, but only because Melissa insists. I'm just going through the motions. I had most of the work for the semester done before Jennifer died, other-wise, I would not have finished. No way!

I'm not going back to pottery class. I don't care if I get an F. My friend Lisa went to Washburn and got our boxes of pottery, one of Jennifer's and one of mine. I put them in the basement. I don't want to open them.

Every day, Melissa helps me figure out what I need to do to finish school. Step by step, she tells me what I should do. I'm supposed to be student teaching next month. There's no way. Melissa is going to tell them so.

Melissa makes my bed, gets groceries, picks up the house, and organizes my school-work. It sounds simple enough, but it's not. Stepping into someone else's life is complicated. She's done it without wavering. That's unconditional love—strong, unexplainable, to-the-bone love.

She seems to know what I need before I do. This afternoon I asked her how she knows what to do, and she said, "I didn't set out to step in and take over anything. I do what needs doing. If you or Jim don't know what to do in a situation, I just take care of it. If it's something I think you can handle, I step back."

DECEMBER 5, 2002

When I find myself thinking of anything besides Jennifer, I feel like I'm betraying her. If it had been me who died, I would not want anyone consumed over my death. I know Jennifer would feel the same.

I have to force myself to remember that she has everything now, more than we can imagine. And while that makes me happy, I can't stand the thought that I'll never get to see her grow into the wonderful adult, wife, and mother I know she would have been. I must let her go, but I don't know how to do that. I loved her so much.

I tell myself, "Life is unfair, get used to it. God never promised any of us an easy life." It's easier to utter those words than to live them.

I'm comforted by something Jim said to me last night. "Lori, Jennifer has gone to a place where angels soar. She can't come to us, but we can go to her if we keep our faith."

I know Jennifer is in Heaven and with Jesus. I can't wait for the day when we'll sing, shout, and dance with Him together.

Jim

DECEMBER 5, 2002

Everyone faces hurdles. Before Jennifer died, I could get over most of mine with ease. Now, all of life has become an endless mountain of them.

Hurdles like trying to fall asleep at night, knowing I have to face the morning with Jennifer still gone. Hurdles of having to go back to church and see people who want to help but don't know how. Hurdles of having to talk to people everywhere I go and reassure them that we're doing okay. It takes all the energy I have not to let them see how I'm really feeling.

Jennifer's death was a head-on collision for all of us. Our pain, every minute of every day, is an impossible hurdle. We can't run from it or leave it at home for a few hours—it's part of us, it comes with us and stands in front of us wherever we go.

A friend from our church told me that she thinks I'm crying on the inside. She's right, but I was surprised when she said it because I try not to let anyone see me breakdown. That's just the way I am.

Lori

DECEMBER 5, 2002

Another day. Jim's gone hunting with a friend. Mom and Dad came over yesterday to spend the night. It's morning. Dad's gone to get coffee, and Mom is still asleep. It's probably a good thing she's here. I'm on edge.

I have a new mantra, "You have to go on."

It's been almost six weeks since I've seen Jennifer. And that is precisely what we've done, "gone on." *What a farce!* Someone dies, and everyone goes on. That's it. Some have "gone on" a little too quickly, and that makes me angry. I don't even know if angry is the word. Stunned? Surprised? Are they insensitive? Did they not love Jennifer? Are they so shallow that Jennifer's death is, "Just another person gone?" If so, they don't really know or love me.

I hate going on. It seems so...so...I don't know. Can a mother really live without her child? People have done it forever. But are they merely walking shells? How can a person give birth to a child, as I did with Jennifer? And nurse her, nurture her, love her, teach her, watch her grow into a wonderful young woman and then bam! In two and a half hours, she's gone! And now, I'm just supposed to go on living?

I was asleep, got a phone call, and within two and a half hours, I was back home, and Jennifer was dead.

Dear God, Give my family the wisdom to handle this. Give us strength. Shower us with hope and love. In Jesus' name, Amen.

DECEMBER 6, 2002

I actually woke up this morning thinking of something other than Jennifer. It was only for a split second, but it happened. In that briefest of moments, my all-consuming grief vanished.

And then I remembered the call. I remembered that I'm not supposed to be happy. *How can I be? Jennifer is dead!*

Jim, Justin, and David, and I are all changed. Our positions in our family, our roles—the whole dynamics have changed. Jim and I no longer have a daughter to love and worry about and plan for her future. David no longer has a twin that he can call whenever he wants to talk. Justin no longer looks for a light on in his little sister's room. Neither has their sister to protect, tease, and confide in.

David has left to go back to school in Houston. He's so worried about us that he calls every night.

My sister, my parents, and my friends Chris and Lisa are all on-call 24/7. They keep in constant touch. Other family and friends would be there if we asked, but I can't ask for anything right now.

Decisions are still hard. I can do the things I've always done, like brushing my teeth and putting on makeup. But if I have to make any decisions, I can't do it, even simple things like going to the store. I can't do it. I can't concentrate long enough to know, or care, what to buy.

DECEMBER 7, 2002

Last night, in the middle of the night, I sat straight up in bed and realized what I need to do: I need to live a life that honors Jennifer. A life that benefits my boys, my husband, and myself. Anything less will dishonor all that was important to her. Anything less will dishonor God.

I want to live a life honoring her—a life worthy of being Jennifer's mom!

Dear God, Thank you for helping me realize a purpose for my life. Give me the strength to live it. Give my family the wisdom to handle our grief. Give us strength. Shower us with hope and love. In Jesus' name, Amen.

DECEMBER 8, 2002

I do cry for Jennifer. Even though I intellectually know she's in Heaven, my emotional side is different. I miss her. I miss her calling out, "Mom." I miss her calling my cell phone just to see where I am. I miss her very presence. I tell people that I cry for us, but my tears are for Jennifer and the longing I have for her. I close my eyes and can hear her coming down the stairs calling, "Mom." I envision her coming into my room and saying, "Mom, I'm okay."

Last night, right before I fell asleep, I had a vision of her pushing open my bedroom door to tell me she was home like she always did. I jumped up and asked her where she'd been. She looked at me surprised and said, "Out with Carolyn." Then, I realized that all of Jennifer's death was just a deep, dark dream. *Jennifer's not dead! There was no accident!* Then I fell asleep.

Now, it's morning, and it's real once more, so real—so very, very real.

Jim

DECEMBER 8, 2002

I went to southern Kansas for a few days to go deer hunting with a couple of buddies from church. It took everything I had to go. Several times on the way there, I just about turned around. Once we got there and hiked into the woods, the cold air in my lungs felt good. I thought about Jennifer, and for the first time since she died, I thought about her in a good way.

I have always loved to be in the outdoors, where I can see so clearly what God has given us. Since she was a child, Jennifer felt the same. The times we were together outdoors were the times I always felt closest to her. I think that's why, even at home, I yearn to be outside.

Overlooking a breathtaking valley, I watched a doe walking far below and was struck by the beauty of God's creation.

My friends even made me laugh, which I needed.

I found myself not wanting to go home. I knew Lori needed me but going meant going back to a house filled with pain—a house without Jennifer.

While walking in the woods through the snow that last morning, I thought of the poem, "Footprints in the Sand," about how some of the times in our lives there are two sets of footprints behind us: ours and God's. But when things are the worst for us, there is only one set of footprints—when God carries us.

God has been carrying me since Jennifer died. There's no other way I've survived losing her this long on my own. No way.

Lori

DECEMBER 8, 2002

The anger inside of me is growing like a cancer. I don't want to become bitter, but I am—toward everyone in our extended families because they all have a daughter, and we lost ours! Every time I'm with them, it's a reminder. I hope they value what they have. I just want my family back. Intact!

How do people survive when they lose an only child? My God! My only focus now is my boys, even though they are not as receptive to my love as Jennifer was. She wanted me. The boys need other things. *My God, my God, why did this happen?*

I talked with my father-in-law last night. He said they have backed off somewhat from us because he sees my family taking good care of me. Situations like this can cause misunderstandings, and I don't want that. He said I was like a daughter to him, and I know that's true. He said he doesn't call often because he doesn't know what to do or say. He thought I was pulling away, not needing them. Oh, how wrong they were! I need anything anyone wants to give, and I told him so. I will have to make an effort to keep communication open.

It's getting harder, not easier. I feel so lost. I'm leaning on people so heavily that I feel them struggling. My sister and two friends are here so much that I'm afraid it will hurt their marriages.

I've never been one to wallow in self-pity for long. But this is different.

I'm trying to fill the void of Jennifer, but I can't. *How can something so deep, with no bottom, be filled? I have no idea.*

Dear God, Help me to fill my empty life with positive things and be a better person. In Jesus' name, Amen.

DECEMBER 9, 2002
There's a sadness so deep inside of me that is so strong that it feels like it's pulling the rest of me into it. I fear I'm literally going to implode, when all of my body collapses in on itself—until there is nothing left of me except a hole filled with grief.

DECEMBER 10, 2002
My mind is starting to go far into the future, in the years ahead of my life without Jennifer: without her ever getting married, without her ever having children, and the void of it all. How in the world we are going to survive her being gone—forever?

It's my birthday today. I don't even care. *Why would I?*

There's no happy in this day.

Jim

DECEMBER 10, 2002

Impact is when you hit something, or something hits you, hard. Death is an impact.

I'm stuck in a zone of time that goes nowhere. I'm not getting any worse or any better. I can't see anything past this moment. It's like I'm standing in a round room with no doors. I move along the wall looking for the door, but I find that after searching and searching, I'm right back where I was before, with nothing behind me, and nothing before me.

The other night I walked past Jennifer's room, and I opened the door. I shouldn't have done it. My body went limp. I felt lightheaded. A terrible feeling of death hit me head-on.

No one is in the mood for Christmas. I don't think I have the strength to go through it. *But what can I do?* Nothing. It's coming, and I can't stop it. All I want is to go outside, dig a hole, and crawl into it until Christmas is over.

Lord, help my family for what is about to hit us.

DECEMBER 11, 2002

Am I destined now to live in the dark forever? I hope not, but I don't know how to stop the darkness. I just want my life back the way it was before!

Lori and I were sailing along really nicely in our lives together. Our kids were nearly grown. We had more time to ourselves. We were making more money than ever before, beginning to really travel, and enjoy this new life with grown kids. Now, all that is gone. We've been forced into a cave where all the oxygen has been sucked out. The candle flame is gone out, and we're in complete darkness. There is no light where we are and no way to turn it back on.

DECEMBER 12, 2002

Living under the same roof with two people with broken hearts is very hard. How can we share our love for each other when our only daughter is dead, and all either of us feels is pain?

I think this has been even harder on Lori than it has been on me if that's possible. A mother carries her child for nine months, night and day, always with her. She had a connection with Jennifer that I will never know.

There is very little talk in our house. Neither one of us knows what to say. When I do speak, it seems to make things worse.

I think we are in for a long, long haul.

We tried to do everything right in raising our kids and living our lives. I want it to go away.

Lori

DECEMBER 11, 2002

I keep forcing myself to concentrate only on what I have to do today to get through it. When I look at it like that, each day and each moment at a time, I can function. But I have to keep control of my mind, every second. That's what makes me so tired. If I lose control, I truly feel I might leave and never find my way back. The intensity of my grief is stronger than it was before. I don't know how that's possible, but it is. I wonder if the protective fog I've been in is lifting.

Acceptance is moving in, and I fear it might hurt as much as the news of Jennifer's death. I don't know anything anymore.

Nothing is definite now, except that there are no guarantees. Anything can happen to anyone at any time.

When I think about the person I was before Jennifer died, I feel sorry for that woman. She died with Jennifer.

DECEMBER 12, 2002

I think Jim has been conditioned not to cry. I've rarely seen him shed a tear in all the years I've known him, even when we've been watching emotional movies that I know affect him.

Since Jennifer died, I still haven't seen him really break down and cry. At her funeral, he remained outwardly composed. And because he's so good at hiding his feelings, I don't think any of our family or friends have any idea how much he's hurting. That worries me. He needs just as much support as I do.

I know that just like me, Jim is dying inside and struggling to survive one moment at a time. But his way of dealing with his pain is to keep busy.

Earlier today, Jim was jittery. He was pacing around the house more than usual. He looked at me and said, "I have to get out of this house. Will you come?" I was relieved. We both needed to get away.

He drove around for about twenty minutes without saying anything. Then he pulled his truck next to a recently plowed field. We sat without talking for a long time, and then he covered his face with his hands, and his whole body started shaking.

It was a long time before he could talk. When he did, he said he thought the anti-anxiety meds he's been taking since Jennifer died have kept him so numb that he can't cry, but because they aren't keeping him from feeling, the meds aren't helpful.

I rubbed his neck and shoulders and told him I thought he was right. He needs to deal with what he's feeling, or he'll be destroyed.

I'm glad Jim was finally able to let his feelings out, even for a few minutes, but it was hard to watch.

We're each just trying to get through every day—any way we can.

DECEMBER 13, 2002

I woke this morning to the sound of my mom's sweet voice singing the song from our kitchen downstairs, "Safe in the arms of Jesus."

Mom has always found solace from the old hymns, especially the ones from her childhood. She has an old, tattered, and extremely thin hymnal book that she's had for as long as I can remember. She even takes it with her when she travels. She told me that after they got the call telling them that Jennifer died, they rushed to the airport in Winnipeg.

While Dad stood in line at the counter to purchase tickets, Mom pulled out the book and started to softly sing the hymn, "Tell Me the Old, Old Story." When she finished, a woman sitting behind her said she and her husband were music professors in Minnesota. She asked Mom why she was singing.

Mom told her they just found out their granddaughter died.

A few minutes, later Mom was told that the woman and her husband had arranged for their first-class tickets to be given to my parents. Mom and Dad were escorted to the more private waiting room. They flew home first class for the first time in their lives.

Jim

DECEMBER 13, 2002
I couldn't sleep last night. I lay in bed for hours looking outside through the French doors of our bedroom.

The night was clear, and the stars bright.

How far would I have to travel to get to Heaven?

It's a journey Jennifer has already done.

Someday I will know.

DECEMBER 16, 2002
It's warm for December. So warm I went fishing the other morning with my brother, Tom.

We were on his pond before sunrise. The sun was still very low, shining through a cloud when a brilliant, red beam of light broke through the clouds. It was unlike anything either of us had ever seen. It looked like it was coming straight from Heaven.

We both stared at it with open mouths. I looked at Tom. "Is Jesus coming down from Heaven?"

He didn't take his eyes off the sky, "I was just going to ask you the same thing."

Within a few minutes, the light vanished. I wish it had been Jesus—coming to take all of us home.

The rest of the morning, the fish were on strike, so I had a lot of time to reflect.

I couldn't stop thinking about Lori, how much I love her, and how much she means to me. She's my wife, my lover, my friend, and even my doctor after having removed a fishhook or two over the years.

I keep thinking about what I would do if she were next to die. I think I would have to follow her. I wouldn't survive losing her too.

Lori

DECEMBER 16, 2002
I was sitting in church yesterday, and one of the leaders started talking about how wonderful Christmas is because we can all be with our families.

My whole body started trembling, then heaving. Jim froze. He didn't know what to do. I didn't know what to do. I felt a hand on my shoulder. Melissa whispered to me to come with her. I had to get out of there, and the quickest way was out through the front of the church. And that's what we did.

DECEMBER 17, 2002
My head is clearing a little now. Clarity doesn't make anything easier. It's just clearer.

Death is a part of our lives now. I'm sure some people are afraid of me because of it. No one wants any part of death.

Death is a part of life. Actually, our time here is just a fraction of our lives, death, an even smaller part. Eternity is the *real* part of our lives.

We put up a Christmas tree. I only put lights on it. I couldn't do anything else.

Jim

DECEMBER 18, 2002

Several years ago, when taking down a dead elm tree on our property, I made a cut clean all the way through with my chainsaw. And even though the tree was cut completely in half, it didn't fall. I pushed against it, but it just stood there like nothing had happened. I shoved it harder. It just stood there.

That's how I feel now—like I've been cut in half, but somehow, I haven't toppled over. I keep thinking that I'm going to fall over at any moment, just like that tree should have done, but instead, I just keep standing...like I'm waiting for something to happen. *Will I stand like this forever?*

I own a roofing company. We have a foreman who, thank God, for the last month has stepped in to help. I've just started back at my job—bidding projects to keep my workers busy.

It's strange because I'll be going about my day, thinking that I'm fine, and then the smallest thing happens, like an unhappy homeowner upset over a minor detail, and bam! It hits me so hard I can't deal with it. I want to yell at them and tell them to take a hike. But I can't, or nobody would be working. Instead, I try to pretend that nothing is wrong, just like that tree.

I think eventually, something has to hit me hard enough that I will finally fall over.

But for now, I just keep standing there, cut clean—all the way through.

DECEMBER 19, 2002

It's as though I'm walking blind, searching for a light switch that I can't find.

I keep thinking of the phone call that night—a call that killed our lives.

I went to the gravesite today. I felt sick to my stomach, knowing what was lying beneath my feet. I felt so utterly empty and helpless. *What happened to the little girl that I used to hold on my lap and tell stories to? What happened to my beautiful daughter?*

I stood there for a long time, waiting for a response. I couldn't hear a thing, only silence.

There was nothing I could do except ask, "Why? Why, God? Why?"

DECEMBER 23, 2002

We've been waiting on the police report for two months. It came today. They believe that Jennifer was ejected through the sunroof, not the window.

Alcohol was involved. Both the driver and Jennifer had been drinking. The driver was over the legal limit.

Jennifer's alcohol level was under the legal driving limit, but it may have been skewed because her levels were checked after she had already been given a lot of blood to save her. Regardless, she was underage and drinking. We taught her about not drinking and driving, and still, this happened!

Alcohol is thrown in our faces every day. TV, movies, and commercials all imply the same thing: drinking makes you cool...drinking is normal...to have a great time with your friends, head out for a night of drinking!

I would like to make an ad showing a picture of my daughter lying in her casket.

I had a buddy in high school who got hooked on hard drugs, and his life was destroyed. He permanently fried his brain on drugs and requires care for the rest of his life.

I want to say to those tempted by drugs and alcohol, "Your fun choice may end up killing someone like my daughter. Your fun choice may mean your family having to take care of what's left of your body for the rest of their lives."

No amount of fun is worth that.

Lori

DECEMBER 24, 2002

My anxiety is high. Everyone keeps asking, "How are you and your family going to handle Christmas?" I keep telling them that we have no choice. We can either go on living or we can die.

With my sister's help, I've managed to buy a few presents so my family has something to open Christmas Day, but this year, no one cares anything about gifts.

We're going to have Christmas dinner with Jim's family. They asked Jim if he thought it would bother me if they put Jennifer's picture on the table. Jim said it would be okay. They said that if it started to bother me, they would take it down. Expectations suck. Everyone means so well. They're trying to do this to honor Jennifer. They don't understand that I'm still waiting for her to walk in the door. *Put the picture up! But I'm not ready!*

Jim thinks it'll be easier after the holidays. I don't think so. Christmas, after Christmas, yesterday, last month, it's all the same to me—another day without Jennifer here.

I can't get Psalm 46:10 out of my head, "Be still, and know that I am God." I keep repeating it to myself.

Be still, and know that I am God.

Be still, and know that I am God.

Be still...

Jim

DECEMBER 24, 2002

"It's my turn!" yelled Jennifer. It was Christmas morning. Jennifer and David were little. I think about three. They were both wearing one-piece pajamas with built-in slippers and a zipper from the ankle to the throat. The twins were taking turns running down the hallway. I was keeping them distracted as Lori put out the final gifts. As they got near me, I'd swing a pillow at their legs. Not hard, but just enough to knock them over. They'd go down like bowling pins on the carpet. They'd squeal, then get up running and shouting, "Do it again, Daddy! Do it again!"

I'd give anything to have that Christmas day back.

DECEMBER 25, 2002

I found a little angel with purple wings and took it to Jennifer's grave. I knelt and touched the ground. I hated that it was so cold. I whispered, "Merry Christmas, my sweet angel."

Lori

DECEMBER 27, 2002

Christmas was a nightmare. Everyone tried hard to make it joyful, but it was impossible. I wasn't able to keep it together long enough to stay at the table, but I tried to stay engaged by at least sitting on a nearby couch. That didn't last long. I ended up in the bedroom.

Everyone, including Jim, came in one by one and sat with me as I cried. All I wanted was for the day to be over.

Jim tried his best to act as normal as possible. He did a pretty good job of it outwardly. Inwardly, I knew he was just like me—dying.

DECEMBER 28, 2002

I can still see Jennifer coming downstairs in her loose pajama pants and tank top. Someday I won't be able to picture her anymore, and when that happens, she will be gone. Completely. I dread that day, so I don't look forward to the future.

Someday even her senior picture will look old. David will have grown into a man, but Jennifer will forever be nineteen in my mind.

I sat looking out the window today, thinking, "I don't know how to do this." Then I reminded myself, "One day at a time. That's how." Someday I hope something— anything— good will come from all this terribleness, but I can't imagine it now.

Our family was so perfect: two boys and a girl. I had my girl and all the hopes and dreams that come with it. Last summer, Jennifer told me that someday when she gets married, she wants her wedding in our back yard with white lights illuminating the trees. She wanted it very simple and elegant. I knew someday we would do that.

I used to imagine that day and how the two of us would be giggling and getting ready for her wedding in my bedroom. Jennifer would look like an angel. I imagined how I would feel when I watched her leave the reception, and how sad and happy that would make me. I dreamed of her having babies. She wanted to have twins. She loved being a twin. Now, there will be no wedding, no twins, and no babies. She was so beautiful, so kind, and compassionate. She was petite, responsible, and walked with such confidence. She wasn't perfect, but who is? Once she hit her teenage years, she could be a little mouthy, but not disrespectful.

One simple mistake, and she's gone. She's gone. All of it is gone. It's all so senseless.

My heart is broken. My very being is shattered. I want my baby girl back, and nothing I can do will change that. Nothing!

DECEMBER 29, 2002
I don't know what to do. I don't want to do anything. I move. I breathe. I still go through the motions of living.

I want quiet.

When I laugh, it startles me.

Jennifer, Jennifer—my precious child. It's cold outside.

Jim

DECEMBER 30, 2002

We made it through Christmas. I'm glad it's over. Opening gifts was painful. Everyone was sad. Lori was inconsolable.

As I looked at the heartbroken faces around the table before we started to eat, I felt so helpless. I knew I had to do something, say something. When we joined hands to pray, I cleared my throat and said softly, "Jennifer is spending this Christmas with Jesus, and what better Christmas gift could we ask for?"

I don't know if it helped anyone else, but it made me feel better.

Throughout the day, I couldn't help wondering how Carolyn was doing. I couldn't imagine how hard Christmas was for her.

JANUARY 1, 2003

A new year, when people think back about their lives and the passage of time. People keep telling me that time will help, and that we'll feel better in a few years. Bull! I don't want to feel better in a few years. I want to feel better now! I want my pain to stop now! I don't have time to wait for time. Time is my enemy.

JANUARY 2, 2003

Lori went to run errands. Her friend Lisa picked her up. When Lisa dropped her back off, I was outside. Lori went straight into the house. I could tell she had been crying.

I asked Lisa what happened. "Lori got really emotional after we went to the bank. I stopped the car. I knew she just needed to work through her grief. She was crying so hard it scared me. She began rocking back and forth. Jim, I didn't know what to do. And then do you know what she did? She started singing the hymn, "Great is Thy Faithfulness!" The wail of her voice is something I hope I never hear again. It sounded like a wounded animal, crying for its young."

Lori

We're already in a different year than when Jennifer died. Someday, it will be two, four, even ten years later. And still, Jennifer will be gone. People say, "Time will help." Maybe, but Jennifer will still be gone.

What will our family be like down the road? Will everyone be okay? Will Jim and I enjoy the empty nest like we had anticipated? An empty nest doesn't sound so appealing when it's empty because one of our children is dead.

I keep asking myself, "How am I supposed to find pleasure in anything again?" Then I tell myself to be patient, that pleasure will come naturally and by itself. But I feel I should be doing something to encourage the process. Not hurry it, but encourage it, and I don't know how.

I don't want to stay in the place I am, but I don't want to let go of Jennifer either. *How do I do both?* My grief is all I have of her, the only connection. She died, and I grieve. The two go together. *Since she's not coming back, do I grieve forever?*

Jennifer's friends are going on to do all the things I wanted for Jennifer. I know someday I will see their faces in wedding announcements in the newspaper. Then the birth announcements of their kids will follow. Maybe they'll even call us from time to time, as they do now. It's not fair! I don't want to know anything about their joys in life. I don't want them to keep in touch! It hurts too much.

Dear God, I'm worried about all of us. Guard our hearts and direct my boys' decisions and actions. In Jesus' name, I pray, Amen.

JANUARY 4, 2003

I know it sounds strange, but I've started sensing that God is letting me know He's with me by putting His hand on my knee. I feel His presence and can hear Him telling me to be patient, that it won't be long before I see Jennifer again. I'm not a patient person.

JANUARY 5, 2003

My best friend, Chris, was with me the night I met Jim. One Friday night, when we were in high school, Chris and I headed out to a local hangout where teenagers in their cars liked to go.

Jim nearly always drove a pickup truck, but on that night, he'd talked his sister into letting him take her car. Jim and another buddy, Don, pulled up in a blue and white 1969 four-door Oldsmobile. Jim was at the wheel. Both guys caught our eye.

A few nights later, the four of us went on a double date. Chris was supposed to be with Jim, and I was supposed to be with Don. As it turned out, I didn't hit it off with Don, and Chris didn't hit it off with Jim. Jim and I couldn't stop looking at each other. And that was it. We started dating after that night and never quit. Since then, Chris and Jim have been friends but have not been very close. She never quite saw in him what I did.

But for every major event in our lives, from that time on, if she could manage it, Chris has been there for us. Just as she was when she got the call in the middle of the night that Jennifer had been in an accident. Chris said before she even hung up the phone, she knew that Jennifer was gone. Maybe that was because of the bond she had with Jennifer. Chris was like a second mom to Jennifer.

When Chris pulled up into our driveway that morning, she sat there for a long time. She said she didn't want to face me and the darkness waiting for her inside. She said she knew that the life of her best friend would never be the same.

Two days later, Chris was still at our house. I was staring out of our bedroom window. I was supposed to be getting dressed for the viewing of Jennifer's body at the funeral home in a few hours.

I couldn't breathe and, suddenly, I couldn't stand my room, my house, my life. I ran out of the room, down the stairs, and out of our front door, screaming.

Chris had been standing on the side of our porch, where she had gone to get some fresh air. I don't remember any of what she said happened.

She said she saw me drop to my knees and Jim running after me, covering my body with his. I was screaming, "She's gone! She's gone! Oh my God, Jim, what are we going to do?"

"We're going to get through this, Lori. I don't know how. But we will. With God's help, we will!"

Chris said it was the most intimate, tender moment she had ever witnessed in her life. It was then she said she fell in love with Jim too.

Jim

JANUARY 5, 2003

People say the pain won't go away but that we'll learn to live with it. I don't want to live with it! *But what else am I supposed to do?*

I'm sensing the devil has moved out of my house, at least temporarily; maybe he found it hard to dwell there when Lori and I are literally on our knees so often in prayer now. Every morning, we pray together for God to give us the strength to make it through the day. At night in the dark, we pray for the peace to get through until daylight.

Everywhere I turn, I keep hearing of more teenagers being killed in auto accidents. So many of them seem to be nineteen! *Has it always been this way, and I'm just now paying attention?* I used to hear occasionally of such tragedies happening to the families of the *other guy,* and I would feel bad. But now, each one rocks me to my core. I know the pain and shock their families are going through. It makes me physically ill.

I met a woman who lost a child several years ago. She said to me, "Jim, I know it's hard to believe now, but one day, life will be good again for you and Lori. I know you're numb now, but someday you won't be. You'll feel alive enough that even the sun will feel warm on your faces again. I promise."

A good life again? I can't imagine it.

JANUARY 10, 2003

Being in good health, I've never really thought much about death. It seemed far off—something we wouldn't have to deal with for a long time.

Now that death has come through my front door, I'm forced to look at it in a new way. When the God that made us calls our name, we'd better be ready, because life is short, any way we look at it. Our clock starts ticking the moment we're born.

I can't get the song "Lightning Crashes" out of my head about the circle of life. Like the song, I know that when Jennifer was closing her eyes in death, somewhere, a little angel was born.

JANUARY 11, 2003

It's like I'm being killed from the inside out and becoming a person I don't like. There are only a few friends that I can stand to be around, and only for a short time before I want to be left alone. And that isn't like me. I've always been the happy-go-lucky one.

I'd be happier if I could go live in a cave and never have to talk to anyone.

I am beginning to wonder if I'm going insane. Nothing seems to make sense or matter. All I know is that my only daughter is a ghost to me. It scares me how low I am.

Lori

JANUARY 11, 2003

All my emotions are exaggerated. Every possible emotion is jumbled inside of me: calm, rage, sadness. I can't stop them, and I can't separate them.

Yesterday, I cried and screamed—all morning. I screamed at Jennifer for the first time. I'm so angry at her decisions and for putting us through this.

Anyone looking at me today might think I'm at peace. I couldn't be farther from it. I'm emotionally and physically drained.

Just when I was sure I was going to collapse from weariness, Jim's sister called. It's remarkable how often, when I most need it, the right person comes along. I thank God for Julie. Just talking to her helped restore my energy. Everyone needs someone like her.

JANUARY 13, 2003

I bought a quilt today and dropped it off at the hospital. I added a note that it be delivered to the surgical floor to replace the one they had given to us after Jennifer died. I told them how much it meant to us and that we hoped this one would be of comfort to someone else.

JANUARY 14, 2003

Two days ago, I decided to go to the grocery store. I parked the car in the lot, opened the door, stepped onto the pavement, and thought, "How do I walk?" I couldn't remember how to move.

How can I not remember how to walk? Can grief do this?

I didn't know, but, as I moved toward the store, I had to concentrate on putting one foot in front of the other. I finally made it, but it took forever.

I kept looking at the rows and rows of stuff. I couldn't remember what I needed or what we had at home. I picked up a box of cereal and just stared at it, then put it back.

After I got a few things in my basket, I made it to the checkout line. I started shaking, and I couldn't stop. All I could think was that I had to keep it together long enough to get back to my car. A woman in front of me turned around and said, "Hi, Lori."

I looked at her. She was just a blur. Everything was a blur. I said, "I'm sorry, I…I don't you. I don't know who you are."

She told me her name. She was someone from church that I would normally know well. But I was in such a state that I hadn't recognized her.

I could tell by her reply that she was offended. To her, I must have looked normal. She'd probably forgotten that I'd lost Jennifer.

When I got to the car, I just sat there, not driving, not moving. *Have I gone insane, or is this just grief?* Someone who isn't insightful about grief would say that I've gone insane. Maybe I have.

JANUARY 15, 2003

"Someday, I'm going to marry you!" I couldn't believe it. That's what Jim blurted out to me on our second date, just after he kissed me, which was shocking enough. I was fifteen. He was seventeen.

But he was right. A month after I graduated from high school, Jim made good on that promise in the living room of my parents' house. I think of it now and can hardly believe it. My parents weren't happy. They loved Jim, but they thought we were too young. I remember walking down our stairs to the living room. Chris was my maid of honor. We were giggling like the teenagers we were.

Jim jokes a lot about his declaration of marrying me, saying with his big, toothy smile, "Lori, if nothing else, you have to admit that I'm a man of my word."

I was nineteen when Justin was born, and we packed up and moved to Midland, Texas. Our parents were horrified when we told them we'd bought a trailer at 25 percent interest! I can't believe we did that.

Justin was still a toddler when I was pregnant again. I told the doctor I had to be having twins. No way I could be that big that fast! He said nope, he didn't think so but agreed to do an ultrasound. I was right. Two babies.

Jim and I were terrified. We were already overwhelmed with one baby, and we were soon going to have three! We sold the trailer and moved back to Kansas.

When I was in labor, Jim got it in his head that since he was in the delivery room for Justin, he ought to try, as he called it, "the old-fashioned way," and wait in the waiting room with Justin and my parents. The delivery nurse saw Jim sitting there and said, "What are you doing out here? Your wife is having twins! You get back in there." When my mom told me about that later, I laughed. I could have hugged that nurse.

Half an hour later, Jennifer was born, then David. Each over seven and a half pounds. I had been carrying fifteen pounds of babies! No wonder I was huge!

When we left the hospital, we went to my parents' house instead of ours. We needed help.

Three weeks later, my mom came with us to our house to help us unpack and get settled back in. I'll never forget watching the taillights of her car as she drove away, thinking, "How am I going to manage this?" Then I started to cry.

Jim

JANUARY 15, 2003

I feel like I have to learn how to live again, from the very beginning. Outwardly, everything looks as it did the afternoon before Jennifer died: our house, my car, my clothes, and my job. And yet, everything is different. The Jim living here before we lost Jennifer could put on his socks without thinking about Jennifer. That Jim could go to work and concentrate on work. That person could get in his truck and had somewhere he wanted to go.

The Jim who did all those things evaporated the night Jennifer died.

JANUARY 16, 2003

In 1 Peter 5:8, the Bible says, "Be sober and self-controlled. Be watchful. Your adversary, the devil, walks around like a roaring lion, seeking whom he may devour."

It also says to put on the full armor of God in order to resist evil. I believe there's a devil wanting others to join him in darkness, and he's after every one of us. He's not selective. God could destroy him in an instant but instead lets us choose how to live our lives.

I hate cockroaches. They're dirty and sneaky. I don't know anyone who tolerates them in their homes. We go out of our way to kill them. The devil is a million times worse than any cockroach. Why do we permit such evil to hang around, tempting us when we could chase it from our lives by praying to God?

I think it's because the devil is good at disguises, often coming in the form of someone, or something, we trust. He delights when anyone gives into temptation. He wants us to live our lives in the way of the world. He loves us abusing alcohol and drugs.

He feeds on distraction, defamation, and deception. I know because I can feel him, tugging me toward darkness.

I heard from a friend that a childhood girlfriend of mine had also lost a child.

I called her, and we talked for quite a while. It felt good to talk to someone who has been through what we've been through and has learned how to live again.

Is it so wrong that I want to talk to another woman about how I'm feeling?

It doesn't feel wrong. But I don't want Lori to know I made that call.

The devil loves darkness. I know that, and it scares me. But I think Lori would be hurt if she knew, and I don't want her hurting any more than she already is.

Is that so wrong?

Since writing the question and looking at it, I think I know the answer.

Before I make any calls like that again, I'll talk to Lori about it first.

JANUARY 17, 2003
I've taken a lot of things for granted in my life. Even things like being able to walk. If I became paralyzed today, that would change in a heartbeat. *Why does it take losing something for us to realize how much we treasure it?*

I should never, never have taken Jennifer's life for granted!

Some days I start off feeling pretty normal, and then...BAM...something hits me. Sometimes it's seeing something of hers, even though I've seen it every day since she died, but for no apparent reason, something about it suddenly reminds me that she will never use it again. And without warning, my day is shot. I can't think. I can't work. I can't do anything.

All I want is to have one good day.

73

JANUARY 20, 2003

It's 4:30 a.m., and I'm enraged. Last night, I actually had a family member tell me how much fun they had getting smashed the weekend before ... and then drove home!

How could this person tell me this after I just buried my daughter?

And this person had been at Jennifer's funeral!

How could they be so clueless—so insensitive? "Drinking and driving don't mix, you idiot!" That's what I wanted to shout, but I didn't.

"What if you killed another kid, like Jennifer?" That's what I should have said!

People would have said, "It was just a bad accident." No! That would have been no accident! Accidents are something that happen by mistake. No one makes drivers drink like a fish, then start the car. Give me a break! It was a decision they made!

I know this person has driven drunk before, and I'm sure they thought they could handle it. That's what everyone thinks until they can't.

What's it going to take for people to wake up and quit drinking and driving?

I'm just so mad this world can't seem to face the truth! A lot of people die because someone else thought they could handle drinking and driving.

Why did Jennifer get in that car with her friend who had been drinking? Was she too impaired herself to make that decision?

Why didn't she call us? WHY DIDN'T SHE CALL US?

All the time parents tell their kids not to drink and drive, and then the parents go and do so themselves. Two-faced hypocrites! I can't stand people like that. I just hope they don't call me when they're on their knees because their teenager is lying in a casket! I'd better never hear them say, "Why me? I didn't deserve this!"

I don't want to hear about anyone's great night of stupidity. But that is all I can think of now, lying in bed at 4:30, when I should be sleeping. I think I'd have felt better if I had punched him in the teeth. Maybe I'd be able to sleep.

Right now, I'm too angry to sleep.

Lori

JANUARY 20, 2003

Jim asked me if I would mind if he called an old girlfriend from when he was young to talk to her about losing a child. He said he already called her once before about this. I told him if he thought it would help, to go ahead. When he went outside to the back of our house to talk, I went upstairs to work on the computer. I could hear Jim talking on the phone through our open window.

I could guess from his responses what she was saying. It didn't seem like any big deal conversation. But toward the end, there was something in his tone that bothered me. I perked up when he said something in a macho kind of way. I thought, "Mental note... watch this relationship."

When he got off the phone, he said it was good to learn about how she has handled her grief. He said she's coming to town in a few days and asked if I cared if he talked to her in person. I told him I didn't care. But I'm not sure I really meant it.

I hope he knows how vulnerable he is right now. We're both vulnerable.

Two men that I know have each offered to get together with me privately to talk about my grief. I have declined both. I don't think having either of those men put their arms around me, comforting me, and letting me cry on their shoulders would be good for me. I know it would feel good. I just don't want to be tempted.

I don't need to be playing with that kind of fire right now. I have enough on my plate. And so does Jim. And so does our marriage!

I think people need to think long and hard about the destruction they would cause if they encourage or take advantage of others when they're hurting. It's not okay—not for them, and not for those they claim to want to help.

Jim

JANUARY 21, 2003

I should have gone out tonight and jumped off the roof of our house headfirst instead of going into Jennifer's room. The pain would have been less.

I felt like I had been punched in the gut when I saw her shoes, knowing that she'll never walk in them again.

Pictures of her friends line her bedroom walls, smiling and laughing.

Pictures are all that we have now to capture her life, moments frozen in time, capturing what was, but what never will be again.

There are pictures of us there with Jennifer too. Pictures of when we didn't realize just how blessed we were.

Lori

JANUARY 21, 2003

We're planning a trip to Aruba to get away. I can't wait to be there and be just like everyone else—tourists—and not the parents of a daughter who just died!

The enormity of our loss is just now hitting me and how astronomical it is. Justin told me the other day that he and his fiancée went looking for her wedding dress. They want to get married once things settle down. I'm happy for Justin, but his words hit me hard. I will never help Jennifer pick out a wedding dress! I'll never watch her walk down the aisle with Jim. I'll never get to meet the man she would choose to spend the rest of her life with.

A friend from church told me that her pregnant daughter asked her about hormone changes she can expect. I stared at her, realizing that I'll never have such a conversation with Jennifer. I'll never get to hear the emotion in her voice when she tells me that she's pregnant, I'll never get to hold any of her babies, make them cookies, or watch as they get on the bus for their first day of school.

I'll never do any of these things with Jennifer! *How do I accept this and go on?*

How can I be happy for anyone getting to do all these things when I never will? Smile? Pretend? Fake interest? Perpetual smile?

I'm sure that's how. I don't think I'll ever have a real, genuine, involuntary smile again. *How could I?*

I'm most comfortable with no one around except my family. People make me nervous. They all talk, talk, talk. They know nothing about what I'm going through. I've been where they are, feeling badly for those who lost a loved one, but not knowing what to say or do.

I'm so angry and sad.

People say I'm supposed to accept this and find joy. *Are you kidding me?* Acceptance and joy don't fit together!

I think I'm going to die from a fatal disease. My mind and body cannot handle this!

I've got to remember and thank God for what I have. If I can't focus on the good things I have, I will die. I've got a wonderful husband and two beautiful boys.

Dear God, Help me to focus on what You have blessed me with and take comfort that Jennifer is with You, and I will see her again. There are things worse than death, and I still have a perfect family, albeit without my Jennifer. Help me to realize this every day. In Jesus' name, I pray, Amen.

JANUARY 22, 2003
Oh, God! I'm so sick of being dead inside. I just want to feel alive again! But I don't see how that's possible.

God, help me feel alive again!

JANUARY 23, 2003

"Be grateful you had nineteen years with your daughter," she said. "Be grateful you got to hear her voice as an adult."

If anyone else had said that to me, I would have been offended. But those words sounded a lot different coming from someone who had earned the right to say them—someone who had lost a child much younger than Jennifer.

Her name was Stephanie. I met her yesterday. I had gone to my mom's house. I walked in the door and burst into tears. I couldn't stop. Mom didn't know what to do. Finally, she took me by the hand and said, "I want you to meet someone."

We walked across the street and knocked on a neighbor's door. A beautiful woman greeted us. Mom said she wanted the two of us to talk alone, then she turned and left. Stephanie knew about Jennifer's death. One look at Stephanie and I knew I could trust her.

We had a lot in common. We were about the same age. She had had twins too: a boy and a girl. They were born about the same time as Jennifer and David. She showed me their pictures. Then she told me that her beautiful daughter aspirated and died in her sleep. That was seventeen years ago. She was three years old.

I had had so much more time than that with Jennifer.

I told her that I didn't know how to get through each day.

"You get up in the morning. You take a shower. You put on your makeup. Then you do whatever you have to do to get through the day. And the next day, you get up and do the same. And every day—every day, be grateful you had nineteen years with her."

Stephanie opened her china cabinet to show me her collection of angels. She laughed, "I never really thought about it, but I guess when you're white like you, you collect white ones. When you're black like me, you collect black ones. "

She handed one to me. "It's the only white one I have. It's also my favorite, not because of the color, but because it plays one of my favorite songs. I want you to have it, in honor of Jennifer, so that you remember the joy she brought to your life. Listen…"

Stephanie turned the crank. The angel slowly began to spin. As it did, a Christmas song began to play. It was "Joy to the World."

Jim

JANUARY 23, 2003

I don't even want to talk to my friends. They ask me how I'm doing. *How am I doing? Really? How can I answer?* I could lie and say I'm fine, or I could tell them the truth, but that would get real old, real fast.

I just want to be left alone. I don't want to answer any questions. I don't know if that is right or wrong, and I don't care.

JANUARY 24, 2003

My dad loves cars. He had had an amazing collection over the years. None has he loved more than his '31 Model A Ford Convertible Cabriolet. With its sky-blue paint and shiny chrome, it looks like it just rolled off the lot decades after it did. The classic car is the talk at car shows where dad spends a lot of his free time. He's often asked to drive it in local parades.

Mom used to say, "That car is the other woman in his life." Then, she'd laugh. "Although she's older than me! She was born in 1931, and I'm a 1936 model. And she's a lot more expensive to maintain than I am."

All three of our kids used to love to ride in that car.

Dad showed me a poster he made with Jennifer's picture on it. It said, "*This is the car Jennifer Dultmeier used to ride in.*" Dad said he was going to mount it on the back of the car and keep it there.

Dad misses his granddaughter. He may not seem like a sentential guy, but he is. It'll show now—every time he drives that car.

JANUARY 26, 2003

A few days before she died, Jennifer drove over to my parents' house to show them her new car, a used '96 black Dodge Avenger. She had worked several jobs to save money to help buy it.

When she got to their house, Dad wasn't home. Mom was in the basement, sewing. She heard someone walking around upstairs. She assumed it was Dad.

I imagine Jennifer looked around their first floor, walked out back to their pool, and then to Dad's shop where she would normally find her grandpa working on one of his vehicles. Not there, she probably walked into the garage. Seeing my dad's car gone, she likely assumed they had gone somewhere together.

When Mom went upstairs later, she saw that Jennifer had written them a note. "Sorry I missed you, Grandma and Grandpa. I wanted to show you my new car. I'll come back later. Love, Jennifer"

There was no later. They never saw Jennifer again.

I don't know if Mom will ever quit beating herself up that she didn't call out when she heard Jennifer's footsteps.

Lori

JANUARY 27, 2003

I had a dream last night. I was holding young Jennifer on my lap—pleading to God to let me keep her.

I woke up exhausted and crying.

God knew my prayers for her before the accident too. I wanted to keep her! I wanted to watch her grow up and grow old. *Why did he take her from me? Why?*

JANUARY 28, 2003

Oh my God! Did I cherish Jennifer enough? Did I ever just stop, look at her, and thank God for this precious gift I was given? Did I take for granted that I had this perfect little child and would always have her?

JANUARY 29, 2003

Grief is like holding my breath underwater. I'll be okay for a while, but when I come up for air, it's violent. Then I start to cry, knowing that I'll soon be forced back under.

Every day I do what Stephanie said I should do. I take a shower, fix my hair, put on makeup, and take deep breaths. I look okay in front of my family and friends until I'm alone, and that's when I fall apart.

Often, I just sit and stare. I'm worn out from thinking. I can't believe this has happened. I actually thought this morning, "Maybe it's me who is gone! Maybe I'm in a coma, and I will wake to find that it had actually been me who had an accident. Jennifer is really okay!" *Oh, how I wish that were true!*

JANUARY 30, 2003

I got my grades for last semester. I got an A in pottery. I couldn't care less.

JANUARY 31, 2003

I've always been close to Melissa, even though she's three years older, but we have very different personalities. Our dad worked for the railroad, and we moved a lot.

Once, when we moved to California, away from Kansas where most of our family lived, Melissa took it very hard. She accused me of being like a duck, with the pain of it just flowing right off. It was true. I've always been pragmatic and a realist. I've just dealt with whatever happens.

When we were still living in California, we got the horrifying news that my dad's parents were killed in a car accident. They were hit by a drunk driver!

I was devastated. We all were. I couldn't believe that, just like that, my grandparents were gone. My mom kept saying that we'd get through it because of our faith and because strength was in our DNA. We came from a line of seriously tough ancestors.

My mom's parents lived in New Mexico and lost three of their fifteen children in one year! One died at birth, and two more died from illness. I may be from hearty stock, but I can't imagine losing three children! I don't care how many others you have. I don't know how they survived. I really don't.

Jim

JANUARY 31, 2003
I want to go back to the life I had before! Before, when I looked forward to some-day taking Jennifer's kids fishing. I would clean the fish for them to take home and surprise their mom. Jennifer would have been a great mom.

Instead, I force myself to focus on the good things I have: two sons, a wife, and a place to rest my head at night.

FEBRUARY 2, 2003
I've never liked this cold time of year when I'm trapped inside. This year it's much worse. The lakes are covered with ice, but the layer is too thin to walk on. Hunting season is over. Even my business is slow. It's hard to replace roofs in the dead of winter.

It seems all I'm doing now is waiting for something to change—the weather, my pain—anything!

When my kids were young, I couldn't wait until they grew up. How stupid of me! Now, all I want is my kids back!

FEBRUARY 3, 2003
Little things have started to get to me. I hate waking up. I hate trying to think about something else all day. And worst of all, I hate the long nights, trying in vain to sleep.

I've had it with most people right now. They're testing my nerves, and my nerves have very little patience for stupidity.

I try not to, but I get so mad thinking of the accident that I want to hit something. Drinking and driving at a high rate of speed don't mix! I keep asking myself, "Am I so old that I've forgotten how fun it was to go fast?"

When I was young, I loved to drive fast. When I got older, I was sick of paying for speeding tickets, and finally realized that speed could kill me. *So why didn't it? Why was I spared from my stupidity, when Jennifer wasn't?*

I want to run away, but I don't know where I can go that will take away my sorrow and my rage. *Where is that place?*

Lori

FEBRUARY 5, 2003

Jim is not okay. I know him well enough to know when something's up, and it's obvious things are very wrong with him. He talks and laughs too much in front of others, and all of it's a mask. He's good at hiding his pain. Too good. He's in trouble. I'm not sure anyone else realizes how badly he's hurting.

How can I help him when I don't know how to help myself?

FEBRUARY 7, 2003

My dad grew up in an era of no seat belts, and it bothered Jennifer that he often didn't wear his. Since she was young, she'd told him so.

When she was in junior high, Jennifer made him a poster that still hangs in his garage. She'd pasted family pictures all over it. One was of herself wearing an Easter dress that I made for her when she was eleven. The brim of her straw hat was flipped up.

In bold colored letters, she wrote, **"We love you, Grandpa. Wear your seat belt!!!"**

How could she not have had hers on?

FEBRUARY 8, 2003

Jennifer, David, and their cousin Brooke were together so much it was like having triplets. Jennifer and Brooke could not have been closer if they had been sisters.

Jennifer loved all her cousins, and there were a lot of them. Most were younger. She'd spend hours playing with them in either our swimming pool or the one at Jim's parents' house where we'd all get together for birthdays and the Fourth of July. I can still see the younger kids taking turns jumping off the diving board, shouting to their teenage cousin, "Watch this, Jennifer!" Then they'd sputter up for air. "Jennifer, did you see that?"

She was so patient with kids. She would have made a great mom.

If anyone had asked her philosophy in life, I think she would have said, "Be good to people. Be nice. Be kind." That wasn't to say she was perfect. She could be stubborn and belligerent. There were times she would have terrible fights with me, with Jim, her brothers, and sometimes her friends. If she thought she was right, she'd say so. But mostly, she was very quiet and content. She was happy being so. To her core, Jennifer was a sweet, tenderhearted, and loving person. I think those traits would only have intensified as she grew older.

Jim

FEBRUARY 9, 2003

I went to Jennifer's grave today and just stood there and stared at the cold, hard gravestone.

She had so many dreams for her life. She loved to make pottery, and she was good at it. Our bookshelves are lined with pieces she made. They're still here, but she's not. She wanted to get married and raise a family. She wanted to travel. She wanted to have a big wedding in our backyard. She wanted to dance to a slow song with me at her wedding.

This just isn't fair to any of us.

Lori

FEBRUARY 9, 2003

Jennifer's things are everywhere. I can't open a drawer without finding something of hers—pencils, notes, hair clips—things she used as she lived. Now, the things are here, but Jennifer isn't. *How is that possible?*

FEBRUARY 10, 2003

Jim's sister picked me up last week and took me to Lawrence to buy yarn. It's been years since I've knitted, but Julie has encouraged me to start making scarves.

I'm nearly finished with my first one. Just doing something with my hands has made me feel better. I need to remember to thank Julie.

FEBRUARY 11, 2003

Lately, I'm seeing glimpses of the old pragmatic Lori. At least it's a glimmer of hope for the future.

It's strange, but sometimes I feel like I'm watching myself from afar, thinking, "Her will to survive is stronger than she believed possible. She's even feeling a little excited about going on a trip. But those feelings don't jive with the situation she's in. She feels she should be dead, but, surprisingly, she's not. That's the survival instinct, the innate part of her, that one that wants to survive."

FEBRUARY 12, 2003

Until Jennifer died, I don't think I really knew the enormity of the gift of children. Jim and I were talking about this last night. Did we ever really grasp and appreciate how good we had it?

The week she died, Jennifer and I were driving home from our pottery class. I told her that I knew as a parent, I'd made some mistakes. She turned to me and said, "Mom, I couldn't ask for a better mom."

I have to hold on to those words! She had no idea what a gift they would be to me...for the rest of my life!

Dear God, Help me. Help me find peace and joy in memories. Help me to live free of pain. In Jesus' name, Amen.

Jim

FEBRUARY 15, 2003

I can no longer stand to be around teenagers.

Before Jennifer died, I loved having them over to the house, listening to their laughter, and enjoying their young antics. Now, their laughter and their voices are poison to my soul. All I can think whenever I see a group of teenagers is, "Where's Jennifer?"

Friends keep inviting us to their homes for parties and gatherings. Every time, I want to ask, "Are there going to be any teenagers there?" If so, then, "No, we won't be coming." But that's unfair to everyone. So, instead, I tell them that we'll come. I just wish I could go without dreading it.

FEBRUARY 17, 2003

I can't sleep, so I'm writing out my thoughts. Sorrow has no bottom. I want Jennifer to come home so badly that I can't bear it. I keep staring at the driveway, praying that I will see the headlights of her car.

It's getting harder and harder, not hearing her voice. I look at the empty couch, and she's not there. We should be playfully arguing what TV shows to watch. If she were here, she would be telling me her car needs to have the oil changed. I miss driving past her on the highway near our home, and her brilliant smile as we waved to each other.

I'm fighting a madness growing inside of me. It scares me. I don't want to talk to anyone about my feelings. I have to figure out how to deal with my pain, in my own way, not someone else's.

I've always believed that if I wanted something badly enough, I just needed to work harder to get it. But I can't work harder to bring her home.

I keep hearing that phone call. I keep asking myself what I could have done to stop this. I keep seeing her dead in that coffin as I kissed her goodbye.

I have to be strong for my boys and my wife, but it's getting harder and harder to hold my head up in front of them. When I'm alone, off hunting or fishing, I can let it out. I'm fighting to be strong in front of them instead of doing what I want to do, which is to yell and kick down every tree I see.

I'd be lying if I said I haven't been having thoughts of killing myself, just to end this pain. But while that would be the easiest way out, it would be unthinkable for what it would do to Lori, my sons, and everyone else I love. Ending my pain to create more of theirs isn't the answer. I have to be more of a man than that.

Lori

FEBRUARY 18, 2003

I don't know what started it, but I was standing in an aisle at the grocery store and started to cry. I couldn't stop. I was so mad at myself, not because I was crying, but because it was embarrassing, inconvenient, and I couldn't control it. This wasn't the type of crying that the people around me could ignore. If I had seen someone crying as hard as I was, I would have thought I had to do something. And that's what I was afraid of. I was afraid someone was going to come up and try to help. I knew I had to leave, groceries and all. I tried to keep my head down as I rushed out, but I know it was obvious that I was crying.

I kept thinking of the people I was passing. I'm sure they were all carefree and going about their lives without having to deal with the grief of losing a child while they were shopping.

I really think this grief is going to kill me. Physically kill me. I have to be dying.

FEBRUARY 19, 2003

I need to do something about the situation with Jim and his old friend, but I don't know what, without sounding paranoid and demanding. I'm aware they're talking a lot on the phone.

I know what the problem is with our relationship; I'm no longer exciting. That's an understatement. I'm hardly present in anything, including my marriage. It's like just the outside of me is here. On the inside, there's nothing—just nothing.

We're going on a trip to get away. Jim thinks it will help us heal. I don't even care if we go or not. He says it'll be romantic.

How am I supposed to deal with a romantic getaway when I don't care about anything?

Jim

FEBRUARY 26, 2003

The island of Aruba is thousands of miles from our Kansas home. The ocean view from the balcony of our hotel room is spectacular. For millions of years, the waves, with their brilliant tones of light and dark blue, have rolled in. I can't stop staring at them.

We came here to get a break from our sorrow. *What a joke*! Lori was right! No matter how far we go, our grief won't be left behind.

I went deep-sea fishing yesterday, and all I could think of was how much Jennifer would have loved it.

Last night, we went to the far side of the island where huge waves smashed against the cliffs, and all I could think of was how I wanted our kids to see it…all three of them! Lori was so sad. She couldn't stop crying. I put my arm around her, but it didn't help. I think it made it worse.

We stayed there for a long time, watching the ocean change colors from blue to green to red to orange, mirroring the setting sun. I had a hard time enjoying the beauty. Lori finally stopped crying. She was worn out.

Lori

MARCH 2, 2003

One day on our trip, while he went fishing, Jim surprised me with a spa day. He was trying so hard to find something…anything…that would make me feel better.

My first stop was a saltwater bath. Four women had me crawl onto a large tarp that they lowered into this pit of water. Then they left me. I felt trapped. I couldn't get out on my own. All I could think was, "My God! How long are they going to leave me here?" I couldn't stand the smell of the saltwater or the music that was playing. I started to call out, softly at first, "Hello? Anybody?" No response. They had vanished. Soon I was yelling, "Get me out of here!" A couple of women came in. If they were surprised by my shouts, they didn't show it. Very cheerily, one of them said, "Now it's time for your massage. You're going to love it."

I didn't think anything could be any worse than the bath. I was wrong. I don't really like people touching me anyway. When they had me lie down on my stomach, with my face through an opening, I started to cry, and I couldn't stop. This wasn't the little sniffles kind of cry. This was full-on, full-body wailing. Once I started, there was no stopping. My eyes were running. My nose was running. And it was all going through the little hole to the floor. It was a mess. I was a mess.

The woman was trying to massage my back like nothing was wrong. Finally, I blurted out, "I just lost my daughter three months ago! Can you please turn the music off? I just want to lie here and cry." And she said, "Okay." And I cried and cried and cried as she massaged my back.

I don't ever, ever want another massage.

That evening, Jim and I walked out onto a rocky shore. I started bawling again. He just waited for me to stop. I knew he felt terrible and helpless. There was nothing he could do to help.

Once back at our hotel, I called my sister. I had to call her collect. I know it cost a fortune for her to listen to me crying.

The entire trip, I just kept thinking, "Jennifer's dead." It didn't matter if I was on a beach or at home; Jennifer was still dead. I couldn't get away from that reality.

Jim

MARCH 3, 2003

The last day on the island, I got up early to watch the sun come up over the water. Lori walked out on the balcony with me. I knew we were both thinking the same thing. We were wishing that Jennifer was there to see it.

89

Then it was like I got hit by a lightning bolt. "Lori! What if, right now, this very minute, Jennifer's standing in Heaven and thinking, 'Man, I sure wish Mom and Dad were here to see this! They'd never believe it!'"

Lori looked at me and grinned.

My coffee that morning tasted better than it had in a long time.

MARCH 5, 2003

I'm not afraid of death. When it comes, I'll take the same journey Jennifer has already forged. Looking down at the ocean as we flew home, I knew that at any moment, something could go wrong. In a split second, I could die and be with Jennifer again. How glad I would be to see her and leave all this pain behind.

But as I took Lori's warm hand in mine, I thought about my wife and our sons. It was a good reminder, too—of this part of my life—the one that still needs me at home.

Lori

MARCH 8, 2003

I had a breakthrough of sorts. For the last few days, I've been on the verge of completely losing it. But I didn't want to spoil Jim's mood that has seemed better since we've returned from our trip. I've been forcing myself to hold back my emotions until I'm alone. Finally, yesterday after breakfast, I waited for Jim's truck to leave the driveway. As soon as he was gone, I put on the music again from Jennifer's funeral and allowed myself to grieve—wholly and completely grieve.

For hours I walked around the house screaming for God to help me.

When I finally calmed, I was able to hear the words of the songs that were important to Jennifer. I closed my eyes and tried to convince myself that she was there listening with me. Maybe, even from Heaven, some part of her was.

As I listened to all these songs in our family room, it was impossible to imagine that the singers' voices that Jennifer loved were still there, filling the air, but she was not. The thought made me cry again.

Afterward, I was so exhausted that I slept until early afternoon. When I awoke, I was still tired, my voice was hoarse, and my eyes and face were puffy and swollen, but I had won a private battle! For the first time since Jennifer died, I'd taken some measure of control over my emotions. I hadn't stopped them, but I had decided when I would allow them to flow.

It may seem like a small thing, but it was huge to me.

Thank you, God!

MARCH 9, 2003

It's hard for me to think about how close I came once to losing David and my dad. It's even hard to write about, especially now. I get sick to my stomach just thinking about it.

Just before David's sophomore year of high school, he went with my dad to watch a tractor pull race in a small town not far from where we live. When it was over, Dad started the car. David buckled his seat belt and looked at his grandpa. Dad shrugged, then did the same. Just as they got up to speed on the highway, an oncoming pickup truck crossed the center lane right in front of them.

David said Dad slammed on the brakes and turned the steering wheel toward the ditch in an effort at evasion. His front tires had reached the shoulder when Dad shouted, "Oh no!"

David said he remembered hearing his grandfather shout.

The pickup slammed into them, head-on.

David recalls being propelled forward and the sound of breaking glass. He was briefly knocked unconscious.

When he roused, he looked over. My dad was slumped in the seat, covered in blood. David was certain he was dead and tried to get out of the car. His door was jammed shut. He crawled into the backseat and opened the door enough to squeeze out. He collapsed on the pavement. A woman two cars behind had stopped. In the car behind hers was an off-duty police officer who called the ambulance. While he attended to both my dad and the other driver, the woman pulled David into her arms and put his

91

head in her lap. She stroked his hair and told him everything was going to be okay. She waited with him until the paramedics arrived.

The other driver was killed on impact. We were told later that he had just come off a series of long shifts at work. The officers think he had fallen asleep.

The Jaws of Life were needed to extract Dad from the car. He was flown by helicopter to the hospital. David was taken by ambulance. After getting the call from the hospital, Jim and I raced to the ER. We found David alert but with a broken collarbone. He also had broken his jaw, but no one knew it at the time. My dad had a cracked sternum and a severe gash on his neck that just missed his jugular vein. His chest injuries were especially scary, for he had recently had open-heart surgery.

When I saw the vehicles a few days later, I nearly fainted. They were a crushed mess of metal. I don't know how they all weren't killed. Dad's Audi was designed to absorb head-on collisions. The hood looked like a piece of cardboard folded in half, but thank God it protected the passenger compartment, even though it had no airbags!

The investigators determined when they hit, the pickup was going 60 mph. Dad had managed to brake to about 40 mph. The officers said if Dad and David hadn't had their seatbelts on, they likely would not have survived the 100 mph impact.

David had to deal with a broken jaw for weeks, not being able to open his mouth and only able to drink liquids through a straw. While he recovered physically, I'm not sure he ever fully recovered from the trauma of looking over and thinking his grandfather was dead.

My dad felt terrible that he hadn't been able to do more to prevent the wreck. But the investigators said there was nothing Dad could have done differently.

I think it was doubly hard for my dad because he experienced nearly the same thing that killed his parents years before when their car was hit head-on. Dad knew his mom and dad must have felt that same helpless terror as he did. That was hard on him.

After David came home from the hospital, he fell asleep on the couch. I curled up in a chair across from him and stared at him for hours. I couldn't take my eyes off his chest, rising and falling with each breath. I kept willing it to keep moving because it meant his heart was beating. I was terrified to realize how, in one instant, I nearly lost my father and my son. That was unimaginable.

How could I have known that less than four years later we would lose Jennifer in a wreck when she wasn't wearing her seatbelt?

Jennifer knew full well that accidents happened when people were least expecting it. Mom told me after Dad and David's accident that she believed my dad's life was saved because of the poster Jennifer had made for him about wearing his seatbelt. Dad walked past it every time he left his garage. Mom thinks Jennifer helped save Dad's life, and yet, she removed hers, and a split second later, she was killed.

That is still very hard to come to grips with. I don't know if I ever will.

Jim

MARCH 8, 2003

There are a lot of people who came to Jennifer's funeral that we haven't heard from since. They may not know what to say or how to help, but not hearing from them hurts. I've learned something that I never really understood until now. No matter our pain, we have to be there for each other. From here on out, if anyone I know loses someone they love, especially a child, I will be there for them in any way they need.

And no matter how painful it is for me, I will never stop talking about Jennifer. I will do so until my last breath. If I ever have grandkids, they will know about her. I can't let her be forgotten. Not ever.

MARCH 9, 2003

A group of teenagers passed me on the highway today. The driver was weaving in and out of the cars in front of me, barely getting back in time to avoid hitting the oncoming cars, racing up quickly, and then tailgating the car in front of him. I wanted so badly to chase that punk down and shout at him to grow up and quit driving stupid. There was no way to catch him, so I just went home.

Tomorrow we go to court for Carolyn. Lori and I have been asked for our input on her sentencing. I'm going to tell the judge that two girls died that night. One is at peace. The other has to live with what happened for the rest of her life. I'm going to request the judge consider community service instead of jail time. If Carolyn were to talk to teenagers at schools about what happened, and if that could save even one life, it would be the greatest gift to us, and the greatest way to honor Jennifer's memory that we know.

Sometimes I think the world is losing its battle for our kids. Movies, commercials, and TV encourage stupid behavior. Kids think they need to drive nice cars. They think it's cool to stay out all hours of the night.

When I was young, I used to love the nightlife. Now, I couldn't care less about it.

My dad used to tell me that nothing much good happens after dark. I think he was right.

Lori

MARCH 10, 2003

Today we're headed to court. I'm numb. I can't believe what has happened. It is so catastrophically huge. I can still imagine Jennifer coming downstairs and lying on the couch to watch TV. But she's not ever coming downstairs again.

We are getting ready to go to court for Carolyn because Jennifer died in a car wreck. It's so unbelievable. I just want to get this over with.

Jim wants to tell the court not to have Carolyn go to jail. He said that two girls died that night. I don't want anything bad to happen to Carolyn, as Jennifer wouldn't want that either. I want the justice system to decide what's best for everyone, including Carolyn. I just don't know what that is.

Everyone is taking off work and has changed their plans to go today. I just wish they were doing their own things and not having to change their schedules. I wish Jennifer and I were going to school together, that Jim was headed to work, and we were all looking forward to spring. But we're not. We're going to court.

Jim

I don't think we'll ever know for certain who supplied the alcohol at the party where Jennifer and her friend were that night, much less prove anything against them. I have a pretty good idea who they are, but the young men have claimed the girls had the alcohol when they arrived. If they did it, I wish they'd be real men and step up and admit it. Hiding from the truth will not be good for their souls or their peace of mind. And they're missing the chance to help others not make the same mistake.

I have a good friend who's fearful I'll take matters into my own hands. He's afraid if I confront the guys I have suspicions about, I'll end up either being shot by one of them or land in jail for beating the tar out of them. He's probably right. I'm so angry. I keep envisioning driving my fist through their teeth, but that would only make things worse for Lori. And in the end, what difference would it make? Unless they confess, which they haven't, we can't prove they did it. Either way, Jennifer is still dead.

I just wish they could see the pain they've caused so that they never let this happen to anyone else. I know I can't touch these little chicken punks, but I want to. They took away so many dreams from so many people by their stupid decision to provide alcohol to those girls. Jennifer knew better than to partake, and I hold her accountable also. Still, if there weren't people like those young men making it possible for underage teenagers to get a hold of alcohol, we wouldn't be living this nightmare.

My friend said that I have to leave it up to God to take care of them. I don't like it, but I know he's right.

MARCH 14, 2003

I believe in prayers and that miracles can happen, so it's hard not to keep asking God why he didn't perform a miracle and save Jennifer's life.

I believe God loves everyone on earth, but He hates sin, and He hates our bad choices. He knows how painful the consequences will be to us. He wants us to make better choices and live better lives—but He lets us decide. My head knows it, but my heart is another matter. Only God knows why Jennifer died so young when so many others make just as bad, or worse decisions, and are spared.

Part of me is so angry with God for not saving her. But what good does that anger do? Every time I feel my anger rising, I keep focusing on Jesus, opening his gentle and loving arms to Jennifer. Maybe he said something like, "Jennifer, that was a stupid way to die, but I still love you." That's what dads are for.

MARCH 16, 2003
Over the years, we captured some of the fun times on videotape of our three kids. Maybe someday we can bring ourselves to watch them. Right now, I can't even think about ever doing so.

MARCH 17, 2003
I used to come home after dark, and Jennifer's light was almost always on. Tonight, her room was as black as night.

MARCH 19, 2003
From the time she was an infant, Jennifer was a beautiful girl. When she walked into a room, heads turned. She was shy most of her life, but if she felt she was right about something, look out! She could be fierce.

She liked to test me on my rules, as so many teenagers do. As her dad, there were times I was scared, especially when I saw the expression on some of the faces of boys when they looked at her.

She dated boys and had a steady boyfriend until the week before she died, when she decided that since she was in college, it wasn't wise for her to be tied down. We all thought she would have plenty of time for that later.

I learned from Lori, after Jennifer died, that she had broken up with one of her boyfriends, not the most recent one that we liked a lot, but an earlier one, because he wanted to have sex and she wouldn't do it. Jennifer was a sensible girl. It was a good thing I didn't know about this earlier guy who was pressuring her to have sex, or we would have had a more than uncomfortable come-to-Jesus moment. It turns out she handled that situation well on her own.

Jennifer loved all her relatives, especially her grandparents. My dad's nickname for her was "Sugar." When Jennifer was a young girl, he said to me one day, "Jim, you're going to need to keep her safe."

Now, I'm haunted by those words because Jennifer died, and I didn't keep her safe. I feel I've let not only Jennifer down, but also my dad. I know he doesn't hold me responsible, but I can hardly look him in the eye.

I tried to stay on top of what was going on in her life, but at nineteen, I felt that I had to let her fly a little farther from us. I had just started to think we could sigh a bit of relief that she had survived her teenage years unharmed.

Sometimes I'm afraid I failed her by not getting in her face enough before she went out with her friends. But she was growing up fast, and the road in front of her was wide. I was excited about her future, and I knew that one day before too long, I would be walking her down the aisle to begin a new life as a wife to a man she loved.

All that changed on an October night. What really hurts was that I was just starting to really see her as the beautiful young woman she had become.

All I want now is to tell her how beautiful she is. Instead, I have to live with the last conversation I had with her and what I said to her. I can't bear to think of it.

Oh, what I wouldn't give to be able to tell her that I love her—more than she ever knew! And I can't. And that is what hurts the most.

Lori

MARCH 25, 2003

Our friends, Lon and Christine, came over last night and brought their little boy. Lon owns a BBQ restaurant and insisted on bringing dinner. I didn't feel like talking. I think Lon realized it. He said there was a new season of *The Bachelor* on TV and asked if we wanted to watch it while we ate. I'd never seen it but was glad because it meant I wouldn't have to sit at the table pretending to have fun. I spent the night lying on the couch. They didn't seem to mind. I know Jim was glad they came. They asked if it would be okay if they come next week. I told them that was fine.

I'm grateful for so many of our family and friends who've spent so much time with us. I hope I never get so caught up in my own life that I don't do the same for others.

MARCH 30, 2003

I've started exercising. My energy is slowly returning. I can't imagine the toll this has taken on my body.

I just keep going, trying to remember my sweet, precious baby girl and how she now has everything she needs. Her journey is complete.

The Bible says, "Be still and know that I am God." So that's what I'm doing...one step at a time.

Dear Savior, One step at a time.

APRIL 1, 2003

When we were dating, Jim worked as a DJ. The first time I saw him working at a wedding, I was impressed. He always had two turntables going and would start a new song just as another ended so that dancers wouldn't leave the floor. When things needed to be livened up, he'd crank up rock and roll. When he sensed people were growing tired, he'd slip on a slow song. If he thought the dancers were ready to leave the dance floor, he'd play something everyone wanted to dance to like "Proud Mary," and people would say, "Oh, I love this song! We can't stop now."

I was dusting today and picked up an old photo of us the day we were married. I couldn't believe how young and naïve we looked. Good grief! I had only graduated high school a month before!

No wonder my parents were having a fit. I would have, too, if Jennifer had wanted to get married a month after graduating high school!

Jim

APRIL 1, 2003

I thank God every day for my sons.

David came home for a weekend. We were sitting around a table, trying to talk about the good times with Jennifer, but it was like trying to enjoy a puzzle with half the pieces missing.

For nineteen years, we've worked this life puzzle—a puzzle with millions of pieces, beginning the moment she was born. How can we now share the good times of her life when the puzzle isn't complete?

Some part of me wishes I could tear the puzzle apart, put it back in the box, and never look at it again, but I can't do that. The truth is, I'm going to have to learn to live with it, as it is, incomplete and holding on to the belief that one day when we're in Heaven, the puzzle will be complete. Until then, a partially done puzzle will have to be enough.

APRIL 2, 2003

Pictures are great until you lose a loved one. Now, pictures of Jennifer are only an empty reminder of life when it was good, a snapshot of a moment of how things were. I don't care if I never again see another photo of our kids when they were young.

The only picture I can see in my mind is the one I wish I could forget—the image of my daughter lying in her casket.

Today was a bad day. When I came in from work, Lori took one look at me and said we needed to talk. I admitted how hard it was coming to a home without Jennifer. Lori said, "Jim, this is no longer Jennifer's home. Home for all of us is in Heaven, and that's where Jennifer is now."

APRIL 3, 2003

I'm scared every night when I go to bed, knowing that our phone could ring at any time again, telling us another one of our kids has been in an accident.

I wish all teenagers knew what a parent goes through when they lose a child. Does Jennifer know the minute she died that our whole world changed? Does she have any idea how deeply we ache for her? Does she know that the lives of her many family and friends changed forever too? Does she know that for all of us, nothing will ever be truly right again?

Lori

APRIL 3, 2003

Five days before she died, I took Jennifer shopping for college clothes. It was a beautiful fall day. The air was crisp and warm. The leaves on the trees were turning gold. The sky was bright blue, without a cloud in sight.

Jennifer tried on all sorts of clothes. She bought a couple of blouses, some sweatpants, and two pairs of jeans. After we finished, we went to lunch. She talked a lot about David and how much she was going to miss him being in Houston for school. We talked about Justin. She was so happy that he was doing a lot better.

As we were leaving, we walked past a photo booth. Jennifer's eyes lit up. "Mom," she said mischievously, "let's get our picture taken." We laughed, making silly poses. Afterward, Jennifer scanned the options for a frame. She laughed out loud when she found one, "Okay, since we're both college girls, this has got to be the one!" On the frame was one word: *Hotties!*

I laughed as she slipped the photo inside.

I'll cherish that picture for the rest of my life, even though I can't bring myself to look at it now. In it, the two of us were smiling and laughing. We had no idea it would be the last photo we'd ever have taken of the two of us.

Jennifer walked out of the mall with bags full of new clothes she would never wear.

APRIL 4, 2003

I can't believe that I'm still alive when the healthy, beautiful daughter I gave birth to is dead. Something is very, very wrong and not okay with that.

APRIL 5, 2003

Some friends ask me how I'm doing because they really want to know. Others, those who don't know me well, ask out of courtesy, but I don't think they really want to hear anything more than, "I am fine." They walk away, feeling better, that all is well. If only that were true.

So, to those people, I tell them I'm fine. But the ones who are really asking, I tell them the truth about how I'm actually feeling that day.

There are some days when I'm surprised to realize that I am truly feeling okay. I know that I have to enjoy those moments because soon, the pain pendulum will swing back. It always does.

Jim

APRIL 5, 2003

David came down for breakfast. He didn't look right.

Lori asked him if he was okay. He looked at the floor. "I ran my car off the road last night. It rolled."

"It rolled?" I couldn't have heard him right.

"Yes."

I looked at Lori, then turned away. I could not believe what I was hearing—or feeling—shock...horror...disbelief...relief. All in the same instant. Each to its fullest comprehension: the beginning, the middle, and the end. Life. Accident. Death.

One look at Lori and I knew she felt the same. Another dead child. Another phone call in the night and dash to the hospital. Another funeral. Another burial. Another beginning of the horror—all over again.

We could not have survived it. No way.

The air in the room was like a building collapsing in on itself; all the energy was sucked out.

No one said a word. Not for a long time.

Lori hadn't moved. Not a sound. Not a movement. Nothing. We were both paralyzed, incapable of responding.

"David, what in the world?" It was all I could say.

Finally, he told us the rest. He had been at a friend's house. They had been drinking. Later, he decided that he should drive to Lawrence and talk to his former girlfriend to see if they could talk about their recent breakup.

He thought he was fine to drive. Instead, halfway there, just before a sharp curve, David fell asleep. He said he didn't know if it was because of the drinking, being tired, or both. He woke when his tires left the pavement and hit gravel. He overcorrected. The car spun, hit the opposite ditch, and rolled.

Airbags burst open. David was hanging upside down, and he wrestled his way out of the seat belt.

No one else was with him. A passerby stopped and gave him a ride home.

If he hadn't been wearing his seatbelt, we likely would now have lost both Jennifer and David.

I stormed out of the house and stood outside on our front porch. My eyes stared as hard as they ever had—at nothing and everything. David's words settled in. Hot anger flooded every cell in my body, replacing the horror. I've never been angrier in my life.

I was shaking with it.

How could this happen? And to David of all people? David, who had always been so responsible?

What part of pain doesn't he understand?

Haven't we suffered enough? Wasn't one death in the family enough? Did he think he should add his also?

I fought the urge to march back into the house and scream at David, "When we go retrieve your car from the ditch, how about we stop at your sister's gravesite? You can stand next to her headstone and tell her how safe a driver you are when you've been drinking! I'm sure Jennifer will be impressed!"

I shoved my hands into my jean pockets.

I couldn't believe David allowed this to happen—not after losing his twin, and not after the terrible accident he went through with his grandfather!

I'd have bet my house that David would never have gotten behind the wheel impaired or too tired to drive. I was wrong!

If David can succumb, anyone can!

What is it going to take for people to learn—for my own family to learn? Apparently, a lot!

APRIL 6, 2003

Every time I think of David drinking and driving, I keep thinking of a funeral I went to a few years ago for a young man I knew.

The police said that he had been drinking. He hadn't been speeding, but it didn't matter. The car had gone off the side of the road into a ditch and rolled.

After seeing that young man in the casket, I was so traumatized I nearly had to check myself into a mental hospital. When I walked to my truck, a group of the man's family and friends were standing in the parking lot. They reeked of liquor. It was obvious they were smashed. Several of them, including the dead man's brother, had beer bottles in their hands. I'm sure they were going to drive home.

How could they be so stupid? Their brother and friend would be alive if he hadn't been drinking and driving!

Thinking back to that moment today after nearly losing David, my thoughts were dark. I sensed the devil was somewhere near, smiling ear to ear. His work was done with that young man. He had even convinced his family and friends that they could drink and drive and that nothing would happen to them.

Now it seemed he'd been working on David.

APRIL 19, 2003

Lori and I drove several miles today in the country. We couldn't believe all the road-side crosses we saw.

Jennifer now has a roadside cross of her own. Until now, I never gave much thought to the crosses or what happened there. But now, I think a lot about them and wonder who died there: a teenager, young child, a mother or father, or a grandmother?

I will never again just pass by roadside crosses without thinking about the stories behind them, and the lost dreams of each one of them. I pray for all the broken hearts whose roadside markers of love are stained with their tears.

Praise God, we don't have to erect a roadside cross at the site of David's wreck! The incident shook him badly, as it did all of us. He is embarrassed and very upset with himself and has vowed to never, ever drink and drive again. Knowing David as I do, I have no doubt he will make good on that promise.

APRIL 20, 2003

It takes every ounce of strength I can muster to make myself go to work and make phone calls to homeowners.

As the owner of a roofing business, it's my job to keep my crew working. Their families depend on me. Between bidding jobs, making sure we have the right number of people on each site, scheduling work around the weather, ordering materials, handling unforeseen issues, and dealing with employees' issues, it's a lot to handle even when I'm at the top of my game. Since Jennifer died, the tasks are overwhelming. It all seems so meaningless.

Like a dog who'd rather hang out under a porch, fishing is my shelter, the place I go to hide from the world. Being on the water is the one place where I don't have to face anyone or anything. There, I am left alone: to yell, cry, pray, and just be me again.

Before Jennifer died, a day of fishing rejuvenated me and gave me the strength to go back to work. No more. Now, it's hard to find enjoyment in the things that once were so important to me. These days when I go fishing, there is no rejuvenation or pleasure. I go only because it's where I feel closest to Jennifer. It's where I most sense her presence. Maybe it's because she loved to go fishing with me when she was young. Now when I go, I talk to her, and she talks to me through my heart.

I always imagined Jennifer marrying a man that loved to hunt and fish. When they would come to visit, Lori and Jennifer could go shopping and go out for lunch, and

104

I could fish with her husband. Now, I'm left with a far different reality. I would fish every day if I could, just to feel my precious little girl close to me again.

APRIL 21, 2003

I had a dream about Jennifer last night, and, while I was still asleep, I knew I was dreaming. I wanted to wake up because, even in my dreams, thinking of Jennifer hurt.

APRIL 24, 2003

I did it again. I went into that cold room where the emptiness drapes over everything. I knew that once I stepped through the doorway, it would take me days to get over it. I went in anyway.

Why? Is it because, in reality, that cold room is the only tangible thing I have left of her?

"Why *her*, God? Did I do something wrong? I want my daughter back!!! I want my life back, please!!"

Sitting there on her bed, trembling with grief, I heard a little voice from somewhere far away, down deep in my soul, saying, "I'm so sorry. She will never be coming home."

Lori

APRIL 27, 2003

I keep having a recurring dream of being in a bathroom stall with blood all around me. I know that I am bleeding profusely, but I know, too, that I am not going to die from it.

That's how I feel now every day. I know I'm bleeding on the inside and can't stop it, but it won't kill me. It's just what I have to live with.

Not long ago, I dreamt that I had miscarried a baby girl. In my dream, I was telling someone about my miscarriage, and I pointed to Jennifer, who was about three or four years old at the time and said, "It makes me appreciate Jennifer so much more. I need to make sure I take a lot of pictures of her."

In another dream, Jennifer is about seven. She had left her pink Jelly shoes somewhere. I told her I'd get them for her. We started walking to the car, but suddenly she was no longer a child but was about nineteen. I was crying.

She stopped, looked at me, and said, with irritation, "You forgot to get my jellies, didn't you, Mom?"

I said, "No. I'm crying because if I have to lose you again, I won't be able to take it."

Dear God, Give me peace, even in my sleep. In Jesus' name, Amen.

Jim

APRIL 28, 2003
An emergency vehicle with its lights flashing came screaming behind me today when I was driving. My heart started pounding as it passed, and the next thing I knew, hot tears were streaming down my cheeks at the thought of where the ambulance was headed and what they would find there—a teenager who was badly injured, or maybe a mother or father?

Until Jennifer's accident, I never gave a lot of thought to ambulances. I merely wanted to get out of their way. Now, at the sound of sirens, I begin to tremble and pray.

APRIL 30, 2003
Probation was the sentence for Carolyn. I'm glad. They aren't requiring her to speak to schools, but we all hope she will when she's ready. It may take a long time. As hard as it would be for her to do, I think it would also be healing. Helping others can be one of God's greatest medicines.

In October, two teenage girls made a mistake of drinking too much. One got behind the wheel, and the other got in the car with her. That's a heartbreaking burden to carry for someone as young as Carolyn. I feel bad for her, for there's no way to undo what is done. There is only moving forward.

If Jennifer had survived, I believe she would have taken the opportunity from that night to encourage other teenagers not to make the same mistake.

God is a forgiving God. He told us to forgive others. All we can do now is to move on. I had asked the judge to give Carolyn another chance at life, and he did. I hope she makes the most of it and lives, not in sorrow, anguish, or guilt, but in happiness and purpose. Another chance is something that I wish Jennifer had.

MAY 1, 2003

When I go to Jennifer's grave, I know that she's not there. Only the shell of her body remains. That shell is the only tangible thing left of her on this earth. I think that's why I keep finding myself out there alone, even when it hurts.

Lori

MAY 1, 2003

There have been several times when I do what I did shortly after getting back from Aruba. I wait until I'm alone in the house, then start screaming at the top of my lungs for God to help me.

Afterward, with my throat raw and hurting, I collapse on the couch and sleep for two or three hours.

I'm beginning to think that these screaming fits are like a drug for me. It's God's way of knocking me out and giving me a few hours where I don't have to think about Jennifer not being here.

MAY 5, 2003

I saw a poster recently of twins—a boy and a girl. Both had died in separate accidents as a result of someone drinking and driving. The poster left me stone cold. It was unimaginable.

How did their parents survive going through it—not once, but twice?

Whenever I think of David's accident and how close we came to becoming those same parents, it feels like my heart has stopped. I can't even respond. Every part of me is frozen. I haven't been able to even talk to David about it. I have no words. Several times I've started to say something, and each time, nothing has come out.

Jim

MAY 5, 2003

Sometimes when I'm in public, I just sit and watch people as they go about their lives. They're all just on the move. I want to shout at them, "What are you doing? I lost my daughter!"

Instead, I say nothing, and they keep walking.

The world doesn't stop for anyone, not ever, not even for a beautiful girl named Jennifer.

MAY 11, 2003

It's Mother's Day—an impossibly hard day for Lori, just as Father's Day will be for me.

I would give up my life to tell Jennifer face to face that I love her and how proud I am that she's my daughter! I hope all parents are holding their children a little tighter this day.

MAY 23, 2003

Lori is a wreck. She misses Jennifer so much. I feel so helpless. I cannot make her pain go away. I can't make it go away for any of us.

Justin still refuses to talk much about Jennifer. I lie awake at night with a knife of fear twisting in my gut about him.

The other night I told him that I think not talking about her is making him sick. Still, he refuses to talk or even write in a journal.

As his father, how do I get him to talk to me when he doesn't open up to anyone about his feelings?

David came home for the holiday weekend. I picked him up at the airport, and we had time to talk, really talk. He told me how much he misses his sister and how bad he feels about his near-death wreck caused by drinking and driving. I'm glad he learned that lesson and that it didn't cost his life to do so. I'm glad too that he's open about talking about his feelings.

I wish Justin would do the same.

MAY 26, 2003

Until now, Memorial Day meant a fun, three-day weekend; otherwise, I never gave it much thought.

This Memorial Day, we have a grave to visit. I took a bouquet of flowers and put them on Jennifer's headstone. In every direction, graves were lined with fresh flowers and flags.

It never occurred to me how many people, besides military families, actually visit cemeteries on this day. *How could I not have known?*

Cemeteries are a good reminder that death has no minimum age. So many of the graves were of people who died too soon. I thought about each of the stories of the lives lost. How they lived, how they died, and all the heartbroken parents of the children buried there.

JUNE 6, 2003

Lori and I heard the wail of sirens pass our house, then stop a short way down the highway. We jumped in our Jeep to see what was happening.

Two cars had collided head-on and were a mangled mess of metal. Neither of us had heard the crash. Lights flashed, and sirens wailed as more responders arrived. Cars were stopped in both directions. Lori said, "This is what it must have looked like at Jennifer's accident, while we were sleeping."

The driver of one of the cars, a middle-aged man, died at the scene. Two others were taken to the hospital. We heard the ambulance sirens as they left. I hated the thought of the people who would soon be getting that terrible call.

I doubt that the man who died near our house got up that morning and said, "I think I'm going to die today." Death so often comes when we least expect it. I pray he was a man of faith.

Before Jennifer died, I thought I had all the time in the world to correct my mistakes and get things right. I used to think I had all the time I needed to get it right with God. Now, I pray every day for nonbelievers and my own soul too.

JUNE 7, 2003

I found myself just staring at our clock today. I couldn't take my eyes off of it. I would give anything to go back in time to before Jennifer died.

JUNE 8, 2003

I wonder what Jennifer's journey from Earth to Heaven was like. Did she see a great and welcoming light? Did she see us weeping for her in the hospital? Was she trying to comfort us?

We'll never know, not until it's our turn. But we do know, because of God's promises, He was and is there for her.

Lori

JUNE 10, 2003

I don't write much in my journal because quite literally, there are no words to describe what I'm going through. The only way is through metaphors. I thought of one today.

In everything I do, it's like I'm walking through thick mud. I struggle to keep my balance with each step and fight not to get sucked into the darkness.

I keep telling myself that sooner or later, I'll make it to dry land. So, I just keep moving.

What choice do I have?

Jim

JUNE 12, 2003

A longtime client called me today about his roof, and he started the conversation by asking, "So how have you been, Jim?"

Well, what was I supposed to say?

I told him that it is as good as it's going to get for now, after having all the wind knocked out of me in October.

"Oh, what happened in October?"

I told him I lost my only daughter.

"Oh, I remember reading about it. I'm sorry about that."

He's sorry about that? Well, thank you very much!

In less than eight months, the world, and even those I know, had forgotten "about that."

What's going to happen in five or twenty years from now? Is she only going to be remembered by us? I don't want people ever to forget her!

I don't expect people to keep sending us cards, but it hurts when people can't even remember that our daughter died!

I guess I'm going to have to get used to it.

People are going to forget. Just like I did when it happened to the *other guy.*

JUNE 13, 2003

I feel like I've been thrown into a roller coaster with no seat belt. I am all over the place.

Mostly I'm mad and don't know what to do with my anger.

Will this roller-coaster ride ever end? Am I on it for the rest of my life?

Somehow, the devil has managed to worm his way back into my head and is saying, "What you need right now, Jim, is a little fun." Some part of me thinks he's right.

I've spent the last couple of weeks daydreaming about running away with my old girlfriend. It sounds crazy—crazy, stupid, and cruel. I just want to go somewhere with someone, where there's no pain.

It's like I'm living a scene from a movie with the devil saying, "Leave, go have fun!" and God whispering in my other ear, "Trust in Me! I will heal your heart and soul. Trust in Me. You will see your daughter in a second because that's all earthly life is, a second in time. Trust in Me! I'm your seat belt."

JUNE 15, 2003
My foreman said Justin had been showing up late for work and not doing much while he's there. I talked to Justin about it this afternoon. He said he's been really tired and having trouble sleeping because he's thinking about Jennifer.

I can relate!

Justin told me not to worry about it and that he can handle it. I hope so!

Lori

JUNE 15, 2003
Jim rarely carried his cell phone until lately. He used to leave it sitting on the counter when he was outside working in the yard or in his workshop. Recently though, he's taking it with him everywhere and making a lot of calls outside the house and in the garage.

Yesterday, when he was outside mowing, I saw his phone on the bed. I picked it up and went to his recent calls. The same number appeared over and over. I didn't have to ask him whose number it was.

I don't know what to do.

JUNE 16, 2003
I can't believe what I heard today! Jim was talking on the phone with his old girl-friend. He was on the front porch. I was in our bedroom above and opened the window. I could hear every word he was saying. It was clear that nothing had happened between them, at least not yet! But just like before, it was his macho tone that bothered me. *Why was he doing that?*

I know why he's making these calls, even if he doesn't! And I know his heart. I don't believe he has any intention of being physically unfaithful, but he's vulnerable. I just want him to wake up before he does something stupid. I think he's in more trouble than he realizes.

I heard Jim ask her if she wants to go out on our boat when she comes to town next week.

Our boat? That's where we go to have fun!

He said it would be fun. They could have a little wine, and he could show her around the lake.

I couldn't believe what he was saying! I'd planned to let this thing go because I'm pretty certain he will come to his senses before anything bad happens. I don't think from what Jim has said the woman has any motives other than trying to be a good friend to someone who is hurting. But if they go out on that boat, whether Jim thinks so or not, he's setting himself for temptation beyond what he may be able to handle!

I've been stewing all night, barely sleeping, thinking about what to say to him. It's 4 a.m., and I still don't know what to say. I feel sick and shaky, the more I think about it. I need to talk to him about this before she comes to town. I just can't stand the thought of doing so right now. I don't have it in me to fight.

JUNE 17, 2003

I'm so upset. Jim has been spending a lot of time on the computer, which isn't normal. He'd rather do anything than sit at a computer. We share the same one so it's easy for me to check what emails had been deleted and sent to the trash. It's clear he doesn't understand he also has to empty the trash for them to completely disappear.

I can't believe what I found today. I should be angry.

I'm not. I'm scared to death.

Jim

I'm so mad right now I can hardly see straight. It's the middle of the night, and there is no way I can sleep.

I came home today and found Lori standing in our kitchen, arms crossed with a stack of papers on the counter—copies of the emails I sent my old girlfriend.

I glanced down at them but refused to look any closer. "You've been spying on me?"

"It's not hard when they're on the computer we share!"

We stood there glaring at each other, her arms still crossed, mine now on my hips. I felt like a little kid being confronted by his mother, and I didn't like it one bit.

"I haven't done anything wrong!"

"Really, Jim? You want to read what you wrote and then tell me that?"

My face and neck felt hot with anger and embarrassment.

"And now you're making plans with her to go out on our boat?"

"Yeah, and what's wrong with that? Nothing has happened! Nothing's going to happen! I just want to go out with a friend for a couple of hours on our boat. The same boat where we take lots of our family and friends. It's not like we're going to have sex! She's not like that, and neither am I!"

"You're playing with fire!"

"Yeah? Well, I know how not to get burned!"

"You have no idea what you're getting yourself into! This has to stop before something happens that can't be undone."

114

"Lori, you can't tell me who I can and can't be friends with. She's a friend. That's all! A friend I like to talk to, someone who has been through the same thing we have. Having her as a friend is helping me—helping us!"

"Yeah, right, Jim. Helping us?" She scoffed. She literally scoffed. "Well, let me tell you, this isn't helping us! Not at all! This thing you have going with her has to stop."

"I don't have a thing going with her or anyone else. I'm not going to stop talking to a friend just because you're feeling insecure about it. I told you, nothing happened! Nothing is going to happen!" As I spoke, I thought my words sounded shallow, even to me.

"You don't know that!"

In our many years together, I've seen Lori mad at me, but never more than she was tonight when she said, "And I'm telling you right now, you're not taking her out on our boat. That isn't going to happen!"

"Lori, I don't tell you what to do, and you're not going to start telling me what I can and can't do!"

JUNE 18, 2003
When I got home from work today, Lori's car was gone. I found a note on my pillow.

Lori

JUNE 20, 2003
I keep asking myself, how'd we get to this point? *Are we going to be like every other statistic...just another marriage that fell apart after the death of a child?*

Ever since Jennifer died, one of my greatest fears has been losing Jim. Not because he doesn't love me, but because there isn't enough left of me to love. And the truth is, I don't have the energy to do anything about it, even if I knew what to do.

I left him a note saying I didn't want to see him until I had time to think. I didn't tell him where I was going. I told him that if anyone asked, to tell them that I went to see

Chris in Wichita. Instead, I'm holed up in a hotel in Kansas City. I called Chris and told her everything. She agreed to cover for me if anyone asks.

If I thought for one moment that Jim actually loved this woman, and he would be happier with her, then I would let him go. But I know him! He's just as lost as I am and grasping for anything that can make him feel better—and right now, that's her. But if he were to leave me for her and turn his back on his life, it would destroy him. I know it.

I'm also too sad and hurt to stay in the house with him. I just can't stand the thought of it.

Jim

JUNE 20, 2003
Two days ago, I thought to myself, "Fine! If she's going to leave, then I am too!" I threw a few things into a duffle bag and went over to where my old girlfriend was staying. I picked her up, and we drove around town talking.

At one point, I pulled the truck over, looked straight at her, and thought, "What am I doing?"

I knew what I had to do. I turned the car around and took her straight back to where I had picked her up. I let out a huge sigh of relief when she got out of the car and walked away. I think she was glad too.

I'm just happy she didn't know about the packed bag in the back seat.

As she walked away, I felt like I was looking at the backside of the devil. Not that the woman as a person was the devil, but that he had used her to get to me. This had nothing to do with wanting anything from the woman, even sex. It had everything to do with escape, and the evil one knew it.

JUNE 23, 2003
Lori's been gone for five days. She won't take my calls. I don't know where she is. She promised me in the note she wouldn't do anything to hurt herself. I believe her;

otherwise, I'd have the police searching for her. She said she just wanted time alone and didn't want anyone bothering her. She said she'd contact me when she was ready.

I can't sleep. I can't work. I can't do anything. I'm so mad at her for leaving and not telling me where she is and if she's okay. And I'm so mad and embarrassed at myself for causing this. I just don't know what to do to fix it. *How can I begin if I don't even know where she is?*

I'm so mad. I feel like stomping outside and kicking down the nearest tree. I don't know what else to do.

I'm too humiliated to call anyone and explain what has happened. *How could they possibly understand?*

Lori

JUNE 28, 2003

The last few days have been a blur of crying. I've barely eaten. I feel sick. All I've done is stare at worthless TV programs, pray, and sleep. I put a *Do Not Disturb* sign on my door, and for days I've barely said a word to anyone. I haven't let the maids clean the room since I got here. I'm just glad no one has called the police or welfare services.

It's been ten days now since I left. I finally took Jim's call and told him where I am. He's on his way over.

Jim

JULY 1, 2003

When Lori opened the hotel room door, she looked terrible. Her eyes were red and swollen. She looked like she hadn't slept in a long time. Her hair was tangled. I don't think she had brushed it since she left.

What have I done to her? How could I have done this? She, of all people, doesn't deserve this!

I walked in, but neither of us knew what to say. I should have just taken her in my arms, but I didn't. I knew I was wrong, and although I didn't mean to, I found myself acting defensive. My arms were crossed, and I was shaking my head.

"So, this is how it's going to be?" she said. "We're going to be just like all those other couples who didn't make it after their child died?"

I moved to the window, opened the shades enough to see outside. "I don't know, are we?" I didn't want our marriage to be some sad statistic, but I didn't say so.

"I called her," Lori said.

I turned around and looked at her in disbelief.

"I told her that you're confused. She told me she didn't know what you wanted. She said that she was worried about you. I told her that she didn't need to worry about you. I would take care of you."

"I don't need you to take care of me! I'm fine."

"You're not fine, Jim!"

I turned again to the window. I couldn't bring myself to look at her. I thought of the emails and phone calls I made to the other woman. I hadn't been fair to her either. She thought she was counseling a friend through a hard time when, all the while, I was fantasizing about running away with her. I didn't even know who that man was.

"You're right." I finally said, "I'm not okay—and Lori, neither are you."

I sank down on the bed. I didn't have the energy to fight, argue, or even talk. I knew that whatever it was I had been seeking from this other relationship no longer mattered. I wasn't going to find it.

Lori sat down next to me and took my hand. Hers was wet with tears. "None of this is going to bring her back, Jim. None of it."

"I know." And I did. In the last few days, it was clear that I had no choice but to move forward, living with my grief. There was no hiding from it. There was no running from it. There was only living through it.

"Jim, something came to me this morning. There's only one way that we're going to survive losing Jennifer—and that's when we get used to living without her. When we get used to her not being here. When we get used to knowing that all that we will ever have of her is what we had. And the only way any of that is going to happen is with time. Time doesn't heal wounds. Time is just going to give us a chance to accept what is—our new reality.

And, Jim, the only way we are going to survive long enough to get to that point is by the grace of God and holding on to each other. When Jennifer died, the first thing you said to me was to hold on to my faith. You were right. It's what is going to get us through this."

Her words were the most painfully honest words I had ever heard.

I pulled Lori into my arms and held her as tight as I could.

Then we sat holding hands for a long time and prayed as we never had before.

We were both exhausted. I knew that this thing with the other woman, whatever it had been, was over, and I told Lori so. I knew I would never contact her again. Lori knew it too. It's why she agreed to come home. The boat ride never happened, nor would it ever.

Before we walked out of that hotel room, Lori picked up the stack of emails she had brought from home ... the ones I had written to the other woman. She dumped them in the waste bin. I glanced at them, and thought, *Good, and the devil can stay in there, too, along with the rest of the trash.*

Watching Lori's car taillights ahead of me as we drove home, I found myself praying the whole way, thanking God that I had never crossed the line of being physically unfaithful. Some couples find a way of coming back from sexual infidelity. I don't know how, but they do. I don't know if Lori and I would have recovered if I had done so or not. I just thank God we didn't have to find out.

Thank you, Lord, for not letting this go any further. Thank you for my loving wife, who is willing to give me another chance! Forgive me for hurting her. Let me never fall into such temptations again.

Lori

JULY 6, 2003

When Jim came into the hotel room in KC, he was drawn and pale. He was hurting. When he finally told me that he was done with the woman, I knew he meant it.

The truth was, I felt sorry for him. I felt sorry for me, for all of us. We just wanted our pain to be over.

I realize now why marriages fail so often after losing a child. Staying together means not only dealing with our own grief but each other's. It would have been easier for me to stay mad enough at Jim to walk away from him forever. Fighting for our marriage, and working through our issues, requires more energy, and we have so little of it.

JULY 9, 2003

We've got to stop saying we "lost" a daughter. Lost implies we did something wrong. You can't lose a child without some neglect. Jennifer died. Our/my daughter died. And lost can also imply never finding. WE WILL see Jennifer again. She is not lost!

JULY 10, 2003

I found a school paper in one of Jennifer's notebooks today. She was writing about her family for an English class last year. I don't think she was in a very good mood when she wrote it. She wrote that she used to fight a lot with her mom. She said she thought I was, "Pretty cool for the most part and that she loved me a lot, but that I was way overprotective." She said, "she wished I'd get off her back."

I wonder what she would have written had she known what was coming. I don't think it would have been that.

Jim

JULY 12, 2003

When I think of all that happened recently, I cringe. It wasn't fair to Lori. It wasn't fair to my old girlfriend. It wasn't fair to our sons and our families—and it wasn't fair to God. Leaving wasn't the answer. It never was, and I knew it all along, but just thinking about it gave me an excuse to think about something besides facing the empty pit inside of me.

I wanted to go somewhere, anywhere, back to the time before I had a sword piercing my heart.

I'm ashamed of what I did. I know it will take a long time to heal what I've done to our marriage and for Lori to be able to trust me again.

I thank God for the wisdom and understanding of my wife! *What a fool I've been!*

JULY 13, 2003

When I looked at the clock last night, it said it was way past midnight.

The moon was so bright it looked like midday instead of the middle of the night.

People have been looking at that moon forever since humans have been on this planet. Thousands of years separate my eyes from others who have gazed upon it. Along with the sun and the stars, it is one of the few experiences we all still have in common, binding us with those far away and those long, long ago.

I haven't been out to Jennifer's grave for a while. I fought the urge to get up and go, even if it was the middle of the night. I imagined standing in the cemetery with the moonbeams reflecting off my shoulders and onto her grave.

Instead of getting up, I rolled over in bed. I couldn't bear the thought of standing out there, knowing she could no longer see the same light as me.

Lori

JULY 13, 2003

Jim sees Justin at work, but he rarely comes here. When he does, he either heads to the basement to watch TV, or he goes outside. I don't know if he's tired, depressed, or what, but it isn't normal, even for him. I've tried to talk to him, but he doesn't have much to say. I've asked him to come to church with us, but he won't. I told him I'm worried, and he said that I worry too much. "I'm just tired from working all day in the heat. I'm fine, Mom."

I don't think he is.

JULY 20, 2003

Jim and I have talked about seeking professional grief counseling. If we didn't have the support we do, we would go.

I have my mom and sister, who are as insightful as anyone I've ever known. Chris and Lisa are there for me at every turn. Our family has our church community, which upholds us every week. And we have our good friends, Lon and Christine, who come every week to spend time with us.

Jim and I have each other, and, most importantly, we have God. If we didn't have these areas of support, we would seek professional therapy.

If I ever decide to go, I'm only interested in talking to someone who's lost a teenager, especially a teenage daughter. Otherwise, how could they have any idea what we are going through? They couldn't. So, what would be the point?

I've told Jim that if he wants us to go, we can. We've told the boys that if they want to go, we will make that happen. As it is, we all agree that no amount of counseling is going to change why we are sad.

Jim

JULY 24, 2003

Lori found a paper Jennifer had written describing us. Her words about me nearly broke my heart. "My dad is real laid back and is always busy with work and hunting. He doesn't pay a lot of attention to us kids. But I know he loves me because he buys me roses, or if my car breaks down, he always fixes it. I do wish I had a closer relationship with him."

Hearing those words with her gone is hard to take. I feel like tearing up that paper and never letting anyone see it, but I can't do that. I need to tell others not to be like me. It's too late for me, but it's not too late for them.

"I wish I had a closer relationship with my dad." Those ten words eat at me.

I used to listen to the song "Cats in the Cradle." It is about a dad who was so busy with his life he didn't take time for his son. Somehow, I never made the connection that I was the dad in that song.

I was just trying to take care of my family, keep a roof over our head, and food on our table. I worked really hard to make that happen. But I was so busy building a life for our family that I lost sight of what was most important. I wasn't there for my kids like I should have been. When I had free time, I was mostly out hunting and fishing. I spent more time with Justin and David because they helped me on the job.

Jennifer would occasionally come out with me to fish, but as she got older, she had other interests. For a lot of her life, I thought, "I have the boys, and Lori has Jennifer." Looking back, all I can think is, "What a crock! What a stupid thing to think!"

JULY 25, 2003

I'm pretty sure I had a hammer in my hand before I could walk. I grew up working for my dad's construction company. When he retired, I worked for my uncle's construction company.

After we got married, I worked construction during the days and as a DJ in the evenings, making $250 a night. That was big money for us then.

When Lori went into labor with Justin, I was doing a private party at the country club. Lori was worried I wouldn't get there in time. As soon as the gig was over, I bolted out the door and got there in time to see my first son born. It was a new start for us, just like the fresh snow blanketing the hospital's parking lot when I walked out the next morning.

My work as a DJ was helping buy baby supplies, but it cut into my time at home. I was either swinging a hammer or spinning a turntable. Most of the time, Lori was taking care of Justin by herself. It was hard on her.

In the early 1980s, I heard the railroad in Topeka was hiring welders. I'd helped Dad weld over the years and was pretty good at it. I was thrilled when I got the job. I didn't have to work in the rain and cold as I had most of my life in construction. I worked forty hours a week with the railroad and then could go home. It was great until the railroads started laying off workers. I was one of them.

I had a lot of sleepless nights worrying about paying bills. I heard the oil fields in Texas needed welders, so we headed south. We'd barely hit the Texas border when the oil industry tanked. While oil was struggling, construction was booming, so I strapped on my nail pouch and went back to framing houses. That worked for a while until the company began laying off workers.

Lori and I had just bought a trailer. The morning after I was laid off, I put on my painting overalls and told Lori I was off to try and get a job painting.

"Why are you wearing your paint scrubs now? Even if you find a job, it'll be a while before you start."

"If I find something. I want them to know I'm ready to go to work right now."

Lori kissed me as I walked out the door. "Wearing your paint clothes is smart."

I walked into the largest paint store in town and explained to the man behind the counter that I was looking for work. I asked him which of his customers was buying the most paint. He looked at me and laughed. "You're in luck. He just walked through the door."

I introduced myself to that man and told him that I needed a job. I told him I had a wife, a young son, and was good with a paintbrush.

It was late that night before I got home. Fresh paint covered my overalls. I had worked all day.

After several months, I was painting the inside of office buildings. We didn't wear respirators, and there was no way to open the windows in the tall buildings. We worked with all kinds of chemicals. One of my coworkers got really sick and ended up in the hospital with breathing issues. The doctors said they didn't know what was wrong with him. I went to visit him in the hospital. As I stood looking at him wearing his oxygen mask, I thought to myself, "I know what's wrong with him. He's breathing chemicals all day long, just like I am."

I went home and learned that Lori was pregnant...with twins!

I didn't want to end up like my painting buddy, too sick to take care of my kids. We sold the trailer and moved back to Topeka. The town had a lot of damaged roofs from a recent hailstorm. My dad and uncle owned several rental properties and asked if I'd roof them. The next thing I knew, there'd be a neighbor standing under the house, hollering up at me, "Hey, you want to do my roof next?"

I realized I couldn't do it all myself. I looked for the hardest working and nicest guys I could find and hired them. We set about doing things right. We got a lot busier. Some more new guys started showing up wanting to work. A couple of them were just out of prison. I told them I believe in second chances and agreed to hire them so long as they were very clear about what I expected of them. I never had any trouble.

I expected all my workers to show up, work hard, and not be jerks. I worked alongside them through every kind of weather. If it was too hot or too cold for me, it was for them as well. I never wanted to be the boss who would drive up in a big fancy truck and yell at them to work harder.

With my crew, they never had to worry whether or not I'd pay them on time. I always did. If they needed a little extra money to carry them through, I'd make sure they got it. Most of the time, I was repaid, but not always.

I wanted to prove to our community that roofers weren't all foul-mouthed shysters out to rip people off. I'm not a rough guy. I wanted to be the roofer people could trust and count on. And I was. Soon we were working two crews.

I loved roofing and working with people. I'd go crazy if I had to sit in an office. I can't be locked up. I loved the end of a project, knowing I'd made something that would last a long time, and that I'd helped a homeowner. I loved hard work and the accomplishments that came with it.

For nearly eighteen years, I worked alongside my men. We often worked from sunup to sundown, including many Saturdays. In the early years, I also took care of all the bidding, bookkeeping, ordering supplies, marketing, and talking to customers.

I knew I was working too hard, but I felt that I needed to keep everything going. I felt responsible for our family and responsible for my crew and their families. I knew what it felt like to be laid off, and I never wanted to do that to anyone. So I made sure we always had enough work, except in the winter when no roofers were working.

Physically, I began to hurt. All over. It went on for a long time. Then one winter several years ago, it got really bad. I thought I had a weird stomach flu. I started to take aspirin for the pain. The more it hurt, the more I took.

I got up one night to go to the bathroom. Just as I was returning to the bed, I collapsed, landing on the end of the mattress. I thought I was dying. I called out for Lori. She was sound asleep. I said I needed to go to the hospital. She murmured something, then rolled over. I was too sick to say any more, and I either fell asleep or went unconscious.

When I opened my eyes, it was morning. Lori was standing over me, her eyes wide in horror. "Jim! You're white as a ghost! Get in the car." I was doubled over in pain all the way to the hospital with Lori apologizing the entire trip for falling back to sleep. I felt bad that she felt bad.

The staff took one look at me, started an IV, and then began pumping blood into me—a lot of blood. I could feel the fluid as it entered my system; it felt ice cold. I ended up needing nine pints of blood. I had a bleeding ulcer. The physician said he could not believe I was alive. He said it was lucky I had not had a heart attack or stroke.

No one could figure out how I could have lost so much blood without knowing it over a long period of time. We finally figured out how it happened. It was always at night when I had to go to the bathroom. Not wanting to wake Lori, I'd keep the lights off. If the lights had been on, I would have seen black stools and, later, as it got worse, a toilet full of blood. As it was, I had no idea.

After several days in the hospital, I knew I couldn't continue doing all I was doing. I turned over all the on-site work to my foreman. I concentrated on doing the bids, ordering supplies, and working with customers.

But instead of using the extra time to be more with the kids, I did more hunting and fishing. *Oh, God! What was I thinking?*

Lori

JULY 26, 2003

Several months ago, I woke up overwhelmed with grief. I was scared. If I didn't do something, I was not going to survive the day. I got in the car.

Mom saw my car pull into her driveway.

She took one look at me, took me by the hand, and led me to the couch. I was so emotionally exhausted I couldn't stay upright. Mom pulled my head into her lap and began stroking my hair, just like she used to do when I was a little girl.

Mom didn't say anything to me, only to God. I heard the aching pain in her voice as she talked softly to God. I hated how much pain she was in and how there was nothing I could do about it. She was grieving losing Jennifer and losing the happy daughter she had always known. I hated the pain we both felt, but I didn't know how to stop it. Neither of us did.

And so began the pattern of what I did when I didn't know what else to do: I went home to my mom. Sometimes I would close my eyes, and I'd listen to her softly singing old hymns.

Occasionally my dad would join us on the couch, but it was clear he had no idea what to do when I was upset. Sometimes, Mom would ask him if he'd like to pray out loud for us. She was wise in that way, letting him know that he was needed.

Yesterday I was really in bad shape and found myself standing at my parents' front door, where my dad looked at me with panic in his eyes. Mom wasn't home.

He sat with me on the couch, looking around helplessly. I hated that he was so uncomfortable, but I couldn't help him any more than I could help myself. And I couldn't stop crying.

"Lori, how about we go somewhere and get some coffee."

I didn't want to go anywhere but knew my dad was desperate to do something. I shrugged and said, "Okay."

I'm sure those sitting near us must have wondered what was going on with this elderly gentleman and the emotional wreck of a woman he was with, but if it bothered Dad, he never let it show.

On the way home, when I finally had quit crying, he said proudly, "Don't you feel better now." It was a statement, not a question.

Before I could stop myself, I said, "No!" Then I saw his expression. He was crushed. I felt horrible and said quickly, "Yes." His expression changed to relief. "I really do, Dad. Thank you." I meant it. I did feel better. His solution was to change my focus, even if only briefly, and it worked. But I still wanted to see Mom.

Last night in bed, I pulled the covers over my shoulders and realized that everyone, including Dad, was coping in whatever way they could. There's no handbook for fathers on how to deal with a daughter who has lost her only daughter.

And though it hadn't been much, I realized that sometimes the best help is just a cup of coffee offered by a loving father.

Jim

AUGUST 5, 2003

I was called out to a home to look at a leaking roof. It turned out that the homeowner was one of the nurses in the operating room the night Jennifer died.

She told me the surgeon had worked on Jennifer for a long time trying to save her. She said he continued long after everyone else in the room knew it was no use. The doctor refused to stop until another physician came in and told him gently that it was time to stop. Jennifer was gone.

When the doctor finally came into the waiting room to tell us that he had done everything he could for Jennifer, he meant it. I didn't realize then the terrible toll it had taken on him and the entire hospital team.

It was a relief to hear these details. I realized that once the accident happened, if Jennifer could have been saved, she would have been. The first responders just happened to be around the corner from the accident, and the top surgical staff was on hand when she was brought in, but still, none of it was enough to save her.

AUGUST 10, 2003

Some days it feels like my heart has turned into iron and now it's reinforced and immune to pain. But then I feel it—a twisting, searing pain so deep, impaled like the blade of a sword, embedded so deep it can never be removed.

God, how am I supposed to live with a sword piercing my heart?

AUGUST 12, 2003

Sometimes I'm amazed at how well we've been able to hide our pain from others.

Last night I woke to the sound of Lori crying again.

I was so tired at that moment that I thought there is just no way we could continue on. Every time she cries like that, it is as though we're reliving again the night Jennifer died.

I shook Lori and asked her to come with me outside on the balcony and get some fresh air. She didn't respond; it was as though she was still asleep, yet crying.

I was suddenly enraged at something I couldn't define. I wanted to carry Lori out to the car and drop her off at the home of anyone who was thinking of drinking and driving, and say, "Look what I have for you now! A mom crying for her daughter! A wife that I can't help!"

Instead, I just rubbed her back, not knowing what else to do. Lori whispered something. I moved closer. "What's happened to us? What kind of people have we become?"

Lori

AUGUST 14, 2003

One of my uncontrollable crying fits inexplicably hit me earlier this week while we were at Jim's parents' house. Jim's mom sat with me on the couch. She kept looking around the room. I knew she was hoping someone would come in who would know what to do. My nose was running so badly that she hurriedly left the room and returned with a box of tissues.

It was a small thing, but she looked relieved that she had been able to do something helpful. Like my dad taking me out for coffee, this was her way of offering comfort. I needed something, and she got it. I needed more but what I needed was not something she or anyone else on this earth could give me. I was grateful instead for the tissues.

When I had finally stopped crying, I went outside and found Jim's dad working on his old convertible. The rumble seat was open. I remember Jennifer arguing with David and Justin about who got to sit there. All the grandkids loved to pile into that car with Grandpa at the wheel. Leon took one look at me and motioned for me to sit with him on a bench. His hands began to tremble. I was surprised when he started to cry. "I miss her so much, you know."

I had to look away. It was hard to see this strong man, so capable of fixing almost anything, sitting there, surrounded with tools he loved, weeping. He had nothing to use to repair his broken heart.

"I've been thinking a lot about the day that I die," he said. "I know when it happens, I'll get to see her, my Sugar Jennifer. And I know that my dad and my mom will be there too." I nodded my head in agreement.

"My mom died when I was two years old, you know. I can't remember her. I can't imagine her face."

Not being able to remember my mom's face was something I could not imagine. It struck me how blessed I've been that I'd lived long enough, and Jennifer, too, that we knew each other so well. That was something I hadn't thought much about.

"I like to think about when I die and will see my mom, my dad, and my Sugar Jennifer. I think that will be a really good day."

I liked his smile when he said it.

Jim

AUGUST 16, 2003

Jennifer loved the color purple, so whenever I see it, I think of her. In her room, there is a pair of light purple boots.

Since she died, purple ribbons now adorn my truck antenna. It may not be very manly, but I don't care.

Last month, I went to my first bass tournament of the year. I didn't feel much like going, but Lori thought I should, and I wanted to prove that I'm okay to the people who have been worried about me. Some of the guys there didn't know about Jennifer's death. But before the tournament was over, nearly every boat was decorated with purple ribbons that I handed out.

Before the tournament, I ordered some large plaques to give out to all the first-place winners in the various categories. Jennifer's photo was on the plaque with the words, "In memory of Jennifer Dultmeier."

I was determined that I was going to win one. And I did.

The walls of my study are lined with all kinds of plaques I've won over the years, but none means more, or ever will, than that one with Jennifer's beautiful, smiling face.

AUGUST 20, 2003
It's crazy! Every time I open the newspaper, I read about some other poor teenager killed in an accident. Each one guts me. Another family is having to face that phone call.

The deaths of these strangers are starting to affect me. My friends are growing restless with me. I can feel it. They want the old Jim back. But that good ol' Jim died late one night in October, and he's never coming back.

I can't quit thinking about Jennifer's accident. It's killing me that I can't talk to her about that night.

AUGUST 25, 2003
I don't know what's going on with Justin. He's been driving our big trash truck and showing up late. He was late again today. I tried to talk to him about it, but he shrugged it off. "It's only half an hour late, Dad! It's no big deal."

"No big deal? I had eight guys standing around waiting for you! They couldn't start tearing off the roof without that truck. Half an hour—eight guys—that's four hours of work between them! Four hours that I have to pay them, not only their hourly wages, plus nearly double that when I figure in worker's comp and taxes! How about I start taking that time out of your paycheck, and you can see how long you can afford to be half an hour late!"

I know Justin's grieving, but this is ridiculous. I don't want to have to fire my own son, but this just can't keep happening.

AUGUST 27, 2003
This morning I wished I could call 1-800-GOD and ask him a few questions. God must have been laughing because I looked down and saw my Bible. He was probably thinking: You don't need a phone. I've already given you the manual on how to live your life!

I opened it up and started reading. I've read more of the Bible since Jennifer died than I have my whole life.

132

I know God answers prayers in His own way and on His own time. I don't think we are meant to like or understand many of his answers.

I can't imagine what would have happened to our family if we hadn't had our faith or hadn't been surrounded by friends of faith who helped carry us when we were too weak to go on.

AUGUST 28, 2003

Recently, I met a man who lost his young son decades ago. He was shaking with rage when he told me about it. "How could a loving God allow him to die?"

I know how he feels. I've often been angry with God. I felt sorry for the heartbroken man.

I've been thinking about that guy all day. The intensity of his emotions bothers me.

Please, Lord. Don't let me be that man—still angry, decades from now.

Lori

SEPTEMBER 2, 2003

Jim has been beating himself up over how much time he spent away from the kids and me.

Looking back, I had no idea the pressure Jim must have been under to keep us afloat. There were times when I would say, "Jim, we need more money." And somehow, he always found a way. He always had. His mom told me that one summer when he was a boy, he started selling tomatoes he had grown at home. He piled them in his red wagon and took them to one of the busier streets in Topeka. He set up a card table, and instead of lemonade, he sold tomatoes.

His dad gave him a scale and told him that he should sell them by the pound. What Leon didn't realize was that Jim didn't know how to read it. So, when a customer stopped by and selected their tomatoes, Jim would carefully set them in the scale, write down a number, any number, and then randomly tell them the price. That was

Jim. The "fake it until you make it" motto could have been written for him. It's what I've always loved about him. He makes things happen.

Jim has always been generous with his time and money. He's the helper in our family. Whenever it snows, I know where to find Jim. If he isn't out shoveling our driveway, he's at one of the neighbors doing theirs.

SEPTEMBER 3, 2003

It's been eleven months. I can honestly say, right this minute, that I can think about things other than Jennifer for a while. For the first time, I can actually say, "It's a nice day today," and mean it.

Even though I don't always want it to be so, my life is going on. It will never be as good as it was, but it will be livable. And I guess that's okay. Jennifer is not here, and that's a fact. But I've changed. I will never be the same. I have a much deeper understanding of my spirituality. But I'm not as full of life as before. Maybe that will change.

I still isolate myself a lot, and my tolerance for people is short. When I'm alone, there is no one to impress, entertain, or think about. It's easy. Unless it's with Jim or the boys, being with people is hard work. I know people see a change in me, and the people closest to me just go with the flow. Others will just have to take me or leave me. Either choice is fine with me. I don't have the energy to try to please anyone. I'm just taking care of Jim, our sons, and myself. Jim still comes first. I'm doing all I instinctively know to do to keep us from falling apart.

Each month I feel a little less numb, and I have a little more of me to give.

Dear God, Thank you for helping me. In Jesus' name, Amen.

SEPTEMBER 4, 2003

Sometimes I wish I lived on an island where there were no people and no expectations of us. Even going to church is hard. My saving grace has been that every Sunday, we arrive late and leave early. It allows us to go, listen, and leave. I need my church family more than they will ever know. I don't think we could have survived without their love and support, but it's all I can do to show up each week. It's all the energy I have.

On the days we've lingered after the service, some people approach me with puppy dog sad eyes, pitying me. Others tell me of their struggles as if it might help me to

134

know life is hard for them too. I should be asking them if they're okay. I should be saying, "My daughter is fine! Her journey is done." I should be rejoicing that she is in Heaven with no more struggles. *Is that something I will ever really grasp?* At times I do; other times, I collapse at the thought that she isn't here.

As I was leaving church last Sunday, I walked toward a group of my friends who were laughing and having a good time. As soon as they saw me, their expressions dropped. They stopped talking. They looked at me with remorse and pity. One of them said solemnly, "Oh, hi, Lori. How are you?"

I was mortified that I'd suddenly become this person where everyone feels like they are walking on eggshells. I felt bad for them. I felt bad for me. I wanted to scream, "Just get me out of here!"

When did I become this downer of a person?

Jim

SEPTEMBER 4, 2003

It's hard to do, but I look back at that man who fantasized about running away with another woman and shake my head. Thank God I have a wife who helped me walk away from that madness before it destroyed us.

That's what it would have done if I had followed through and left. It would have destroyed me. It would have destroyed Lori, my relationship with my kids, and our families. *How would I ever have faced any of them again? How would I have ever looked at myself in the mirror?*

I wouldn't have been able to, not without complete loathing.

Lori told me the other day that she thinks she's suffering from PTSD because of all that happened with the other woman. She wasn't joking. That's on me. Knowing that I caused my wife to feel that way—that one's a hard thing to take.

SEPTEMBER 5, 2003

Today was a good day until I thought I was having a heart attack. All it took was one wrong look at our bookcase, loaded with family pictures. And there she was, the face of my beautiful daughter.

Time stopped.

It hurts the most when the sword of pain twists without warning. I felt the room spin.

Like a wound waiting for the seal of a scab, it took over an hour for my heart to calm enough for me to breathe normally.

What happens if the scab won't form? Will I bleed to death from this broken heart? Sometimes I swear I will.

SEPTEMBER 6, 2003

I'm shaking so hard that I can hardly see straight. Justin came home and told us that he's hooked on meth. *My God! Meth! Are you kidding me?* I feel like I'd been smashed in the gut with a crowbar.

He's been working for me for several months, and I had no idea. I knew he's been struggling but thought it was from depression over Jennifer. *How could I not have known? How did he hide this?*

SEPTEMBER 7, 2003

Justin said he wanted to go to rehab, so we've made some calls and dropped him off. We are reeling. The counselor we met at rehab said that people do recover from meth, but how? Justin has to kick this! WE CANNOT LOSE ANOTHER CHILD!

SEPTEMBER 8, 2003

I can't quit thinking about Justin and how he's doing. He looked so sad when we left him. I couldn't sleep all night.

I couldn't feel any worse than if he'd taken out a two-by-four board and hit me over the head. Lori isn't sleeping either. I want to hold her in my arms and tell her that everything will be okay, but I don't know that it will.

Dear God! We've already buried one child. We cannot do it again!

SEPTEMBER 9, 2003

"Justin, you're a bigger fool than I thought!" That's what I want to shout at him for having gotten himself in this mess. We all lost Jennifer due to alcohol, and now you're dragging us into the world of drugs? You've got to be kidding! That's a rat hole we don't want any part of! *My God! What did we do wrong?*

SEPTEMBER 10, 2003

Meth! I still can't believe that's what Justin has been taking! This isn't like getting hooked on diet Pepsi. This is major. I don't know if he can kick it. Once something like that gets it hooks in you, it's going to take a lot to get it out. I pray he's got the strength.

I should have listened more closely to my foreman when he told me things that were going on with Justin. I've seen this sort of thing in other men I've worked with over the years who have gotten hooked on drugs. But with most of those men, it was obvious. Justin just didn't seem that bad to me. I just thought he was grieving.

I feel so sorry for Lori. She is exhausted, and the shaking in her hand seems worse. *How much more can she take?* We just keep asking ourselves, how did our lives come to this? This is not how we raised our kids! We've warned them of the dangers of drug use. I've seen it first-hand being around the construction world. Guys get hooked, and it's nothing but bad after that. They end up unreliable, out of work, and then God knows what happens to them. So, over the years, we've tried to protect the kids from the ways of the world, but here we are, staring at the worst of it.

First, we lose Jennifer, then David rolls his car, and now Justin's hooked on drugs? Oh, dear Lord, what did we do wrong? I don't want that for him! I want him to live to be an old man, looking back on his wonderful life. Don't let him throw his life away!

Lori

SEPTEMBER 10, 2003

I haven't been able to bring myself to write about what's happening with Justin. I'm worried sick about him.

I don't understand how this could have happened! Ever since they were young, we've talked to our kids about the dangers of drugs.

I keep thinking about last spring when Justin drove to Houston to see David. I got the sense from David that things hadn't gone well, but I had no idea how bad it was. I don't think David wanted to burden us with anything else, so he didn't tell us much of what happened. But when Justin went to rehab, we called David and told him about Justin's meth addiction. When he got over his initial shock, David said that explained a lot of what happened when he was in Houston. He couldn't understand at the time what was wrong with Justin. He thought his brother was upset about Jennifer, and that was why he was being a jerk.

I know part of Justin's problem is his sorrow and anger over losing Jennifer. He's been so withdrawn ever since she died. We knew he was hurting, but his being on meth never entered my mind.

Oh, dear God, we can't lose him too!

Jim

SEPTEMBER 12, 2003

I'm so angry right now I don't know what to do. Justin got kicked out of rehab! If it were for abusing drugs, I could understand, but for talking? You've got to be kidding me! They have strict rules. I understand that. But, wow, this is Justin's life we're talking about! One of the rules is that the guys and girls in the program aren't supposed to talk to each other. They want them focusing on drying out, not figuring out who they can date. I get that. Justin and a young woman broke that rule, and that was it. They both had to leave. I'm scared to death! I don't know what we're going to do now.

SEPTEMBER 15, 2003

The last few days have been a nightmare. Justin moved back home as he tries to dry out. We can hear his heart-wrenching anguish coming from our basement as he fights to suppress his urge to give in and take just one more hit.

We go to him, hold him, and pray with him to talk him off the edge of the abyss. Justin's fiancée, Danae, has been staying with Justin now, trying to help him as best she can. It's got to be so hard on her.

So far, Justin has stayed clean, but my God, at what cost! I'm not sure Lori and I can take much more of this. We are literally on our knees in prayer every day, begging God that Justin finds the way to open the door to a new life; we're asking Jesus to walk with him every step.

Lori

SEPTEMBER 17, 2003

I know it used to irritate some of my friends that Jennifer was my shadow. They'd want to talk to me alone, but Jennifer would often be there, usually on my right side, just sitting quietly, taking it all in. I don't know if it was because she liked the adult conversation, whether it was a chance to be rid of her teasing brothers, or because she felt so bonded with me that she just wanted to be where I was. I think it was all of it, but mostly because she wanted to be with me.

Most of the time I was glad she was there, but there were times when I just wanted to be alone—like walking down our long driveway to get the mail. I'd sometimes try and sneak out quietly out of the house. Just when I thought I'd succeeded, I'd hear our front door open and close, then the sound of soft footsteps running to catch up.

More than once, I almost said, "Jennifer, I'd really just like to be alone." It's odd, but every time I was just about to speak, something in my head said, "Don't say anything. Someday she'll be gone, and you'll miss this."

I assumed my thoughts were because she would grow up and get married, and then I would miss her company.

I shiver every time I think about how close I came to telling her to leave me alone for a while. I'm so glad I never had to see the look of disappointment and hurt on her face that I know I would have seen. That memory would have haunted me for the rest of my life. I'd give anything to have even one of those moments—and my shadow—back.

Jim

SEPTEMBER 17, 2003

I'm proud of Justin. He voluntarily checked himself into a thirty-day, all-male rehab facility near Kansas City. Lori and I are relieved, but we are still so worried about him. He almost never talks about Jennifer and doesn't want to be around anyone who does. We know his sadness is a big part of his drug problem. I don't think he realizes how much.

He did tell us that while he was clean when she died, afterward, he felt so lost and just wanted his pain to stop. Doing drugs was the best way he knew how. I asked the rehab counselor how we could have been so blind to his addiction, and he said that Justin is a "functioning addict," someone who can go to work hiding it pretty well, as long as no one looks too closely. We've been so pounded with grief that we haven't been aware of much else. I wish we'd pushed harder to get Justin to open up, but we've both been so worn down we didn't have the energy to fight as hard as we should have. *God, help us! God, help Justin!*

SEPTEMBER 18, 2003

I'm under sniper fire from a pain sniper waging war against me. Shots are coming in from every angle: shots of how I'll never see my only daughter again on this earth, shots of knowing Jennifer will never have kids, shots that I failed in teaching our kids about drugs and alcohol, and shots that my marriage isn't what it should be.

I'm so full of holes; I'm convinced I'm slowly bleeding to death. I keep actually touching my side, expecting to see blood. I must be bleeding internally.

When a bullet hits, I force myself to remember when things were better. That works for a while, but the sniper is good at adapting. He just finds another angle.

Sometimes the sniper comes disguised as a well-intended friend. Like yesterday when I was filling up my gas tank. I ran into a guy who said that I was in his prayers. "I can't even begin to think how hard it must be to lose a child."

I appreciated that he took the time to say something. So often, others don't know what to say, so they pretend that nothing has happened.

But yesterday, my friend's comment was all it took. After he drove away, I barely had enough strength to return the nozzle to the cradle. My legs were as heavy as lead as I tried to lift them enough to get into my truck. I sucked in for air, but it didn't feel like any came.

I was near a small lake. I drove my truck over to it, sat there, unable to move, and just stared at the small waves.

Lori

SEPTEMBER 18, 2003

When I was young, our family lived in Clovis, New Mexico. My mom's sister and her family lived not far from us. My mom and her sister had taught themselves pig Latin when they were children. When they became mothers, it was useful when they wanted to say something and not have any of us children know what they were saying. It took a while and a lot of practice, but I eventually learned it too. Mom could speak and understand it at lightning speed. She usually talked so fast that I had no idea what she was saying. I'd have to ask her to slow down.

When my kids were young, Mom and I would occasionally slip into the secret code when we didn't want Jennifer, David, or Justin to understand what we were saying.

One afternoon, when Jennifer was about eight, she walked into our family room just as Mom was asking, "What does Jennifer want for Christmas?" I said, "An utay-utay." Jennifer looked at me, perplexed. She had told me earlier that one of the things she wanted was a tutu for ballet. Jennifer looked away. I knew by her stare that she was thinking hard. She was quiet for a few minutes, and then blurted out, "Tutu! Utay-utay is tutu!"

141

Jennifer was smart. It had taken me a long time to figure out pig Latin. Not Jennifer. And once she got it, Mom and I were no longer able to keep secrets from her. Our code was broken.

SEPTEMBER 22, 2003

I'm flying to Houston today to be with David on his first birthday without Jennifer. I didn't want him to spend it alone. I don't know how either of us will be able to face it.

For nineteen years, I've made two birthday cakes: one for David and one for Jennifer. They got to pick the kind. Each year it was different.

This will be the first year I will make just one.

Two was better.

Jim

SEPTEMBER 22, 2003

I'm glad Lori will be with David, so he doesn't have to face this first birthday without Jennifer alone. His twentieth birthday will be nothing like what any of us could have imagined a year ago.

Jennifer's birthday is one more mountain we have to climb, along with October 26, the day she died. Life is completing its circle. It's a cycle that I don't like.

I think I'll go someplace where there are no phones that night. I know I'm going to need to cling to Jesus to get through the next few weeks.

I'm taking purple balloons to Jennifer's grave tomorrow and will let one soar. I know Jennifer's not in the grave, but it's the only way I know how to celebrate her birthday with her.

I remember the first time I held the twins and how proud I was at being their father.

Tomorrow I should be watching her open presents and eat cake. Instead, I will stand over her grave, tell her again how sorry I am for my last words to her, and say how much I wish I had been able to tell her goodbye.

SEPTEMBER 23, 2003
By noon, I'd had enough of this day.

I went to the crash site and put some purple balloons on Jennifer's roadside cross. Then I went to her grave with purple balloons and a purple "love" teddy bear.

When the day was half over, I thought, "I can do this. I can make it through."

Then, I came home and opened our mailbox. It was full of cards from loved ones. I read every word and fell completely apart. *Jennifer should be here opening birthday cards, not me!* I never dreamed this would be how we'd spend her twentieth birthday.

While the rest of us are getting older and grayer by the years, she will be young, with blonde hair, forever.

Happy Birthday, Jennifer—from a dad who loves you. I know you're with Jesus, and I know you're happy. Knowing that is the only way this day is bearable.

Lori

SEPTEMBER 26, 2003
This birthday week of Jennifer's has been harder than I expected and really hard on David. He looked so sad when he was opening his presents. "It's so odd not to have Jennifer here opening hers too."

"I know what you mean, David. Earlier this week, before I came to Texas, I was standing in a department store and thinking that I wasn't shopping for birthday gifts for Jennifer for the first time in twenty years. There wasn't anything I could give her. But then I passed the bedding department and realized there was something I could do.

I dropped off a new quilt at the hospital on the way home with a purple ribbon tied around it. On it, I scribbled a note: "In honor of Jennifer Dultmeier's 20th birthday. May it bring comfort to someone who has lost a loved one."

"I'm so glad you did that, Mom!"

It was great to see David smile on his birthday. That was gift enough for me.

SEPTEMBER 28, 2003

Jennifer's dear friend Kelly came over to the house. What a paradox of emotions! I love that she took the time to come. She wants to make sure that I know how much she cares for us, and how much she loves and remembers Jennifer. That means so much. But her visit took a lot out of me.

Carolyn had been Jennifer's first best friend, but she was not her only one.

When Jennifer was in the seventh grade, she met Kelly. They became really close. Jennifer adored her.

Kelly said that Jennifer was the best friend she ever had. I believe it. Their friendship always reminded me of my lifelong friendship with Chris. Like the two of us, I know Jennifer and Kelly would have remained close all their lives.

While she was here, Kelly told me how she learned about Jennifer's death. Her words left me shaking.

Kelly said, "I'd spent the day shopping with my mom. We were at the mall in a clothing store for teenagers. I opened my purse and saw that my phone was off. I didn't even know it. I turned it on. I had missed more calls than I could count. Then it started ringing.

It was my boyfriend, Nathan. 'Where are you?'

'Shopping, why?'

'Shopping?' He sounded surprised.

'Why'

'Who are you with?' His tone was tender.

'My mom.'

'Can you put her on?'

'Why?'

'Kelly, please, just let me talk to her.'

I handed Mom the phone, confused at Nathan's insistence. He didn't sound alarmed, but his voice sounded different. My heart started beating faster. 'Is he trying to find out my ring size? Maybe this is about a wedding proposal!'

My mom pressed the phone harder to her ear, 'Please repeat that.' Her face went white, ashen white. This was not a proposal. She closed the phone and said quietly, 'We have to go now.' She started walking.

'Mom, what's wrong?'

She didn't answer as she left the store, heading to JC Penney's to get to the parking lot. 'Mom, please stop. What's wrong?'

She wouldn't look at me. She kept walking. 'We just have to go.'

I stopped in the middle of the lingerie department. 'Mom, please, you're scaring me. What's wrong?'

'Please don't make me tell you now. Let's just get to the car.'

I'd never seen my mom act that way. I knew something terrible had happened.

'Mom, please. Tell me what happened!'

'Jennifer and Carolyn were in a wreck. Carolyn's in the hospital.'

'Can we go there to see her?' Then it hit me. 'Where's Jennifer?'

'Kelly,' mom said softly, 'Jennifer didn't make it. Honey, Jennifer died.'

I didn't know that I had collapsed on the floor of J.C. Penney's. All I knew was that I could hear someone screaming. I didn't realize for a long time that the screams were mine."

Jim

OCTOBER 7, 2003
The moment I saw them, I knew.

I had just stopped in a monument store to see when Jennifer's updated headstone, with her photo on it, was going to be delivered. At the counter was a man and woman with their backs to me. Without even seeing their faces, I knew they'd lost a child.

I had to say something. After talking to both, the husband came outside with me. His daughter and her boyfriend had been riding on his motorcycle when it broke down. They'd pulled it off to the shoulder of the road and a drunk driver hit them.

The man was so angry; his words sounded like hisses. He didn't know how to go on living. I knew he was in shock. The worst was still coming.

The man told me about the nightmare call. While he was talking, I saw in him the mirror image of myself, both fathers who were now shattered.

"How do you sleep knowing she's not coming home?" That's what he asked me—no, he didn't ask—he demanded it.

I bear-hugged the man, and he broke down, hard, right in my arms like a baby. It took a long time before he could talk. Then he asked me a question I couldn't answer. "How long will it take...how long before we can go on?"

I told him time would help, but I really wanted to tell him the truth. His broken heart would not heal completely until it stops beating for the last time.

I asked him if he was a man of faith, and he said no.

146

Lori and I talked about the couple as we drove home. They gave us their phone number. We're going to ask them to come to church with us. It'll be their call, but I hope they come. They're gonna need all the help they can get.

OCTOBER 8, 2003

The couple we met yesterday had just come from the local MADD office. They told me where it was located.

Mothers Against Drunk Driving sent us a card after Jennifer died. We were so over-whelmed with people trying to help that MADD wasn't in the mix.

As I walked away from that couple, I was shaking. I realized I really wanted to talk to someone about my anger and grief.

I walked into the MADD office today. A kind woman named Karen walked me back to her office. She had a soft way about her and was a good listener. I stayed for a couple of hours. I was really glad I'd come. If we hadn't had the family support we did, we would have needed MADD sooner.

OCTOBER 9, 2003

I'm restless today. I keep thinking about my conversation with Karen yesterday. What is it going to take to stop people from drinking and driving?

How about we start with the alcohol companies offering to pay for the funerals of every person that's killed by someone else driving drunk?

I know they would argue they didn't make them drink and drive, and their ads encourage people to drink responsibly. That's true. And it's also true that people are responsible for their own actions. That's a good thing. But what makes me so mad is that so many of these companies pitch alcohol at venues appealing to kids, like sporting events and concerts. Funny, I've never seen an alcohol company sponsoring funeral homes!

Until Jennifer died, I never paid much attention to these ads. Now, I see them all over. Beer commercials are great at making us laugh and tugging at our hearts, especially ones using animals.

I wonder why they don't show us the funny commercials of a family standing over the graves of their teenagers killed by a drunk driver.

Why don't they show the funny side of a driver waking up in a hospital or jail, knowing they had been driving a car that killed someone the night before, maybe even someone they loved? Or the funny side of a husband watching as his wife collapses on the floor, sobbing for her dead child.

It's all fun and games until someone gets killed, and then it's the teenager's fault for not saying no to alcohol. It's the parent's fault for not doing enough to educate their kids about the dangers of alcohol.

If the person is older, they say, "Well, they knew better than to drink and drive," all the while shoving it in our faces to go out and get a cold one.

OCTOBER 12, 2003

Lori and I drove out to Jennifer's grave today to see the picture of her on her headstone. I told Lori, "Why are we going to a graveyard? We shouldn't have to! We should not have a daughter there!" I was so mad I could hardly contain my rage.

While we were standing there, a man came over. I recognized him. He'd lost his son in a car accident a couple of months before Jennifer died. They'd been friends. Jennifer had gone to the boy's funeral. I looked over at the young man's grave, yards away from Jennifer's, and I couldn't help thinking that Jennifer had stood there on the day he was buried, right near the very site where she, too, would soon be laid to rest. She had no idea. None of us did.

Lori

OCTOBER 12, 2003

Jennifer used to hold my hand when we were at church. She did this all her life, even as a teenager.

Sometimes when I am sitting there, I close my eyes and imagine her hand in mine. I feel her soft, warm skin and her long, slender hands.

OCTOBER 13, 2003

Jennifer was so beautiful, so petite. She was kind, but, like other teenagers her age, she struggled at times with peer pressure and finding her place in the world.

Before Jennifer died, Melissa told me how excited she was that Jennifer had asked her for quilting lessons. She was excited to have time alone with her niece. For so long, Jennifer had been one of the many "gaggle of kids," as Melissa called them, between our two families. All our kids were about the same age and had been one big group all their lives. It was hard sometimes for those who weren't their parents to see them as distinct individuals. Now, each one was developing into who they would be as adults. Melissa told me she liked what she was seeing in Jennifer. I did too.

Melissa confided in me that the timing of her death was heartbreaking because she felt that Jennifer, having just started college, was at a pivotal time in her life. Melissa said, "I think Jennifer was just now truly coming into her own, discovering who she was, and what she liked to do. She had found her wings and was about to soar."

OCTOBER 14, 2003

In the year since she died, several people have asked me about the prayer I said when we were waiting in the hospital during Jennifer's surgery. Everyone was praying for Jennifer to be healed. I said, "No, we need to pray for God's will to be done."

People ask, "How could you have asked for that prayer, then, of all times?"

The truth is, at that moment, I couldn't ask God to heal Jennifer because I couldn't bear the thought of being let down by God if she didn't survive. I couldn't bear the thought of asking God for something as important as saving Jennifer, and then not have her live.

That disappointment would have been too much to bear.

Jim

OCTOBER 16, 2003

I met a woman the other day who said she lost her only son several years before. She asked me how I was really doing, deep inside.

I told her, "Day by day."

She looked at me, her expression dark with concern. "Jim, I don't want what happened to my husband to happen to you. After our son died, he was never the same."

She explained that they would be out for a nice dinner, and he would get up and walk out. She said that after her son died, she never saw her husband smile again, not ever—not even with his grandkids.

Her words hit me hard. I don't want to be like her husband and let Jennifer's death destroy the remaining time we have on this earth. Jennifer would never have wanted that. She would expect more of me than becoming a destroyed man. She'd tell me that Lori and the boys deserved more than that from me.

OCTOBER 19, 2003

I can't stop thinking about the last day of Jennifer's life on earth. It seemed like such an ordinary day. I'd changed the oil in her car. Lori had taken her shopping. Justin had lunch with her. David was away at school, and she tried to call him.

If only we'd known what was coming at us. But it was all just so normal. If we had known, we would have locked up the house. No one would have left that night.

Then I think of the people who go to bed at night, thinking they're safe. But people die in their sleep all the time. The reality is, there is nowhere that we are safe when death calls.

I went to bed that night, thinking I was safe, then the phone rang.

OCTOBER 20, 2003

The countdown is on to the anniversary of our lives being changed forever, and we can't stop it—just like we couldn't stop it that night, either.

I don't believe in ghosts, but sometimes I see Jennifer lying on our couch or sitting at the table doing her homework. It's not her ghost I'm seeing, but a memory of her being around here, doing her everyday things.

OCTOBER 21, 2003

I hadn't been in Jennifer's room for months until today. It would have been better to let my truck run over me. I stood there for the longest time, just staring at her stuff. *What happened to this beautiful young woman who called this her room? She has not been home for a year. Why?*

Her pictures and clothes were just as she left them. Her sunglasses were lying on the bed as if she casually tossed them aside after realizing she wouldn't need them for the evening.

I picked up a bottle of her perfume and inhaled. It smelled just as it did when she wore it. *Had she worn it the night she died?* I imagined her spraying some on her wrists the way Lori does, then flipping a strand of her long, blonde hair over her shoulder, getting it out of the way before she sprayed a little on her neck.

Out her window, the trees were in full fall color.

The sun was shining in her room, but there was no feeling of life there.

We still can't bring ourselves to clean anything out of her room, including the open can of pop sitting next to her bed that she hadn't finished.

OCTOBER 25, 2003

One year ago, was Jennifer's last day on earth.

Today was a long day. I went to purchase roofing material. I had just entered an intersection. The light was green. Out of the corner of my eye, I saw a truck coming from my right, racing through his red light. I stomped on the brakes. His truck blew through the intersection. He never even slowed down. I sat there in stunned shock. Adrenaline pulsed through my hands and legs. If I hadn't hit my brakes when I did, he would have plowed right into me!

I learned long ago never to trust the other guy. *My God! Of all days!*

I'm certain I would have been injured, maybe fatally. I would have been taken to the hospital. Lori would have gotten a phone call on the last day she'd ever want to get a call, telling her that I'd been in a wreck. I shuddered at the thought and then blew out a long sigh. *Thank you, Jesus!*

OCTOBER 26, 2003

I worked hard all day yesterday so that I would be too tired to think about a year ago when we got the call.

Lori had a friend over last night, and I was glad she did because I was no help. I just went to bed. I didn't think I would be able to fall asleep, but I was so tired that it came easily. I don't know how it went for our sons. They didn't call. Thankfully, the phone never rang after supper. I think everyone knew it was a bad night to call.

I've had a lot of time to think about this past year. At first, I had no idea what was coming at me. It was like trying to drive at night with no headlights. Now, with this year behind me, it feels like maybe I can at least turn on my fog lights. A year in total darkness is enough.

I know we have more sad times coming than I can imagine, but I pray I will be better at knowing how to handle what's ahead.

OCTOBER 27, 2003

The times I lost my cool with Jennifer now haunt me. I know I was a good dad, but there were occasions where I would get angry and yell at her. I would grab her arms and make her stare at me while I was trying to make my point.

Jennifer was a very strong-willed person, and she knew how to push my anger buttons.

I never hit her, but there were times I made her cry. As her dad, I felt it was up to me to make her understand that she had to follow our rules. I didn't want her to think she could run over me. I've seen the destruction of families where the kids have too much control.

We had so many great times with our kids but now, at night when I'm trying to sleep, what I remember most are the times when I got angry with her. Those memories are a poison. They make me physically sick. I want to be rid of them, but they are part of a past I can't change.

I'd give anything just to tell Jennifer that I love her. I would shout it, whisper it, and cry it. "Jennifer, I love you! I love you! I love you!"

My heart aches, knowing I can't. I tell people now, "Tell those you love how much you love them. There are no second chances to get things right. Take it from a dad who knows, regret is a bitter pill."

OCTOBER 28, 2003
I got scared tonight when I opened the door of Jennifer's room again. The moon was lighting the pictures on the walls, pictures of Jennifer with her friends that are now only cold memories.

There is a scary, empty feeling of death in that room, a room that sits there like a museum.

I remember like it was yesterday when that wasn't the case. If I try hard enough, I can still hear Jennifer's laughter filling the air.

OCTOBER 30, 2003
Last night I woke from a dream. My sheets and t-shirt were wet with sweat. My heart was pounding. In my dream, I didn't want to wake up.

We were all there together: Lori, Jennifer, Justin, and David. All of us, lying in front of the TV, watching a movie and eating popcorn. Someone said something funny that made us all laugh. Jennifer laughed the hardest.

I realized that my dream was actually a glimpse of an actual day of my life. One of many, when the kids were all with us, and we were just together as a family.

How could I not have realized how truly wonderful life was?

I wish I could shout to myself—the one that worried too much about paying bills, the one that got angry over things that, in the end, meant nothing. "Nothing!" I want to yell at the man who wasn't always as kind and gentle as he should have been. I want to tell that man to love and appreciate every moment he has with those he loves.

Didn't that man realize that in an instant it could be over, and he would give anything— even his life, for just a moment of it back?

153

Lori

OCTOBER 30, 2003

Justin is doing better, thank God! He called today to tell Jim to turn on the History Channel to watch a show about fighter jets. Then it hit me. I'll never have Jennifer calling me to tell me about girly shows.

I know I've got to get busy, or my life will take forever to end. I don't want it to end any time soon, but I don't want it to drag on either.

Justin is well enough to start a new job. I'm so relieved. He looks better than he has in a long time. David, too, is also doing as well as he can.

Jim's been dragging this month. We try to push ourselves to do things. I guess we'll just keep pushing and eventually get to where we're going, wherever that is. Life isn't as good as it was. I never knew how lucky I was.

But I do know I am still blessed. God is good.

Dear God, Thank you for your strength. Continue to hold us in your arms. Amen.

OCTOBER 31, 2003

Babies—that's what I wanted. I had a beautiful baby boy, Justin. When he was born, he looked like an angel. I never took my eyes off of him in public for fear of someone stealing him.

Then I found out I was pregnant with twins. Two at once! I prayed they would be healthy. "Oh, if only one could be a girl," I daydreamed, "my life will be complete!" I had wanted a little girl for as long as I could remember.

The other could be either, but I just wanted one to be a girl. And then it happened. Jennifer came into the world with her soft, blonde hair and blue eyes. She was so beautiful I was afraid someone would take her, too. Then there was David. He was absolutely adorable when he was young and more so as he got older. I never had to worry about him. He was so mature and reliable that I knew he would always take care of himself and everyone around him.

Even before they were born, I decided that no one would take care of my children but me. I would stay home and raise them. Though it was tough in the early years, I was so grateful we made the sacrifice and that Jim's work allowed me to do so.

My three kids were everything to me. Oh, why did I have to give Jennifer up? What have I done wrong to deserve losing a child?

NOVEMBER 1, 2003
Chronic grief is like living under a never-ending dark cloud. I just want to wake up once and have it be sunny!

NOVEMBER 2, 2003
Justin and Danae are still planning on getting married in December. He told me that now that he's going to be married, there was no way he would ever go back to drugs.

I pray he's right!

Jim

NOVEMBER 2, 2003
On her last day on earth, I said something to Jennifer that will haunt me for the rest of my life. It's been a year, and I don't know how to begin to forgive myself.

I have tried to push it from my thoughts, from my dreams, and from my nightmares, but it's always there—stabbing me in the heart. I would give *anything* to undo what I said.

I had no idea, of course, that I wasn't ever going to see her again, but should that have mattered? *What does it say about me that I said it at all?*

When the memory comes, I try everything to fight it back. I've shoved my hands deep into my pockets and stomped around our property, clenching my fists until they hurt. I've taken an old hammer and pounded it against steel. I've driven my boat as far from shore as it'll go and stood there, shouting at the top of my lungs. Nothing works. Nothing keeps it at bay.

My words were spoken in anger and frustration—a stubborn dad in a heated argument with his headstrong, teenage daughter.

The funny thing is—only it isn't funny at all—I can't even remember the reason for our fight. *Isn't that ironic?* Whatever it was, it was so insignificant that I can't even remember what it was about! And believe me, I've tried to remember!

But I remember my words. Every awful one of them.

I was so angry that I got close to her face so that she would be sure to hear me. "You know, Jennifer, when you're acting like this, you're an ugly person. Why don't you go take a hard look in the mirror, and see how ugly you look right now?"

Oh, God! How could I have said that?

And yet I did. My words still hang in the air I breathe every day.

I had said it, then I stormed into the family room and plopped down on the couch to cool down. Jennifer marched up the stairs to her bedroom to get ready for the night.

A while later, she came back down to where I was watching TV. She was still fuming. Her words were sharp, "Well, Dad, I did it! I looked into the mirror, and all I could see was a beautiful person!"

I looked over my shoulder, shrugged, and said flippantly, "I know that, Jennifer. It's when you're angry that you're ugly."

Five hours later, I stood looking down at the dead body of my beautiful, beautiful daughter. *A daughter who had been beautiful since the instant she was created— beautiful in every way—in every emotion—in every moment of her life.*

Standing over her body, I felt like I was going to be sick. I had so much to tell her, but more than anything, I wanted to tell her how beautiful she was and to tell her how sorry I was.

How does a dad forgive himself for that? Regret is the fiercest of swords embedded in a heart, for its edges are laced in the poison of the most profound truth—the utter insignificance of regret.

Others can only know Jennifer now through photos and stories.

—Jim Dultmeier

Jim 1979

Lori age 16

Jim & Lori's wedding 1979

Jim & Lori 1979

Lori & twins 1983

Jennifer & David 1983

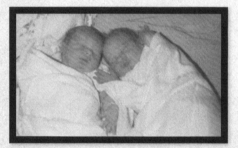

David & Jennifer 4 days old 1983

Jennifer & David 1984

David & Jennifer 1986

Jennifer loves
Tweety Bird 1994

Jennifer (left) & Carolyn 1995

Jennifer (left) & Carolyn 1995

Carolyn (left) & Jennifer
Lake Shawnee 1995

Jennifer tubing 1995

Jim in Aruba 2003

Jennifer, Justin, David 1987

Photos courtesy of the Dultmeier Family.

PART
TWO

THE SAD
SURRENDER

Mom, don't cry for me,
Be patient and you'll see, just how
good life again can be.

—Poem by Lori Dultmeier, May 2005

Jennifer's Fifth Grade Class Journal

10/3/94: The greatest thing this weekend was that my dad was gone so then we went out to eat and got movies for every night. We went shopping for winter clothes.

10/12/94: On Halloween I like to trick or treat. On Halloween I like to get candy a lot.

10/13/94: My favorite book is a book where you can go places and feel write there. I will name the auther Ann A Martin.

This weekend I had a friend over. And I had a baseketball game we lost. We only made 1 point. I think my behavior was a bit bad and a bit good.

10/19/94: I wrote to Saquille O'Neal and I gave him my card to sign. I hope I get it back sign.

10/24/94: This weekend we went shopping for costoms but I didn't find anything. But when I got home I was looking at our Halloween box and I found some thing. But I'm not going to tell you.

10/24/94: We are going on a field trip today. We are going to the zoo.

10/25/94: I like when we where at the Zoo and we got to pet the goats and pigs. And I liked the Park too.

11/1/94: Last night was fun. I did not use my big shoes. I got alot of candy.

11/2/94: This weekend I am going to slep in. I'm going to have my big brother take on sled that is hook up to my three wheeler.

11/10/94: On Halloween I felt so inpresst because I was a clown.

11/11/94: The book I chose is by Ann M. Martin. Then I have some other book I might read.

11/21/94: On friday Tricia came over and she brought her 4 wheller over too. ON Saturday we got a big 4 wheller.

11/22/94: This weekend I am gonna see if me and a friend can go shopping on Saturday.

Jim

NOVEMBER 4, 2003

Raising kids can be a dark road at times, but I can't imagine our lives if we never had them. We would never have known what we had missed. Hard times, yes, but what would have been lost is unthinkable.

I want to do something to help fight the senseless deaths of teenagers from driving impaired, but what can one man do?

NOVEMBER 19, 2003

Justin is doing so much better. He completed his thirty-day stay in rehab last month, followed by a couple of weeks in a safe house under partial supervision with a few other men. He says he's done with drugs forever. I pray that's true, especially now that he has another reason to give his recovery everything he's got. Not only is he getting married soon, he's going to be a dad. Lori and I are going to be grandparents!

Part of me is bursting with joy knowing that we'll have a grandchild to love and spoil, and the other part of me is scared to death, not only for Justin but that we now have another human being to love and worry about.

One step at a time, that's all we can do.

DECEMBER 15, 2003

Justin looks healthier than I've seen him in a long time. I'm proud of him for fighting to get his life back.

Lori

DECEMBER 15, 2003

Finally! Yesterday, Justin talked to me—really talked! He came over to get a picture of Jennifer for the wedding, and, for the first time, he wanted to talk about Jennifer. I think it was really good for him. He's been so unwilling to do so before.

He told me about a time when they were sitting in his truck at a traffic light the week she died. "The song 'Just Like a Pill' by Pink came on. Jennifer cranked up the volume, and we began to sing it at the top of our lungs. When the part about running came on, we started pumping our arms, pretending to run as fast as possible. Sometimes I play it now, and I turn it up as loud as it will go."

His eyes filled with tears. "Mom, I really miss those simple times with her, so much so that I can't stand it."

I told him it's the little things I miss most about Jennifer too. I missed her laughter. I missed having her to talk to when I made dinner. I missed listening to music with her and the way she always was eager to run errands with me, no matter how mundane they were.

It was a relief to have Justin finally open up. He admitted that for a long time, he'd been trying to hide his drug use from us. "I didn't want to be stupid skinny like most addicts are who trade food for drugs."

Then, he said something that surprised me. "When I was high, people would say, 'He's just sleepy, or he's depressed because of Jennifer. He's not acting normal. It must be because of his sister.' All I had to do was blame it on Jennifer's death. And my friends, well, no one wanted to mess with me. I intimidated them. I wanted to scare them, so they'd leave me alone. I've been afraid to be around you and Dad because I didn't want you to find out I was high most of the time."

High most of the time. The thought made me sick. "Why did you do it, Justin? How could you have let it come to this?" I knew the answer before I asked the question, but I wanted him to say it.

"Jennifer's gone. And I didn't want to feel that. High was better."

I closed my eyes. I hated the truth and what it had done to Justin.

"Justin, I wish we'd have talked about this before. Maybe it wouldn't have gotten so bad. I'm so sorry that I've been so…"

"Mom! This isn't your fault! You don't get the power meth has over me. It controls everything. When I take it, I feel like I'm Superman—nothing can hurt me. I know it's not true, but I don't care. It made me feel better, and then I couldn't do anything without it.

"Every day, I'd promise myself that I would just go to sleep without it. And then night came, and I'd do it again.

"I knew if I weren't around a lot, you and everyone else would chalk it up to me being depressed over Jennifer and preferring to be alone."

He was right. That's exactly what we thought.

DECEMBER 16, 2003

I keep reliving my conversation with Justin. I'm so relieved he's at least talking, but he seems so spiritually dead. I'm praying that he finds his way back to God. He needs it, and so does his wife and child! Parenting is hard enough without drugs! I can't imagine it!

DECEMBER 17, 2003

A couple of years before she died, Jennifer and I decided we'd make a gingerbread house for Christmas. Our masterpiece soon morphed into a church instead of a house. We worked on it for hours, carefully bonding the walls with white icing, then trimming the sides with bits and pieces of candy.

While we were working, Jennifer exclaimed, "We can put lights inside! It'll be really cool! It'll shine from within." And so we did. We went to the store and bought tiny battery-operated lights and covered the windows with cellophane.

When we turned the switch on, I couldn't believe it. The windows looked just like stained glass.

We sat there staring at it. "Mom," Jennifer said, draping her arm over my shoulder, "it's beautiful." And it was. "We should do one next year too."

The next year came, but we got busy, and it didn't happen.

We both thought that we'd have many more Christmases to make another.

Jim

DECEMBER 21, 2003

Justin's wedding was great. We're so grateful he's clean and sober. I'm proud of him and his determination to stay that way.

And while the wedding was really nice, it was hard on Lori. She had a tough time keeping it together. It hit me the most when I watched Justin's bride walk down the aisle holding her father's arm.

Jennifer would have loved being part of this day. She would have been so happy for Justin. It pulls my heart out to even think of all the things she is missing and will miss. Justin had Jennifer's picture for everyone to see as they entered the sanctuary. I'm glad he did, but all I could think when I saw it was how she should be here!

Lori

DECEMBER 22, 2003

I was a complete wreck at Justin's wedding.

Of all the voids Jennifer's death has created, nothing has come close to sitting in that church, watching Justin get married. I managed to get through the ceremony, barely, but at the reception, I fell apart. I could not hold back the sorrow. I started to cry, and I couldn't stop. I had to leave.

I felt terrible about leaving the reception before we did the mother/son dance. There was no way I could have stood out there and danced. Leaving wasn't fair to Justin and his bride, but staying would have been worse and ruined their celebration.

It's just so wrong, so unfair.

DECEMBER 24, 2003

I bought another quilt today and left it at the hospital with a note that said, "In memory of Jennifer Dultmeier. Christmas 2003." I just wish no one would die, so it wouldn't be needed. But that's not life. Life is also death.

Jim

Sometimes, lightning strikes twice.

Yesterday, we got another call. I could not believe what we were hearing! Lori's twenty-one-year-old nephew, Nathan, was killed in an automobile accident.

After we hung up, Lori and I just sat on the edge of our bed in stunned silence. Neither of us could breathe or speak. Not for a long time. *My God! Not Nathan!*

He was just here...days ago! At our house!

"Oh, Jim! My mom!" She buried her face in her hands and sobbed. "I don't want her to know!! She can't know! Not another grandchild! It's not fair. It's not fair. It's not fair! She doesn't deserve this! Oh my God! Jim! Brad! Sandra! What are they going to do? NO!!!"

Lori was screaming.

DECEMBER 28, 2003

I still can't believe it. Lori's brother, Brad, and his wife, Sandra, were here two weeks ago for their son Kevin's college graduation from the University of Kansas in Lawrence. Nathan joined the Marines a while back, and he's been stationed in North Carolina. He was given some time off but had to pick between going to Texas to see his parents at Christmas or coming to Kansas earlier in the month for the graduation. Nathan had told his parents that he'd have lots of Christmases with his family but only one chance to see his brother graduate from college.

Nathan was like that—such a great guy with a big heart and a hilarious sense of humor. Everyone loved him. *How can he be gone?*

The day before the graduation, Sandra and I sat in Jennifer's room and talked for a long time. She said, "It looks like Jennifer just walked out the door. It's like this room is frozen in time." Her eyes filled with tears. "I don't know how you and Lori are managing. Losing a child is my greatest fear."

I told her it had been ours too. Now, it's a fear realized for both families.

We're driving to Texas tomorrow morning to be with them. I have no idea how we are going to be able to deal with this. It's a nightmare!!!

The last time we drove to Texas was a month after Jennifer died. Brad and Sandra didn't want us to have to face Thanksgiving at home without Jennifer. They'd done everything to make it as bearable as possible.

DECEMBER 29, 2003

I feel so sorry for Lori's parents. They've now lost two grandchildren in fourteen months! I don't know how their hearts will survive. I'm not sure any of us can. I keep seeing Lori's mom when she collapsed at Jennifer's funeral. She was sickly white for a long time. And now she's going to have to watch another grandchild that she loves lowered into the ground! She doesn't deserve this! She's as kind and gentle as they come. I hate this for her, for us, for everyone! I hate this!

DECEMBER 31, 2003

We learned more about Nathan. At the last minute, his unit had been given a couple of days off on Christmas Eve. Nathan drove Josh, a Marine buddy, to see Josh's family in South Carolina.

Nathan called his parents on Christmas day. Everyone took turns saying what they were most grateful to God for and what they wanted their family to be praying for them in the upcoming year.

Nathan told them how much he loved them and how grateful he was for his family for teaching him to know God. He talked about how much he loved his fiancée and couldn't wait to get married. He asked his family to pray for his fiancée, and he asked them to pray for him to become a stronger man of God. He told them he wanted to be a good husband and someday a great father.

Nathan would have been all those things.

That was the last conversation they had with their son. In a few hours, he'd be dead.

Later that night, one of Josh's friends picked Nathan and Josh up to go to a movie. Afterward, Nathan wanted to go back to the house, but they went to shoot pool instead. He called his fiancé from the bar and told her he had wanted to go home after the movie. After leaving the bar, the driver ran off the road and hit a cement drainage culvert. The impact started the car rolling end over end—three times. The driver survived with minor injuries. Nathan was pronounced dead at the scene. Josh was badly injured and is still in a coma. Alcohol was apparently involved in the wreck.

Why didn't someone call for a ride?

JANUARY 1, 2004
Nathan's body arrived in Texas just before the viewing. His parents, brothers, sister, and fiancée got to see him before the gathered guests. I should have left the building for my own sanity. Instead, I stood outside the door as they went inside. I hope I never hear anything again like the sounds coming from that room.

JANUARY 2, 2004
Nathan's funeral was today. I don't know how much more we can take.

When the song "I Can Only Imagine" was played, I kept wondering if Jennifer was there to greet her cousin. I like to think of Jennifer bear-hugging Nathan, welcoming him home.

Here on Earth I don't have to imagine what his parents are going through. I know, and it makes me sick.

It is all so senseless!

JANUARY 5, 2004
I'm scared his death will set us back.

When the time's right, I'm going to tell Brad that he has to take care of himself and his wife and to give it time. Healing will come slowly, but it will come. And it will come at different times for each of them. Even though Lori and I are changed forever, we're still alive and functioning.

More than anything, I want them to stay strong in their faith and believe God when He says this is not the end.

JANUARY 6, 2004
I hope I never have to go to another funeral because of alcohol. I don't know if I can take it.

I don't have a problem with people having a drink while they are at home, as long as they aren't going to be driving anywhere. The problem is unexpected things happen. If someone's had too much to drink, even at home, and they get a call that there has been an emergency, and they need to go to the hospital, what are they going to do? My guess? Drive anyway.

Lori

JANUARY 22, 2004

I called my brother today. He's numb. He said the military just shipped Nathan's truck back from South Carolina.

Sandra got on the phone. "I couldn't wait to get inside Nathan's truck. It was one of the last places he had been when he drove it Christmas day up to Josh's family.

"Oh, Lori, I just wanted to sit where my son had been... and hold the steering wheel, where he had held it too!"

I knew exactly what she meant. It's what I want every time I wrap myself in Jennifer's quilt.

"Nathan had a CD in the player. I turned the car on and pressed play, and do you know what came on? 'I Can Only Imagine!' Lori, the same song we had played at his funeral!

"I couldn't believe it! I've been thinking a lot about the last time I heard his voice when he called on Christmas Day. And now finding the CD in his truck—it's like he's trying to let us know that before he died, his heart was where it needed to be."

Jim

JANUARY 22, 2004

I can't quit thinking about something. It's a story I'm not proud of, and I still get sick, deep in my gut, every time I think about it.

It was about twenty years ago. I was sound asleep. Lori whispered, "Jim, someone's in the house!"

I grabbed one of my shotguns, loaded it with shells, and walked downstairs thinking, "Someone better have a darn good reason to be in my house." From the time they were young, we've taught the kids that guns aren't a toy. They're to be used only for hunting and for protection.

One of my friends recently had two men break into his house late one night. Like me, he heard them and grabbed his gun. When they came into his bedroom, one of the intruders shot six times at my friend but missed. My friend returned fire, killing the man.

The moon was bright as I walked through my house, throwing light in through the windows. I heard the basement door close. A shadow fell across the floor in the front room.

I stood and waited, trying to still my trembling hands. The shadow moved. I raised my gun. If someone had a weapon, I would get the first shot in.

The person moved into the living room.

The person was my six-year-old son—sleepwalking.

I stood there, aiming a loaded gun at him.

What would have happened if I had been drinking that night? I shudder every time I think of it.

Drinking and weapons don't belong together any more than drinking and driving.

JANUARY 23, 2004

Ever since Jennifer died, I've been obsessed with angel wings. Right after she died, I considered getting angel wings with Jennifer's name in the center, tattooed on my chest near my heart. It would have been my first and only tattoo. I eventually nixed the tattoo after realizing that I don't need a mark on my skin to remember Jennifer in my heart.

During our trip to Aruba last year, I was surprised how talented many of the sidewalk artists were using spray paint. They'd call out as we walked past, "What would you like me to paint for you?" One of them was a young man whose paintings I really liked.

"Can you paint angel wings?"

The man looked surprised. "Sure, *Señor*."

"Can you make the feathers have a lot of detail?"

"Sure. What color wings?"

"I don't know. What do you suggest?"

"Why do you want angel wings?"

I told him. He looked closely at me and said, "I'm so sorry about your daughter. I think the wings should be white."

He picked up a can of paint and began. Lori and I stood there watching in fascination as he pressed long and short spurts from his cans. He worked quickly. Twenty minutes later, he was done. He had created beautiful, white wings against an orange and red sky at sunset. As we walked away with our new treasure, the man shouted his appreciation for the extra money we gave him for his great work.

This year we decided to go to the island of St. Martin. We just got home. While I was there, I found another street artist. His wing painting was equally as beautiful as the one from last year, only this time the sky was blue.

Last year when we were in Aruba, everything we saw we viewed through our tears.

On this trip to St. Martin, despite the terrible shadow of having just lost Nathan, we both were determined to have fun. And that's what we did. I loved hearing Lori laugh again, more than anything.

When the plane took off to return home, it was just about sunset. I had a window seat. The sun shimmered through the clouds. A brilliant rainbow of color painted the canvas sky. I couldn't help thinking how big a difference a year had made.

We spent a lot of that year on our knees in prayer and somehow found a way to live in a new way, with glimmers of joy and laughter. I had not realized until that moment how much I had missed both.

JANUARY 24, 2004

Now that I will soon be having a grandchild, I've been thinking a lot about my folks, and especially Lori's parents, who have recently lost two grandkids. I feel so sorry for them. Their sorrow just seems to be compounding.

I'm scared of becoming a grandfather. I'm scared to love another child all over again. I'm scared of losing them. Lori is too.

JANUARY 27, 2004

I can't even stand the word alcohol! I want to shout at every teenager I see, "If you're drinking and driving because you think it's cool, then you might as well go pick the color you want for your casket! You might be able to get away with it for a while, but, sooner or later, it'll catch up with you or someone you love."

No teenager would ever want their parents, grandparents, and siblings to go through what we have.

Dying of old age or a heart attack is one thing, but an accident involving alcohol is not an accident! It's someone's choice. It can be prevented! Don't drink and drive! Period.

I want to tell everyone, "Next time you think about drinking and driving, or getting in the car with a driver who has been; you'd better stop and think really hard about everyone who loves you.

"Let your life, and the lives of those you love, mean more to you than trying to be cool."

I know Jennifer would say to us, "I'm so sorry for all I've put you through! I could have prevented this had I simply called you. You would have come for me, day or night, I know that. Oh, why didn't I make that call?"

Over and over, I still cry out to Jennifer, *"Oh God! Why didn't you make that call?"*

JANUARY 28, 2004

When does it end? Josh, Nathan's buddy who was injured in the accident that killed Nathan, is still unconscious in the hospital in South Carolina. Another Marine friend of his and Nathan's went to see him in the hospital. On the way home, that young man was killed when his car was T-boned in the middle of an intersection by a driver who ran a red light! That driver was reportedly high on drugs. *You've got to be kidding me!*

The other driver, a man in his forties, will have to live the rest of his life, knowing that he killed an innocent young man.

I would love to ask him now, just one question: "Was it worth it? Were the drugs you took worth killing that young man?"

The bodies of people we know and love keep piling up needlessly.

Unbelievable! Unbelievable!

FEBRUARY 1, 2004

If God knows our pain, why doesn't He stop it? Doesn't He care?

He could make all my pain, and that of Lori and our family, go away in an instant, but He doesn't. I know this is why some people become so bitter towards God.

I know that God hasn't forsaken us. I have to remember where we were a year ago to know that healing is happening. It's slow, but it's there. Lori knows it too.

This morning she said to me, "Jim, when our sorrow becomes unbearable, we need to remind ourselves that the pain we feel for Jennifer is a measure of how much we loved her. And if not for God creating her in the first place, it's a love we would never have known."

FEBRUARY 22, 2004

I went to a class called Impact hosted by MADD. It's a class for people who have gotten their first DUI.

During the Impact class, I sat in the back of the auditorium and listened to a woman talk about her brother-in-law being killed by a drunk driver. This class is a chance to see the side most never see—the victims and their families.

As I looked around the room full of people of all ages, I was shaking with emotion and anger.

I kept thinking, "You all are the lucky ones! You get a second chance to clean up your life and not drink and drive again. It's a chance Jennifer never had."

I fought the urge to stand and tell them about losing Jennifer and what it has done to us.

I hope I get my turn to talk to them someday. MADD is aptly named. I've been mad ever since Jennifer died. Going to the class made me even more so when I saw the room packed with offenders.

As I write, closing out this day, I know I have to start over tomorrow and decide whether I'm willing to let my anger continue eating at me from the inside out. The purpose of MADD isn't for loved ones to stay angry forever but, instead, for their stories to prevent others from having to go through what they've been through.

MARCH 7, 2004
I saw an ultrasound photo of my grandson today in the womb. His mom says he loves to kick, punch, and stretch. So, new life is coming into this world. Wow!

MARCH 10, 2004
Until I can see Jennifer again, I need to keep moving forward, not only for my boys but also for my grandson.

I told Lori that I wished they'd give him the first and middle name of Bow Hunter. She laughed and said she didn't think I would win that one. Regardless of his name, I will have a new little partner to take fishing.

MARCH 16, 2004
Nathan's Marine friend Josh is still in a coma. They don't think he'll ever wake up. I can't imagine the hard road his poor parents are now on. Some things are harder than death. That might be one.

MARCH 17, 2004
I've come to a new place where I'm not afraid to tell others what I think about alcohol.

Driving home tonight, I was yelling at my truck radio, I was so mad. People kept calling in from bars, bragging about how much they've been drinking for St. Patrick's Day—like it's a competition!

No one said a thing about not drinking and driving—not one word about how, as soon as they start up their car, it is no different than aiming a torpedo at others in their path.

I tried to call the show but never got through. No one heard my thoughts. Instead, all they heard was how great a day it was to get smashed.

What a crock. What a farce. What a shame.

Lori

APRIL 4, 2004

I was dreading doing my student teaching and being around high school students so close to Jennifer's age. I put it off for over a year, but it hasn't been as bad as I imagined. It helps that I wasn't teaching at Jennifer's high school.

It's been going well, until last week.

I was standing in front of the class, the only adult in the room. We were listening to a student over the intercom giving the morning announcements. She began a segment on upcoming events. Then she started talking about the prom.

I couldn't help thinking about how excited Jennifer was for her prom. It seemed like it was yesterday.

Most girls Jennifer's age wouldn't consider wearing a homemade dress. Not Jennifer. She asked me if I would make hers. I was thrilled. Thrilled until she tried it on.

She had chosen a silky, formfitting black material with an open back that dipped low. It was simple and elegant, just like her. I couldn't wait for her to try it on.

"It doesn't fit, Mom! It's too low in the back and too big."

I looked at her, exasperated. I had spent hours working on it. I had carefully measured and remeasured it. It had to fit! "It looks fine, Jennifer. It's beautiful, and you're beautiful in it!" And she was.

"Can't you just take it in or something? I can't wear it like this!"

I told her no. Fixing it would mean taking apart the entire dress, including removing the zipper.

Jennifer was mad. She let the dress slip to the floor and walked out of the room. I was mad and disappointed. This hadn't gone anything like I'd imagined.

The next day, after having a chance to cool off, I reminded myself that it was a teenage girl I was dealing with, and her senior prom was a very big deal. I couldn't blame her for wanting a dress that fit. I would have felt the same, but I don't think I would have asked my mom to redo it. The reality was, it was too big. Sighing heavily, I went to work fixing it.

The evening of the prom, we took lots of photos of both Jennifer and David before they left to meet their dates.

I watched them smiling, laughing, and posing, and was overcome with joy and pride at the beautiful people they had each become—inside and out. I was so happy because they were both so happy. David was so handsome, and Jennifer wasn't just gorgeous; she was stunning. I couldn't stop looking at her. I was so glad I had fixed the dress. It could not have fit her any better. She was radiant. I remember thinking, "If she looks like this now, wow, what will she look like on her wedding day?"

As I snapped a photo, she said something to David, and they both laughed. I knew then that no matter what else happened, these twins, along with Justin, would be lifelong friends. I smiled at the thought of how much fun we'd all have in the decades ahead. I couldn't wait.

The classroom was quiet, and I realized the announcements had ended. The students were all looking at me. I couldn't breathe. My throat felt thick and tight. I felt like I was drowning.

I asked one of the students to get the supervising teacher in the next room. When she walked in, I left the classroom and ran down a long hall. I found an unlocked janitor's closet. I pushed my way in as a flood of body sobs overtook me. I sank to the floor, begging God for help.

I don't know how long I was in that closet. When the door finally opened, my supervising teacher was standing there. She hugged me, waited for me to calm, and then asked if she could call someone to come and get me. I shook my head and told her I just needed to leave.

I sat for a long time in the parking lot of the school. I knew I couldn't go home. I could only think of one place to go.

My mom saw my car pull into her driveway. She met me at the door.

Hours later, I mustered enough strength to drive home. I crawled into bed and slept for hours.

When am I ever going to stop having these complete breakdowns? Am I ever going to be able to live life again without being hit by them?

Jim

APRIL 11, 2004
Lori said to me last week, "Jim, there's an angel at this store you may want to go buy to put on Jennifer's headstone. There's only one left."

I've been searching for an angel statue for Jennifer's grave for months. I've seen hundreds of them.

Ever since she was a little girl, Jennifer loved angels, and she reminded me of one! She was just so sweet, so gentle and quiet, and so petite.

We already had an angel engraved on her headstone, but we wanted a statue.

As soon as I saw the statue, my jaw dropped. I stood in the store, staring at it. It was exactly what I had been looking for. So, I bought the three-foot-high angel, put it on the front seat of my truck, and buckled it in.

I turned on the ignition, and the radio came on. "Lightning Crashes" by Live was playing. The hairs on my arms stood on end. I could not believe that of all the songs, this one was coming through my speakers; the same song that repeatedly played in my head for months and months after Jennifer died about the circle of life and an angel's part in it.

I stared at the angel sitting on the seat next to me and shook my head. I couldn't believe that of all the songs in the world, that one was playing at that moment!

I sat there with the engine idling, staring at the angel. Something about it was driving me crazy. It looked familiar, but I couldn't figure out why. The angel had wings as long as her body, with big feathers. I kept looking at it until it hit me. When it did, my heart nearly stopped cold. It was the same angel image that we had carved into Jennifer's headstone over a year ago. The exact one!

I kept staring at the angel, listening to the music, and wondering if I was witnessing the Divine at work. My arms and legs were covered in goosebumps. If that statue angel could have winked at me, I think she would have, with the light of Jennifer's sparkling eyes shining through.

APRIL 22, 2004

In a MADD impact class last night, I listened to the story of a woman who had lost her only child one beautiful summer day, twenty years ago. I could feel her pain from the back of the room as she talked.

Twenty years she's been dealing with her pain.

I looked around the room. I felt like a hungry wolf wanting to talk to the audience about not driving after drinking. I wanted them to hear Jennifer's story and realize that if they had to walk in my shoes for one day, they would never drink and drive again.

MAY 9, 2004

My dad told me today that he just met a man whose young niece had been terminally ill. She awoke one morning, telling her parents that her grandpa, who had recently died, had come to see her in the night. He told her not to be afraid to die because he would be there to take her home. She died later that day.

That story made me feel better, thinking of that girl holding her grandfather's hand as she left this earth. *I wonder who was holding Jennifer's? I don't know, but I know she wasn't alone.*

MAY 11, 2004

It's really hard to be with people who are drinking and not be mentally counting how many they've had. No one should invite me to a party if they don't want me getting in the face of guests who have been drinking and intend to drive home. I don't mean to be a jerk, but I'd rather be a jerk who saves a life than sit quietly and not speak up.

Several years ago, I saw a man who was obviously intoxicated stagger out of a restaurant, get in his car and drive away, going down the wrong way on a four-lane highway. I called the police, but it was too late. He was gone. I have no idea what happened after that.

Since Jennifer died, I often think about that driver. I should have stopped him from ever getting into his car. I will never let that happen again.

If I ever again see someone who is drunk and ready to drive, it won't be pretty, for them, or me, because I won't let them leave, not on my watch. If I'm in a parking lot and have to park my truck right behind them, I'll do it. I have insurance and can get a new truck, but we can't bring back anyone who may be killed by that drunk driver.

I've lost so many people I love to drunk drivers that this is no joke to me. It may be fun and games to a lot of people, but not to me. It's personal, and I've become like a pitbull to stop it.

If I'm ever hit by a drunk driver and live to tell, I don't know what I'll do. God tells us to love our enemies and that he will judge them when their time is up.

I hope I'm never put to this test because I really don't know what I would do. I think the driver had better hope I don't survive. His chances may be better with God than me.

Lori

JUNE 10, 2004

The other morning after Jim left for work, I got on my knees in front of our couch and began to pray. A beam of sunlight blazed through the window, right over me.

I could feel its warmth and imagined that it was the warmth of Jennifer's love.

JUNE 16, 2004

When David and Jennifer got their driver's licenses, we decided to get them a car to share—a decade-old Volvo because it was supposed to be safe. I liked that it had a built-in roll bar in case the car ever rolled. Jim liked it because it only had four cylinders, and he was convinced that the kids would not be able to go too fast in it. I wasn't so sure.

Every day they'd drive to and from high school together. Some days Jennifer would drive, others David would. Once home after school, they'd grab a snack and head to the basement to watch a little TV. Most days, it was an episode from *Full House*. *Power Rangers* came on afterward, but at that point, Jennifer usually lost interest and headed to her room to do her homework. I think they both found comfort in the daily routine of just hanging out and decompressing after school.

On a drive home from school their junior year, Jennifer told David about a guy in one of her classes who kept pestering her. That morning he had been especially cruel. David told her he was pretty sure the guy liked her and was acting that way to get her attention. Jennifer didn't care what his motives were. The next day, David saw the boy in the hall and told him to leave Jennifer alone. The guy apparently listened because David said she never mentioned it again.

While David could be protective of her, he was no saint. After she died, David filled me in on another event that happened after they got the car. One which I knew something about. It had been a snowy Saturday afternoon; David and Jennifer were driving past the high school when David pulled into the empty parking lot. "Hey, check this out." He turned the wheel as far as it would go and began doing doughnuts in the snow.

They were laughing until one rotation, out of the corner of his eye, David glimpsed a green Jeep Cherokee driving past on the road.

"Oh no," moaned David, "that was Mom and Dad."

"Do you think they saw us?"

"Oh yeah. We're in so much trouble."

When they got home, they were met by Jim and me standing in the kitchen with stern faces and crossed arms. Jim said, "Don't ever do that again."

I thought we had handled it pretty well, and that the kids learned their lesson. Apparently not, for after she died, David told me that Jennifer had taught several of her friends how to do doughnuts as well. Parents can try and teach their kids about safety, but in the end, we can't live life for them.

JUNE 17, 2004
Jennifer liked taking photos of David when he was skateboarding. I think it also had something to do with a crush she had on one of the boys he skated with. One day, she showed up at home with a bumper sticker on the back of the car she shared with David: "I love Skater Boys."

David took one look and cried, "I'm not driving around with that sticker on my car!"

"It's my car too, David! I'm not taking it off."

When David tried it to tear it off, the two ended up in a screaming match.

David finally relented as he marched back into the house. "If you want that sticker on the car so badly, then fine."

Much to David's credit and chagrin, he took more than a little ribbing from his friends, but he kept it on the car.

It's amazing what a brother will do for his sister. I was proud of David. He wasn't the only one protective of his sister.

Jennifer's sophomore year of high school, she didn't have a date for the prom. She was planning on meeting a girlfriend of hers there who also didn't have a date. When Justin heard this, he said, "If Jennifer doesn't have anyone to take her to dinner before the prom, I will." And he did. I don't know many brothers, especially one who had already graduated, who would have done that for his sister. *What teenage boy does that?*

JUNE 22, 2004

I'm so proud of Justin. This fall will be a year that he has been free of drugs. That's an amazing accomplishment. Driving to the hospital today, Jim looked at me and said, "Ready or not, life goes on." He was right.

Our grandson, Tyson, was born today. The truth is, I've been dreading his birth because I'm not sure there's enough left of me to give anything to him. But Jim's right, ready or not, life goes on.

As I held Tyson's tiny hand in mine, my heart began melting in love. I stroked his soft, little cheek, and all I could do was marvel at how beautiful and perfect he was. I closed my eyes and whispered, "Thank you, God, for this precious life."

After leaving the hospital and walking into our house, I looked around and couldn't help but smile. For the first time in a long time, our home somehow didn't feel so forlorn.

Leave it to God to tell us life goes on—and show us so with a grandchild.

Jim

AUGUST 19, 2004

I ran into some of Jennifer's friends when I was out doing errands. Kind words were said, and hugs were given. I felt as if I'd been slammed against a brick wall. I could hardly speak. I wonder if they noticed.

Occasionally, I've seen Jennifer's old boyfriend around town. We never seem to have much to say, but it kills me thinking about the good times they had together and what could have been. We liked him a lot, and so did Jennifer.

Lori said to me last week, "Did you ever notice that Jennifer always dated guys a lot like you? They were all hardworking and treated her with respect."

That was one of the most meaningful things anyone has ever said to me.

SEPTEMBER 1, 2004

I've run into Carolyn's father a few times since the accident. Each time, soft words were exchanged, questions about how everyone's doing. He says it is up and down for Carolyn. I can't imagine how hard it must be for her.

I don't point fingers. There's enough fault to go around.

We taught our kids the dangers of drinking and driving and took care never to glorify it. And yet, somehow, the worst still happened.

Lori

SEPTEMBER 10, 2004

In Justin's junior year of high school, he and a buddy were bored one day and came up with the brilliant idea to break into their high school and look around. Once there, they decided to turn on the fire hose, go outside, hide in the bushes, and wait for the fire trucks to come. They turned it on and ran out, but nobody came. Instead of going back in, or calling someone, they panicked and just took off.

Justin said later that he didn't sleep all night, fretting about what was happening at the school. What happened was that the gym floor flooded. The damage was so extensive; the school didn't know if they were going to be able to save it.

The next day, the story was all over our local news. The boys turned themselves in. Jim and I were devastated. Justin looked like a wreck. He felt awful. Both boys wrote letters of apology that were read over the school's loudspeakers, and the letters were published in the newspaper. It was a slow news week. The story was front-page for several days.

Justin was expelled for the rest of his junior year and fined $10,000, which we paid. He spent the next year and a half working to pay us back. And he did, every dime. He had to make up all his schoolwork with tutors coming to the house.

Since the kids were young, I had regularly volunteered at their schools and was often the Homeroom Mother. Jim had an excellent reputation around town as a businessman. Both of these helped the community be understanding. Those who knew us knew that we were good parents. They understood that Justin had made a stupid decision and was working hard, making up for it. It became a very teachable moment for us.

One day not long afterward, Jim went to bid a man's roof, and he said, "I heard what happened with your son." Jim told him how hard it had been on our family. Then the man said, "Whatever you do, don't give up on your boy. Just be grateful you can still talk to him and work through this. If I want to talk to my son, I have to go to the graveyard. Because my son committed suicide."

Jim came home, shaken. After hearing about the conversation, I said, "Wow. You know, Jim, as terrible as it is, this deal with Justin is doable."

And from that day on, whenever something bad happened, or we faced a difficult challenge, one of us would quote our new family motto, "This is doable because no one is dead."

Three years later, Jennifer was dead. We never used that motto again.

Now, when something bad happens, we ask, "Is this doable or not doable?" And for me, death is not doable. Even though we've been through it, it's not doable. It just isn't.

Jim

SEPTEMBER 21, 2004

I don't know what we would have done without Lon and Christine coming over every week. It gives us something to look forward to. I can't believe it's been over a year and a half that they've been coming! Those are good friends. They're so easy to be with, maybe because we've known them so long. We don't have to worry about what we say or do. They come, we eat, and we watch TV. They usually bring their young son Alec. It's hard, but good, to have a kid in the house again. I've nicknamed him "My Little Buddy."

Lon told me last night that he still can't believe our entire family showed up for church the day after Jennifer died and what an example it set for others. I hadn't thought about that. We were simply doing what we had to do to survive.

Sometimes when they come, they'll bring dinner, and sometimes we'll make it. I think it's been really good for Lori. She'll say, "I think I'll make dinner for the Weavers this week." Ever since Jennifer died, Lori likes to watch reality shows because she says, "They aren't real. I've had enough of reality for a lifetime."

When I was walking them to their car last night, Christine mentioned she could tell that Lori was doing better. I asked her what she meant. "I don't know if you remember this, Jim, but the first few weeks we came over, Lori was on the couch, wrapped in a blanket in a fetal position. It was like the blanket was a protective shell she couldn't be without. And every week, a little more of Lori appeared. Look at her tonight; she's off the couch and engaged.

SEPTEMBER 23, 2004

When Jennifer was about thirteen, we were in my old Ford Bronco visiting Six Flags Great Adventure Animal Park in Texas. I was driving, and Lori was riding shotgun. David and Justin were in the back seat. Jennifer was in the back end, facing backward. The rear window was rolled all the way down. Jennifer held a bucket of food we had purchased at the park entrance. I stopped when we saw a small herd of giraffes. They knew what a stopped car meant. One of the larger ones moved toward us. I told the kids to sit real quiet. "Jennifer, throw a handful of that food out the window and see if it'll come closer." It did. But, instead of reaching its long neck to the ground and eating the food Jennifer had just tossed out, the giraffe was no fool! It went for the source. I looked over in time to see the massive animal's head reach far into the car, right into the bucket in Jennifer's lap. I don't know how she did it, but before the sound of her screech hit my ears, she had leaped over Justin and David and landed in the front seat. She was screaming so loud I think her cousins in Kansas could hear her. The rest of us were laughing so hard we couldn't speak.

I could barely see to drive for the rest of the tour because of the tears of laughter streaming from my eyes. I've never laughed so hard in my life. For the rest of the drive through the park, Jennifer sat wedged next to Lori. She was not about to go anywhere near that back end.

Lori

SEPTEMBER 23, 2004

It's Jennifer's birthday. I took a nap and had a dream. In it, I woke up in my bedroom, lying next to Jim. I looked around the room and saw that everything was intact. The room was clean. The sun was shining through our French doors. I felt good. I got up and opened the door into the hall. The rest of our house was in shambles. The roof was gone, and our home was demolished. There was nothing left.

SEPTEMBER 28, 2004

I'm getting to a place I never wanted to be, where I have accepted our fate and where I'm getting used to not seeing or hearing Jennifer. It's a place where I am learning to accept my new relationship with her—a relationship that's not physical, but still exists, nevertheless.

I don't cry as often now, thankfully, because all the tears were for *my* loss. I'm in a place now, for the first time, which feels more real than surreal. Jennifer is a child we had that died in a car wreck.

OCTOBER 11, 2004

Justin reminded me today of something I hadn't thought of in a long time. Her sophomore year in high school, Jennifer was in Big Lots with some friends and saw a headboard and platform bed frame that she really liked. She thought it was more elegant than the one she had since she was young. Jennifer was determined to bring it home, set it up, and then surprise us. With the help of her friends, they got the boxes up to her room. After her friends left, she began putting it together. Justin said she showed up in his room exasperated. "I've spent over two hours, and it won't work! I've done everything exactly right. Exactly what the stupid directions said, and it won't work!" Justin had never seen her so angry. He said he'd come up.

When he took one look at her bed, he burst out laughing. "Jennifer, you've got a full-size mattress and box springs, but the headboard and frame are queen size! You need to take this back and get the right size."

Jennifer shook her head. "I'm not taking it back! It's the only one they had. I'm keeping it."

"Jennifer, you've got at least a six-inch gap between your mattress and the frame on both sides. That empty space looks ridiculous. If you won't take the headboard back, then you need a different mattress and box springs."

"But I like my mattress," she said, even more determined.

"Well," said Justin grabbing a book off her bookshelf, "I guess you could always use this extra space for books or something."

And that's exactly what she did.

Jennifer may have been quiet and accommodating most of the time, but she could also be stubborn. I thought so every time I saw her mismatched bed set.

But I had to admit, it worked pretty well as a bookshelf.

Jim

OCTOBER 21, 2004

I'll never forget the expression on Lori's face when she held our grandson for the first time. It swelled my heart with relief and joy.

We've both fallen in love again with this new baby. Tyson will never replace Jennifer, of course, but he's helping us in a way that we needed.

Our hearts are like broken glass, needing to be glued back together.

Love is the glue for us right now.

When I hold Tyson's little hand in mine, I can't stop smiling. I know there will be other grandkids to come, and with each one, more glue.

NOVEMBER 25, 2004

I used to get stressed over small things, from my job to life in general. As people, we create a lot of self-induced stress that makes life harder.

My outlook has changed since Jennifer died. Or maybe it's my priorities that have changed. I no longer worry much about the "things of this earth."

I look around and see how most of us want for nothing. Some people think they can buy anything. I used to as well. Now, I'm more focused on living a life that honors God and focusing on where I will spend eternity. Money can buy a lot of things, but as the old joke says, "It can't buy air conditioning in Hell."

JANUARY 25, 2005

Just after Jennifer died, a client who had lost a child decades earlier said to me, "Someday, you'll feel the sun shining on you again."

I didn't believe her.

Earlier this week, when I walked to my truck, the air was cold, but the sun was bright. I stopped walking and realized that since Jennifer died, this was the first time I could feel the warmth of the sunshine on my skin.

I turned my face toward it and remembered that client's prediction. She was right. I know Jennifer would be glad. Her smile could light up any room. I wondered if she was smiling down on me.

FEBRUARY 2, 2005

It still hurts to look at pictures of her, and it hurts, even more, to look at all the smiling faces of our family, back when we had it all.

Every chance I get, I remind people to love each other. Husbands and wives need to encourage each other and be more loving to their kids because, in one moment, they could be gone.

FEBRUARY 18, 2005

Lori and I just returned home from a trip to Barbados. We needed a break from the cold. Sitting by the pool one day, we talked to a woman who had recently lost her daughter. She said that she'd been so down that people were encouraging her to take pills for her pain. I think she was wise enough to know otherwise. She said she knew that she would have to deal with it head-on sooner or later. She's a Christian, and she knew Jesus was by her side, helping her.

Any place on this earth we go, one thing is certain somewhere there are others hurting.

FEBRUARY 26, 2005

Lori was cleaning out a drawer and found an undeveloped roll of film. We took it in and got it developed. Yesterday, I was sitting in my truck when Lori opened the package and handed the photos to me. One look and the air left my lungs. I felt dizzy.

More than half were of Jennifer, and several were of her with Carolyn.

These are some of the last photos we have of Jennifer. In them, she is laughing, smiling, and utterly carefree. Both girls are.

While seeing the photos is painful, there is something comforting in them as well. I think it's seeing firsthand that the last few weeks before Jennifer died, her life was fun.

I asked Lori if she thought we should give them to Carolyn. We talked it over and decided that someday we would, but it may be too soon for her now. I can't imagine how hard it will be for her to see them. But in giving them to her, I hope she can find some peace in them too.

Lori

MARCH 1, 2005

I still hate weddings, anniversary parties, family gatherings, and holidays where Jennifer's void remains overwhelming, and I have to worry about whether or not I'll start to cry.

I don't like to go where everyone is happy, and I might put a damper on it. But I feel obligated. I'm supposed to go. They expect me to go. I expect me to go.

They think it'll be good for me. But I don't want to do any of it! How do I explain how I feel without them thinking, "It's time for her to buck up and get over it?" What they might not understand is that my crying still comes unprompted and without warning. And once it starts, it's hard to control. If they think I can just "get over it," they have no idea what a struggle this still is for me, every day.

MARCH 3, 2005

I keep having the same recurring vision of David, Justin, Jim, and me climbing this steep mountain covered in jagged rocks. It's cold, dark, and drizzling. Our hands and knees are bleeding. Jim is leading. He keeps stopping long enough to pull each of us onto the ledge to catch our breaths. We cling to every hand and foothold, pushing toward the top. Every moment we're at risk of falling to our deaths. Exhausted and wet, we all keep helping each other, struggling upward, but we can't get to the top no matter what. Our house is sitting at the peak. It's dark, except for one room: Jennifer's. I know that's where she is now—where it's safe, warm, and dry. The rest of us are not. We're still here fighting through the everyday challenges of life on earth.

MARCH 10, 2005

Before our cat Sweetie came into our lives, we had Sarah, a chocolate and grey calico. When Jennifer was little, she loved to dress Sarah up in baby clothes and push the cat around the house and yard in a baby buggy. Eventually, Sarah would tire of the game and flee.

One morning Jennifer dressed Sarah in a onesie that had been hers as an infant. Later that night, as Jim and I were heading to bed, Sarah dashed up the stairs in front of us, frantically leaping and twisting. She was still wearing the onesie.

"Has that cat been wearing that thing all day?" cried Jim, howling with laughter.

I burst out laughing so hard that I couldn't respond.

Still laughing, we finally made it into bed, and we laughed until our sides ached. Every time one of us managed to stop, the other would start up again, and we'd both end up overcome.

Finally, just as I was about to fall asleep, Jim said, "That cat running around, still wearing that onesie, was about the saddest, pathetic, most hilarious things I've ever seen!"

And it was. And it was a long time before either of us went to sleep that night.

Jim

MARCH 11, 2005

It's been a busy spring for me. I was meeting with a homeowner about her roof. We started talking about our kids, and the next thing I knew, I started to cry. I couldn't believe it. I have outwardly cried so little, and yet there I was, with a person I barely knew, bawling like a baby.

When I was finally able to talk, she asked if there was something she could do to help. I said, "Yes. Would you please tell your husband that someone he has never met has a message for him? Please tell him to remember to hug his kids and tell them how much he loves them."

MARCH 15, 2005

Sometimes, people say the most hurtful things, and they are completely clueless about it. Lori and I have both experienced it when people try to let us know that they understand our pain by portraying theirs.

Lori and I were speaking with a homeowner today. She saw the bumper sticker on my truck dedicated to Jennifer. After asking us a few questions, she said to Lori, "It must have been so terrible for you to lose your daughter. I felt the same when I got divorced."

Watching Lori out of the corner of my eye, I saw her recoil.

It usually takes a lot to offend me. But this did, big time. It took all I had not to say, "Are you kidding me? I know divorce is devastating, but please, if you think it's the same as the death of your child, try telling me that after you've stood over your child lying in a casket!"

When we got into the car, Lori said, "She doesn't know how lucky she is that she knows nothing about how it really feels to lose a child. I hope she stays ignorant forever."

MARCH 17, 2005

I know my family and friends are frustrated with me because I don't want to go to functions where people will be drinking and then driving home. I just refuse to go. I don't get it that our society thinks that we need alcohol to have fun.

At one party, the hostess announced that no alcohol would be served out of respect to us.

It was a nice thought, but we felt like elephants in the room for the first two hours. No one seemed to know what to say. It was quiet and awkward until someone went and brought a cooler full of beer and wine inside. Guests began helping themselves.

I didn't tell anyone how I was feeling, but it was hard to watch. Once people started drinking, the party grew loud with talking and laughter.

It seemed to take alcohol before this group of people could relax enough to have fun. That's sad.

Lori

APRIL 1, 2005

It's been two years and five months now. The pain has dulled, yet anger comes more frequently. I still cry. I miss Jennifer. I have more energy, but perhaps I'm clinically depressed.

I don't enjoy anything. Solitude is still my best friend. I don't have to talk to, smile at, or impress "solitude." I wonder why, if I have so many good things in life, as I do, why does losing one of those things make everything else insignificant.

Jim and me, and our two boys, minus Jennifer makes a family of four. But the reality is five minus one equals zero. *Why? Why isn't four enough?*

APRIL 5, 2005

A couple of years before she died, Jennifer and I went paragliding on a trip to the Caribbean. Our legs dangled like the jellyfish tentacles in the tropical, warm water below. Our hair blew in the wind. With the colorful canopy of a parachute overhead and propelled by a powerful boat, we laughed and screamed with delight as we soared high and free.

Throwing her head back, Jennifer exclaimed, "Look at us, Mom! We're flying!"

I thought we'd have a lifetime of such adventures.

APRIL 20, 2005

I have more and more dreams where I don't want to wake up because I know I'll have to give her up again.

APRIL 22, 2005

I've been throwing a fit inside for two and a half years, and now—I'm done. I give up. It's over. I'm tired. I surrender to the fact that Jennifer is gone.

It's a sad surrender.

Jim

APRIL 24, 2005

We just got back from David's graduation from a diesel/automotive and industrial technology school in Houston. It was a tough program. As we watched him walk across the stage and accept his diploma, I couldn't be prouder of him! He's been hired by BMW to be trained by their mechanics.

It's been a hard road for David. He's had to grow up fast since losing his twin. He broke down last night, wishing Jennifer was there to celebrate.

APRIL 29, 2005

I was driving today and put the CD on that we played at Jennifer's funeral. Music she loved. Soon, I was crying.

Controlling sadness is like trying to chase the wind. You can't see it. You can't grasp it. You can't change it, but you can feel it.

MAY 13, 2005

Karen from MADD called Lori and asked her if she would talk to a woman who had lost her daughter and was really struggling. She said the woman was in crisis.

During their meeting, Lori learned that the daughter had been killed on her way to school when a drunk driver slammed into her. It turned out that the driver and his passenger buddy had been out partying all night. Their night of fun just took the life of a sweet, innocent girl whose only crime was going to school. For a few hours of fun and games, this mother and their family's world has been destroyed.

This has to stop. *What is it going to take to convince people to stop drinking and driving?*

In the wrong hands, a car is no different than a loaded gun. Each can be a killing machine. Pulling the trigger or turning the key after drinking—both are equally dangerous.

JUNE 9, 2005

Our granddaughter was born today: Alexis Jennifer. A new miracle of life. She is an angel with blond hair, just like Jennifer.

My prayer for Justin as a father of this beautiful little girl is for him to be the very best father he can be, so he will never live with the burden of regret.

Jennifer would have loved being an aunt. She would have loved these babies and been so proud of both her brothers.

The circle of life continues.

Jennifer & David 1986

Lori & Jennifer's last photo
together October 2002

Jennifer & Sarah 1987

Jennifer 1987

Jennifer & David 1986*

David, Justin, Jennifer 1989

Jennifer & David age 5

David & Jennifer 1986

Jennifer, David & Justin
off to school 1993

Jennifer 1994

Jennifer with her Grandpa
Dodd "Santa" 1995

Lori's parents Howard & Doris Dodd
1999

Justin taking his sister to
dinner before her
prom 2000

Jennifer's selfie 1999

Jennifer's cousin
Nathan Dodd**

Gingerbread church made
by Jennifer & Lori 1999

*Photo courtesy of Christine Weaver. **Photo courtesy of Brad and Sandra Dodd.
All other photos courtesy of The Dultmeier Family.

PART THREE

HEALING IN ACTION

Mom, don't cry for me,
You've got so many things left to do.

—Poem by Lori Dultmeier, May 2005

Jennifer's Fifth Grade Class Journal

12/7/94: Yesterday I got 1 extra ticket. But I really did not like the sub. She yelled alot.

12/9/94: Today I am having pizza from Pizza Hut. It was good.

12/13/94: Today we are going to my House for Girl Scouts. We are going to decart cookies.

11/14/94: This morning I wrapped presents for my 2 cousin Megan and Matt. I got Megan a Lion King toy. And Matt a batman toy.

12/21/94: For Christmas I'm going to my Grandmas house on Thursday because she going to Texas for Christmas so she wants to see us open the presents.

1/3/95: Over Christmas I went sliding before the snow. And from doing that I got a lot of bruses.

1/4/95: Heather keeps calling me a wolf. I wonder who shes talking to. I wonder what wolf means.

1/10/95: The best thing I did yesterday was going sleding. I had my best friend spend the day and David had a friend spend the night. We all had fun sleding. Just is that we got muddy.

1/11/95: I love it when it rains. Because I can just wach it. Or play in it. And I love hot day because I can swim in my swimming pool.

1/12/95: My favorite board game is Clue because it is mystory. All that you do is see who killed Mr. Bobby.

1/13/95: I'm going to Dr. Z on Monday with my Best Friend Carolyn.

1/18/95: My favorite singer is Fath Hill because I like her singing. I also like Patty Loveless I like her songs.

1/19/95: Today I don't know what I am doing. I just know that I am at school.

1/20/95: My plans for this weekend and tonight I am going to the rodo. And Saturday I might go to my friends house.

1/23/95: This weekend I went to a rodeo. A clown got bucked by a bull. Then I went to Hypermart and there was a casting kids thing and I might been the highest score of a girl. I got 70 points.

1/24/95: The book I am going to read is The Mask. It is good I think. I have not read it.

1/30/95: The favorite dream I ever had I don't know. I don't have dream that much.

1/31/95: I have 109 tickets an I am going to spend, spend. I'm going to diffenly by candy.

Jim

For over two years, several buddies have tried to coax me into going fishing regularly with them, but I've had no interest. They won't take no for an answer. Earlier this year, they convinced me to sign up for the bass tournament circuit. Reluctantly I agreed. Somehow, at one of the tournaments, I found myself in first place, but I couldn't have cared less. It didn't seem fair to the others in the competition who were trying so hard.

I wanted to change my attitude. I decided to set a goal of winning the *Kansas Angler of the Year* in tribute to Jennifer.

Winning is a really tough goal, but I've felt better lately having something to work towards.

A big test recently was a tournament in Western Kansas.

The day of the tournament, it was predicted to be well over one hundred degrees with a stiff wind.

It was miserable. My fishing partner and I fished hard for seven hours without a single bite. At one o'clock, I prayed for just one fish.

Forty-five minutes before we had to weigh and record our catches, I still hadn't had a bite. I made a 911 call to God not to let me fail. I wanted His help in knowing which bait to use. My tackle box was loaded with years of bait. I know it sounds crazy, and maybe it was just the heat going to my head, but I got a sense that God was nudging my hand to one I would normally never use under those conditions.

I picked it up and spun it in the sun.

I was ready to be done. I had made hundreds of casts that day. But this cast had a hard prayer behind it, and I immediately felt something hit. When I reeled it in it was a 16-inch bass. I about fell overboard! Three casts later, another 19-inch bass hit on the same bait.

With the sun still blazing, I looked up toward Heaven and gave a little wink to the One who I think helped me, and to the daughter I love.

I think God knew why something as simple as a fishing tournament meant so much to this father, trying to honor his daughter in one of the few ways he could.

OCTOBER 22, 2005

Last night we got another late-night call. Just like with Jennifer, we raced to the hospital. This time it was my sister's husband. We were told he walked out of a bar after drinking and got behind the wheel of his van. His vehicle went off the road and hit a tree.

Thank God, no one else was hurt! I still can't believe it happened.

Wasn't seeing what we all went through with Jennifer enough?

My sister is a wreck. We all are. I have no idea if he is going to make it. It doesn't look good.

I'm so angry I feel like a coiled rattlesnake wanting to strike at something—anything!

DECEMBER 4, 2005

My brother-in-law was luckier than Jennifer. He didn't die as a result of the accident, but he's paralyzed from the chest down. My sister's family will now be taking care of him for the rest of his life.

He will never be able to walk.

This time, the other guy turned out to be my brother-in-law. *Even after knowing what happened to Jennifer!*

How could he not have learned a lesson from watching us lose our beautiful daughter, and what has become a lifetime of hell for us? Now it seems, he has created his own. All because of alcohol!

Lori

DECEMBER 6, 2005

Before Jennifer died, I selfishly avoided people in crisis. I wanted to be with people who were easier to be around.

Until Jennifer died, I never understood real sorrow. I've come to realize that everyone has painful crosses to bear. Maybe it took Jennifer dying for me to really listen and understand their sorrows. I hear. I listen.

I hope that never changes.

Jim

DECEMBER 19, 2005

I'm so proud of my nephew Daniel and his new bride, Marcy! They got married last week and planned ahead to rent vans to take people home after the reception, so no one would have to worry about having too much to drink and then driving. They just showed their guests how much they value their lives. Wow! We need more people like them!

DECEMBER 30, 2005

We made it through another year without Jennifer. It was a year of more downs than ups, but woven throughout, there were blessings. I'm trying hard to focus on them.

On the shelf in my study is a new trophy: *Angler of the Year.*

Looking at it, I can't help but smile. "This one's for you, Jennifer."

JANUARY 22, 2006

As we walked out of church today with Lon and Christine, a picture fell from Christine's Bible. It was of Lori and Christine the summer before Jennifer died. They had just arrived at a baby shower in Lori's red '63 Ford Falcon convertible. They were smiling big, and their hair was wind-blown from the ride. "Our *Thelma and Louise* days," Christine laughed.

Lori looked closely at the photo. "That's the old Lori. That one's not here anymore."

Christine said, "Yes, maybe not the old Lori, but the new Lori is here, and she's even stronger."

Lori replied, "That's true."

They were right. Lori's stronger now than she was. No doubt.

Lori

FEBRUARY 9, 2006

Every Friday, since my kids were young, my mom, Melissa, and I would take all of our kids for an outing, usually to eat. We'd head over to Mom and Dad's house to let the kids play for the rest of the afternoon, giving the adults a chance to talk. It was great for the kids to be with their cousins and a bonding time for the adults.

My sorrow has been hard on many people, but none more so than my mom. After Jennifer died, Mom was my rock. I spent countless hours with her as she tried to comfort me. But she didn't know how to help me do the one thing she most wanted—be happy again. And over time, her frustration at her inability to help me became a wedge between us.

I couldn't do anything about it because I couldn't make myself happy. And I didn't have the energy to try and pretend. It took every ounce of everything I had just to go on living. Trying to be cheerful for anyone else's sake, even for my mom, was impossible.

Mom has written me several heartfelt letters since Jennifer died for which I'm so grateful. For a while, Melissa and I have encouraged Mom to start journaling about her feelings. She very reluctantly agreed. She recently shared two of her journal entries with me...

FEBRUARY 2, 2006

I do not want to start a journal! Lori thinks this is what I want to do. Because of my age or my personality, I am not prone to spill my guts. People of my generation do not do this very well.

From the very beginning, after Jennifer's death, I have felt like Lori has a script, and I'm never on the right page. All of her friends and acquaintances were on the same page as she was and always knew her needs, but nothing I ever said or did seemed to fit with her. When I went to a counselor at a hospice support group, my subject was: I can't connect with my daughter.

They didn't have any solutions.

For the last few months, maybe for all of 2005, I have felt as though I've lost all connection with Lori. When we're together, it's like two strangers.

FEBRUARY 7, 2006

On Friday, we were talking about the complexity of this grief journey from the mother-daughter standpoint. I said I wrote in my last journal entry that I have a hard time spilling my insides to people, but I don't have a problem baring my soul to God. After fervent prayers about this situation, I believe God gave me an answer. I think the reason I have not been able to reach Lori is that she is in a realm I can't enter.

I can relate to all other realms of her life because I had been there: little girl, teenager, wife, mother, and grandmother. Then Lori entered a realm, not of her choosing, where I cannot enter. And the only way I could go there was if I had lost one of my own children.

Maybe I have been asking Lori to let me enter a place I could never go.

Jim

FEBRUARY 11, 2006

I knew it was only a matter of time. I'm surprised it hasn't happened before.

I was out with a group of men duck hunting. One of them asked me, "So Jim, how many kids do you have?"

I just froze. I could have said, "I have two boys," and left it at that. But that wasn't the truth. I could have said, "I have two boys and a daughter," and left it at that, but that didn't feel right either. And I wasn't in the mood to go into an hour-long talk about losing Jennifer.

Instead, I said, "I have two boys and had a daughter we lost two years ago." God must have been protecting me because just at that moment, a flock of ducks flew overhead, and the man turned to watch them, and thankfully never asked me any more questions.

FEBRUARY 13, 2006

My brother-in-law has spent a lot of time in rehab learning to take care of himself and learning to use a wheelchair. I'm proud of him.

The night of the wreck, he technically died several times, and they were able to bring him back. Later, he told my sister that he saw "gates" and many people he recognized standing in front of them. Some were people he hadn't seen in many years. Jennifer wasn't among them.

Another acquaintance told me the story of a friend who had a heart attack and died on the table. They were able to bring him back. During the experience, he watched himself being worked on. As they were shocking him, he "left" the operating table and "went" to see a man. He didn't know if it was God or Jesus, but all he wanted was to stay with the man. It was so peaceful there, and he felt so warm and safe. Since then, he has been telling people not to be afraid to die.

FEBRUARY 14, 2006

My sister wrote an email to everyone in the family, saying that alcohol is not allowed in her home. After everything she has been through, I understand why.

FEBRUARY 19, 2006

I've been telling my grandkids about Jennifer. I want them to know who she was. As they get older, I will take them to visit Jennifer's grave.

When they're teenagers, I'm going tell them that I don't care what the circumstances are, whether it is day or night, whether or not they've done something wrong, they can call me if they are ever in trouble or at a party where someone has been drinking or taking drugs, and I'll be there to bring them home. I'm not going to bury a grandchild for something that can be prevented. My heart could not take it.

Everything I feel about alcohol has changed since Jennifer's death. I know so many people who think they are pros at drinking and driving. But I've learned there is no such thing. There is only luck. We can all go through life flirting with anything, but sooner or later, if we do it long enough, luck will run out.

I know. There's a double-bladed sword embedded in my heart to remind me.

JUNE 14, 2006

My phone rang. MADD had given out my number, and I was glad. It was a woman calling, crying for help. She had lost her only son compliments of a drunk driver. Her son was twenty-three years old. I knew from her voice she was drowning in pain, madness, and sickness. She was lost.

She told me she thinks her body is exploding from the inside. "Jim," she asked through her sobs, "how can I let this pain out without killing myself? There has to be a way."

I told her to sit down and write about what she was feeling. A few days later, she let me know that she took the advice and that it was helping.

My heart breaks for her.

Lori

Jennifer and Kelly were fourteen when they pledged that when they got married, they would be in each other's wedding.

Today, Kelly fulfilled that promise.

Seated in the church, I opened the program:

Honorary Maid of Honor—Jennifer Dultmeier

Hers was the only name listed.

Jim

JULY 16, 2006
It's baseball season for some of the local youth. We've gone to several games. I cannot believe the amount of alcohol the moms and dads around us are sucking down in front of their kids! *Who's going to drive them all home?* The idiotic parents, that's who!

God help them if they ever find themselves standing over their kid's grave someday, asking, "Why?"

Lori

JULY 1, 2006
I dreamt the other night that I had no head. I was just a stump. I was "looking" in the mirror and trying to put makeup on the scar around the stump. Jim nodded at my headless body, and said, "I don't like playing with that."

When I woke, I realized that my head is everything I am—memories, personality, brain—everything.

JULY 10, 2006

"To fill an empty place in your heart, you have to fill it with something meaningful and productive." I keep telling myself that after realizing I have a huge empty spot inside of me. In the past, I've tried filling it with shopping, spending, and traveling; nothing helps.

The handful of quilts that I delivered to our local hospitals after Jennifer died became dozens, and within a few years, the dozens became hundreds. I started a project called Quilts for Angels. The quilts are used for those like Jennifer, who die unexpectedly, so when the families are brought in to see their loved one, they aren't met with a sterile white sheet.

Many of Jennifer's family and friends are helping to raise funds for the Quilts for Angels project. It's been fun to be together.

In the last months of her life, Jennifer wanted to learn to quilt, so it seems fitting that of all the things I could have done to help keep her memory alive, quilts would be something that she would have liked.

It's a tangible gift of warmth and love. We've started getting letters from people saying how much the quilts have meant to them. I'm glad, but it still does nothing to fill my empty heart. I hope in time that will change.

We've had two grandbabies since Jennifer died. I'm still empty. But I thank God that I am able to extend my love to them. Because of them, I realize that I'm not dead after all.

JULY 15, 2006

When David had his rollover accident shortly after Jennifer died, I had been rendered speechless—completely speechless. Now, another accident has left me equally dumb-struck. It happened earlier this month. I still can't believe it.

My sister Melissa, her husband, Kurt, and their three kids Blake, Brooke, and Alek, were driving home from vacation and had stopped briefly for gas and a restroom break. Everyone piled back into the car. Blake was reaching for his seatbelt just as the car merged back onto the interstate. Seconds later, one of the tires blew out. The car left the road and did a complete roll. It landed with its wheels down.

When Kurt and Melissa looked into the back seat, the space where seventeen-year-old Blake had been was empty.

Kurt and Melissa jumped out of the car and could not believe their eyes: Blake was sitting in the median of Interstate 70! He was alert and talking. No one else was injured. After a trip to the ER, the only evidence of the trauma Blake had experienced was that his ears and belly button were filled with dirt. Blake, a high school football player, was strong and fit for his age, but it took far more than that to save his life.

When we got the news about their accident, we rushed to the hospital. They were all badly shaken and traumatized, especially Melissa.

When she told me what happened, I had no response. I just stared at her in disbelief. I knew I should be saying something, doing something, but I could not form enough coherent thoughts to speak a single one word.

As we were walking out of the hospital a few hours later, Justin turned to me, his tone was indignant. "Mom, why didn't you at least give Melissa a hug? She could have used it!"

I still didn't have the words to explain to him why. How could I? How could I explain that just like that, in the blink of an eye, just like we lost Jennifer, Nathan, and my grandparents, and just like we nearly lost David when his car rolled, we almost lost Blake? How could I respond?

While I was so incredibly grateful Blake was okay, I couldn't help asking God, why? *Why hadn't Jennifer been spared too? Why hadn't she just needed to clean out some dirt from her ears? Why did she have to die?*

Jim

SEPTEMBER 23, 2006
It's Jennifer's birthday. I wish I could know what she would have looked like today.

OCTOBER 10, 2006
I've made a decision. I'm going to join MADD and share Jennifer's story with first time offenders—people charged with DUI. I hope I can make a difference that will save lives. If so, the pain it will cause me to stand up there and tell these folks how lucky they are, lucky they have a chance to go on living—a chance my daughter never had—will be worth it. I just hope I can get through what I want to say.

OCTOBER 15, 2006
The anniversary of Jennifer's death is coming fast. I bet no alcohol company will be showing up to comfort us on the anniversary of her death. It's been four years since she died. I'm still waiting for their sympathy card.

Lori

OCTOBER 18, 2006
The fall air reminds me of Jennifer.

I wish I could sleep until the new year.

OCTOBER 21, 2006
Just after she graduated from high school, Jennifer asked me what I thought was an odd question for a teenager. "Mom, now that we're mostly grown, do you think we'll ever go on any more family vacations like we did last year to New Mexico? Just the five of us."

"I don't know," I answered honestly, "but it will get harder with everyone's work and school schedules, and before you know it, you all will be getting married. I don't know...just the five of us? Probably not."

"That's sad."

I was struck by the disappointment in her voice. Jennifer was right. It was sad. The five of us would never take another trip together as a family, but not because they were all grown.

Jim

OCTOBER 31, 2006

Every time my mom got pregnant, my dad would make her a bet that it would be a boy. He lost most of those bets, as five of her seven children were girls. I was the third, following two older sisters, and shortly after I was born, they nearly lost me.

For the first three days of my life, I wasn't able to keep anything down. Everything came right back up. After three days, I turned yellow. The doctor discovered I had a blocked intestine, just below my stomach. They had no choice but to operate. He said it was that or I would die.

The procedure was very risky for someone so young. Six inches of my intestine would be removed and attached to my stomach in a bypass procedure. Several doctors throughout my life have commented on how advanced that surgery was for 1959. No one could believe I survived, and none more so than the surgeon who did it. Just before wheeling me into the operating room, he said to my mom, "Mary, get out your rosary and start praying and don't stop."

Her prayers must have worked because I recovered fully without any complications.

NOVEMBER 1, 2006

Lori and I were running errands a few days ago. It was a beautiful sunny day. We were driving on a four-lane highway, two lanes in each direction, with most cars going 65-70 mph. We were headed south. Two vehicles were pulled off on the shoulder in the northbound lanes. I glanced over and couldn't believe my eyes. A man was lying face down in the path of traffic. I turned my truck around and pulled up behind the man on the ground to block off that lane and keep oncoming traffic from hitting him. Lori went to help a woman who was kneeling over him. It turned out to be his wife.

They had pulled up behind a car that had run out of gas. When her husband stepped out of his truck to help, he was hit by a passing car.

I wasn't sure if the man was dead. Then I saw him move. I got down on my knees and as close to his face as I could. He was trying to turn over. "Lie still. It's okay. Lie still. Don't move. Help is on the way."

He was trying to talk to me. His lips were moving. I pressed my ear next to his mouth. Only gasps. I knew he was dying—and just like that, he did. One moment he was there, and the next, he wasn't, just like Jennifer.

Now, I cannot stop thinking about that man and how I was the last person he talked to on this earth. That's hard to take and even harder to fathom.

Lori

MARCH 1, 2007
I've spent years trying to learn to live without Jennifer. I think I'm there.

Now, I will learn to be happy without her.

I'm going to focus on being happy that I ever even had a girl.

I will be happy for what I've got, not what I've lost.

This is a journey.

NOVEMBER 29, 2007
I wish I had looked more at Jennifer. Really looked at her. *Did she have specks in her irises, or did she have a dark circle surrounding them?* I just can't remember. I just wish I'd looked—really, really looked.

Her death seems like only yesterday, but 2002 is actually a long time ago.

When does this all end? The pain? The longing? When do the memories become a blessing and not a curse?

MARCH 27, 2008

I watched kids playing on a school playground today. Children's voices rang out with unbridled joy. I thought of my own babies. I cried.

APRIL 9, 2008

"They're so cute!" That's what Jennifer said when she saw the three little statues of children. She was ten. We'd just moved into our new house in the country.

I told the kids that when they grew up and had houses of their own, they could each have one, to remind them forever of our family.

The three statues are still outside the entrance of our home. None of us can stand the thought of those two boy statues leaving the little girl one alone.

Jim

MAY 1, 2008

It's been a long time since I've written in my journal because talking to DUI classes has become my new outlet for expressing my feelings.

I'm sad there's never a shortage of people to talk to. Every time I speak, the room is packed with people who've been picked up for drinking and driving.

I've made people cry while hearing Jennifer's story. Many have told me afterward they will never drink and drive again. For some, I think it's true. If my speaking saves one life, then it's been worth the effort and the pain it takes to do it.

I've found something unexpected about talking to groups of people. I love it because when I do, Jennifer seems more alive.

MAY 29, 2008

When the twins were in fifth grade, we got a gray cat named Sweetie. The kids fought over which of their rooms she got to sleep in at night. In the end, it was mostly up to Sweetie where she ended up. She especially liked Jennifer.

The morning after Jennifer died, I found Sweetie sitting in the hallway staring at Jennifer's closed bedroom door. I picked her up and took her downstairs. When I went back to my study a couple of hours later, there was Sweetie, just sitting and staring at Jennifer's door. It broke my heart. No matter how we tried to distract her, or how many times we carried her away to another room, we'd find Sweetie in front of that door—first for months, then years!

It's been over five years now, and I'll sometimes still find that cat sitting in front of Jennifer's door. Each time, I swoop her up in my arms and say, "Sweetie. She's never going to open that door."

Sweetie doesn't want to believe it. None of us do.

Lori

JUNE 17, 2008

I am missing Jennifer tremendously today. Even my arms ache. She should be here, but she's not. I feel deflated. I'm so tired of trying to make this work in a world without my daughter. My tears haven't stopped all day.

When do memories become less painful? I don't like talking about my memories of Jennifer. People say, "You have so many good memories!"

That may be true, but thinking of them kills me. *When will they stop hurting and become pleasant?*

Life goes on. Yes. And death goes on too.

JULY 19, 2008

A friend suggested I seek professional counseling since it's been years, and I've not cleaned out Jennifer's room. Maybe it's not normal that we haven't done so yet. I don't know what normal is. I'm not sure I care, but if she thinks I need to see someone, I will. I've set up an appointment.

AUGUST 10, 2008

I went to the therapist. She was wonderful. We talked for over two hours. She said she thinks I'm doing pretty well.

I asked her about the room not being cleaned out, and she said, "Lori, whenever, if ever, you decide to clean out Jennifer's room, it's okay. If you find comfort in leaving it as it is, then leave it. If you're ready and want to use the room for something else, that is okay too. Either way, you aren't disrespecting Jennifer's memory. Whether or not you clean it out does not reflect on how you are dealing with your grief."

She believes I'm grief-stricken but not clinically depressed and, while they can mimic each other, there's a difference between them. Grief exacerbates depression, but it's not the same thing. She said something that I've thought all along: she doesn't believe that I need to be taking anti-depression drugs, and I'm not going to be able to medicate my grief away. As long as I'm coping day to day, she thinks it best if I don't. She said that I have to learn to accept and live with my grief. And that's what I'm doing.

Grieving is breathing while my heart is bleeding.

AUGUST 17, 2008

I talked to a woman who lost her son when he was nineteen. Ten years later, she lost her daughter. She had us over for pizza the other night. She cried when she talked about her son and daughter and all the things she misses about them—to this day.

She is eighty-four years old—still grieving—and still crying.

All I could think of was, "That's me in forty years!"

NOVEMBER 30, 2008

My dad's in the hospital.

Mom heard Dad make a loud snore just after they got in bed. That was a few nights ago. It didn't sound normal. By the time she turned on the light, he wasn't breathing. She called 911. They made her pull him to the floor and start CPR. She got him breathing before the paramedics arrived. He had a cardiac arrest from his heart being out of rhythm.

It's been terrible. Dad's been unconscious most of the time.

He woke up after they got him to the hospital. I knew the second he looked at me that he wasn't okay. Now, he's like a little boy. He only recognizes Mom. He doesn't know who I am. They did a scan. He's got extensive brain damage. There is virtually no hope for a full recovery. They're telling us he should be moved to Kansas City. He's hooked up to a breathing tube. The next step is a feeding tube.

Dad would hate that! He would hate living this way! I can't stand the thought of losing him—but I hope he passes before they start the feeding tube.

Mom is beside herself. She's pale and exhausted. I've tried, but she won't leave his side.

DECEMBER 2, 2008
Dad died today. He was seventy-six.

Seventy-six is way too young. So was nineteen.

DECEMBER 9, 2008
Mom and I were with Dad when he took his last breath. He just slipped away. We were in the final stages of having him moved to Kansas City. I didn't want him going through that ordeal. Every breath had been hard for him. I felt so helpless. I kept willing him to just quit breathing, and then he did.

I'm worried about Mom. She's inconsolable.

When we lost Jennifer, my mom kept saying that she felt so helpless because she couldn't do the one thing she most wanted, and that was to take away my pain. Now, I feel the same about her.

DECEMBER 11, 2008
Several hours before Dad died, one of the nurses asked me to come with her. I followed her down the hall to a large storage room. Several of the quilts I had donated months earlier were stacked on a shelf.

"We have a special program here where you can pick out one of these beautiful quilts to cover your father. Once he passes, you may either take it home with you, or it can stay with him."

I reached for a quilt of muted earth tones. The last time I had seen this quilt was in my home, along with the dozens of others I had purchased to donate. I touched the quilted fabric next to my cheek, then traced my thumb over the hand-sewn tag that I had stitched on at some point in the past. I had hand-signed the tag as I do all the quilts. It read, "Donated in memory of Jennifer Dultmeier." Some quilts were donated by others in memory of their loved ones, so I write in those names at their request. I had no idea that when I had this same quilt in my home and signed the tag, it would be for my dad.

It was a few moments before I could speak. "I started Quilts for Angels." The nurse looked at me like she hadn't heard me right. "Jennifer is my daughter."

The nurse cried, "I can't believe it! I've always wondered about the person who was donating all these. Do you have any idea how much it means for us to be able to give these to people when we can no longer save their loved one? It's often the only tangible comfort we can give them. Thank you, Lori, on behalf of all of us on staff. I have no words to thank you enough." The nurse's eyes were filled with tears.

"Dad would like this one. You know, I have the quilts in my home before I distribute them, to sew a tag on each one. With each one, I wonder who it will cover. I always say a silent prayer for them and their families. Until a few days ago, my dad looked like he would live to be an old man. I had no idea this one would be for my dad."

When we got back to the room, I looked at my dad. He looked so pale and fragile. He was in a coma and on a ventilator. I covered him with the quilt and whispered, "Dad, this is going to keep you warm. It's one of our Quilts for Angels, in memory of Jennifer. I think you're going to be seeing her very soon. Will you tell her we love her and miss her every moment of every day?"

I've been told that hearing is the last sense to go. I prayed that Dad heard me. I have no way of knowing, but I like to think he did.

The nurse then lovingly folded back the corner of the quilt, just under his neck, so that the dedication tag was visible. She pressed it gently into place.

"Do you always fold them back like that, so the tag can be seen?"

"Always," said the nurse. "Always."

My dad spent the last few hours covered in the warmth of the blanket, in memory of his beautiful, beloved granddaughter. Under it, he took his last breath.

DECEMBER 15, 2008

I like to think that Dad is with Jennifer in Heaven. I'm no longer certain that once in Heaven, we'll see and recognize those we loved in life.

I don't know about such things; what I do know is that I trust God enough to believe that both Jennifer and my dad are safe.

DECEMBER 20, 2008

Mom isn't handling Dad's death well. Christmas is going to be really hard. Between my sorrow for Jennifer and trying to help Mom get through this, I haven't had time to grieve for my dad. My brother, Brad, said the same. Like me, after losing his son Nathan, we both feel like we've been conditioned to grief and are now almost numb to it.

I know Dad would understand. With his engineer's mind, he was good about seeing problems, fixing them, and moving on. He told Mom a long time ago that he thought I should be over my grief for Jennifer by now. I didn't resent him saying it because I know him. I know he loved Jennifer. When he decided that a sufficient amount of time had passed to mourn, he would say so, and at least outwardly, he would show no more emotion about it. I think he thought the rest of us should do the same. I don't have my dad's personality to do that.

MARCH 18, 2009

I think I'm emotionally paralyzed. I feel no great joy or sadness. Intellectually I know and recognize great joy or sad things, but I do not feel them emotionally.

I was just beginning to feel again when Dad died.

I had a dream last night that I was calling Jennifer's cell phone over and over. She wasn't answering. I left messages for her to call me, tell me where she was, and let me know she was okay.

My longing never ends.

Jim

"You've got to be kidding me!" Lori couldn't believe my plans for the day and why I had wanted her to bring several pairs of her old pantyhose.

"Crawdad fishing?" Are you serious?

"Yup," I said, talking to Lori and the three kids who stood in the driveway after I told them to come outside in their old fishing clothes, "I talked to a guy, and he told me how to do it."

I opened a cooler filled with bundles of butcher paper.

"What's in there, Dad?" Jennifer peered in hesitantly. I could tell she was afraid to look. Even at sixteen, she was cautious.

"Livers... of chickens."

"Oh, gross!" cried Jennifer.

"That's what the guy said, stuff some of these in the pantyhose. Tie it to a pole and plunk it in the water, wait five minutes and pull it up, and you'll have crawdads sucking at it when you pull it up. But you'd better get you some butterfly nets to put under the hose as you pull them up, so you don't lose them.'"

"Yeah, right, Dad," said Justin. "He was pulling your leg."

Even though the entire family thought I was crazy, they all piled into our Toyota pickup. Lori and I climbed in the front seat. David, Justin, and Jennifer were crammed into the little space between the front seat and cab. It wasn't a lot of space for their long, teenage legs, but somehow, they made it work.

Forty-five minutes later, after stopping at Subway to get some food for an impromptu picnic, we parked in a field near the Shunganunga Creek. The Native American-named creek, otherwise referred to as the "Shunga," runs through the heart of Topeka. Each of us spilled out of the truck carrying our own fishing pole with half a pair of Lori's old pantyhose tied to the end, and cheap butterfly nets that I had just bought at the dollar store. Justin carried an extra cooler with food and drinks. David carried a couple of empty buckets, and I brought the cooler filled with chicken livers on ice.

"This is stupid," muttered Justin.

"I hope I don't see any of my friends," cringed Jennifer.

Lori burst out laughing, "We look like the Beverly Hillbillies!" And we did.

David looked around with his shoulders bunched up like he was trying to hide from view. "People are looking at us like we're homeless and out to catch our food for the week." We all looked at each other and erupted in laughter. David was right.

They may have all thought it was stupid, but the first time I pulled my pole out of the water and saw three crawdads attached to the hose, everybody hooted again with laughter.

"You've got to be kidding!" cried Justin.

"Let me see that," said David. I walked the pole around for everyone to see.

"I've got some too," laughed Lori, pulling her pole out the water.

"Me too," gasped Jennifer. One by one, each one of us caught crawdads. Soon it became a contest to see who could pull out the most in one try.

After nearly an hour and a half, Jennifer exclaimed, "Look at this!" She lifted her pole to reveal almost a dozen crawdads clinging to the stocking. "I won! I can't believe it! I won!"

The image of sixteen-year-old Jennifer standing there in her cutoffs and t-shirt jumping around as she shouted for joy is forever branded in my brain as one of my favorite memories of her.

"Jennifer beat us all," I said. "She's the Crawdad Queen!"

"I'll take it. The Crawdad Queen beat you all!" Jennifer was so happy.

We laughed all the way home.

We didn't eat the crawdads, but they made awesome bait for bass fishing for several weeks. And those were fish we did eat.

The next morning as we were eating breakfast, Jennifer said, "Yesterday was fun! When can we do it again?"

I couldn't help smiling at our Crawdad Queen.

Sometimes dads do know best.

Lori

SEPTEMBER 6, 2009
I've set the date, November 7, to clean out Jennifer's room. It's been nearly seven years since she left it for the last time. Jim said he can't face it, so I've asked my friend Diana to help. She lost her eighteen-month-old son, Jamie, to pneumonia decades ago. Even though Diana never knew Jennifer, she knows what it is like to lose a child.

I'm ready to get it done. I want to make the room beautiful again. Jim said that once I get everything out, he will paint it and do anything else that needs doing. I'm not upset at Jim for not willing to help go through Jennifer's things. There have been so many other ways that he's been so strong.

I'm just glad Diana is willing to help. Separation of my heart and brain will need to be in full force.

DECEMBER 9, 2009
It's been seven years since she died, but Jennifer's room is done. I asked Diana to turn the music on, loud. Then we began putting Jennifer's things in boxes to give to her friends, including one for Carolyn, and we donated the rest to charity.

I found a beautiful, hand-decorated box with bold, pastel letters across the top saying, "Best Friends." I remember the Christmas Kelly gave it to her. The box was filled with

223

letters, cards, photos, and trinkets from their many years the two girls spent together. I knew Kelly would want it back.

We kept a few of the items that Jennifer treasured most: her baby book, photo album, stuffed animals, and the two angel collections. We are going to have the room repainted and the furniture replaced. It will now serve as our guest bedroom.

The door to her room has been closed for over seven years, and now it's open. Maybe with the door open, our cat will finally realize that Jennifer is not there. I hope that new memories can be made—of family and grandchildren sleeping and playing in the room. Jennifer would have liked that.

OCTOBER 30, 2010
Our house looks great. We have new carpet. The entire place is clean and decorated for fall, yet I'm completely torn up inside. Everyone has moved on—and I'm missing Jennifer, immensely.

DECEMBER 1, 2010
Every year, the day after Christmas, the five of us would go out for dinner and a movie. Some years it'd be a big blockbuster, like *Castaway* or *Lord of the Rings*. Sometimes it would be a Christmas movie. This simple tradition always meant a lot to Jennifer. A couple of weeks before she died, she said to me, "Mom, *The Grinch* is coming out with Jim Carey. I think we should go for Christmas." I told her I thought it'd be fun.

"Mom, where do you think we should go for dinner?"

I told her I didn't know but that we'd figure out something fun. We never had the chance.

None of us felt like going just after she died. And the next year, Justin was married, and by the next, they were busy with their infant son. Our going out as a family for our Christmas tradition has never come up since.

Jim

JULY 25, 2013
This has been another tough time for our family.

A few months after my brother-in-law was left paralyzed from his car accident, he was excited when he found a way to mow his property using his hands to operate a riding lawn mower. For a while, it gave him a great sense of freedom and accomplishment—until the unthinkable happened.

Since he had no feeling in his legs, he had no idea that his foot had dropped from the foothold and had fallen against the exhaust pipe. While he continued to mow, his foot was being fried against searing metal.

Afterward, and to all our horror, his leg became badly infected. Last week, it all proved too much for him. He passed away. We're still not certain of the details of his death, other than to know the whole affair from his automobile accident through his death was heartbreaking to watch.

What made it worse was that it all could have been avoided if he had never made the terrible decision to drink and drive.

JANUARY 5, 2014
I'm not afraid to die because I believe Jennifer will be there saying, "Hi, Dad! Welcome home."

I wonder how this is going to work. She will probably still be nineteen, and I'll probably be old with no hair and no teeth. When I see her, after I give her the hug of her life, I might wring her little neck for putting us through so much pain.

But then again, none of that will matter—not the pain, not how we look—none of it. The only thing that will matter is our love, unconditional and forever. God taught us well on that one.

MARCH 9, 2014
David was married yesterday. The wedding and reception were held in an old barn in a little town about sixty miles from our home.

Jennifer would have been so happy for David and Becky. The ceremony was beautiful. At the reception, I held it together until the DJ announced the father/daughter dance. As much as I wanted to watch, I couldn't take it. I went outside until it was over.

I stood out there in the country, listening to the music, imagining Jennifer in Heaven, dancing with me. I wondered if she knew.

*Dear God: Help me find peace
and joy in memories.*

—Lori Dultmeier

Jennifer 11th birthday 1994

David & Jennifer birthday 1994

Jennifer & David 1994

Jennifer holding
Sweetie 1995

Lori & Jennifer
Christmas 1987

Lori & Jennifer
Christmas 1987

Jennifer loves crackers 1994

Jennifer holding Sweetie 1995

David & Jennifer 1994

Jennifer & Lori 1995

Jennifer 1999

Jennifer (left) & Carolyn 1999

Kelly & Jennifer 1999*

Jennifer, Justin, David 2001

David, Jennifer, Justin 2001

Jim, Jennifer, Lori
Christmas Eve 1997

Photo courtesy of Kelly Hibbert. All other photos courtesy of The Dultmeier Family.

PART FOUR

INSIGHTS THROUGH TIME

Mom, don't cry for me,
It won't be long 'til we meet
again in eternity.

—Poem by Lori Dultmeier, May 2005

Jennifer's Fifth Grade Class Journal

2/1/95: This morning I tired to sleep in but I could not. I just lied theier doing nothing.

2/2/95: Tonight I am doing nothing. I whould propley ride my 4 wheeler. And clean my room.

2/3/95: This weekend I going to my Grandmas and Grandpa Dultmeier house and spend the night because my Mom and Dad are going to Las Vegos.

2/6/95: My favorite song is Tak me as I am. By Faith Hill. And my other on is How can I help you say good bye By Patty Loveless.

2/7/95: Today I am going to Girl Scouts and we are making mints. Four are parnets for Valentines.

2/9/95: The type of Valentine cards I have are I don't know I have not got them yet. I will get eather Garfield or somethig else.

2/10/95: This weekend I am going to Jennifer my best friends house and spend the night.

2/15/95: For Valentines I got a box of candy and big lips. But Curt stole on purpose or on acctent. I don't know.

2/21/95: The best thing about my 4 day weekend was that I got to have my best friend Carolyn. We rode my 4 weeler most of the time.

2/25/95: This weekend I might spend the night with my friend Megan. Go to my brothers basketball game.

2/27/95: This weekend I spent the nigit with Carolyn. Then we went on the Sunga Trail and roller blade my mom did too.

2/28/95: Spring break will be FUN! I am going to fix my fort. And ride my 4 wheeler.

3/1/95: Our Program will be OK. I am in a dance. MY neighbor is the M.C.

3/2/95: Last night was expost to get some new shoes but no my brother had basketball practes.

3/3/95: This weekend I am going to go to go to my brothers game and then I am going to get new shoes. I hope to get Fila or Nike.

3/6/95: Over the weekend I got new shoes and a went to my friends house then she came over and made a vido.

3/7/95: Last night I watched The Lion King. It was good! I really don't do that much on Monday nights.

3/8/95: This week has ben good for me. Yesterday theier was a robbery and down Hwy 40. I hope the don't rob my house.

3/9/95: All this snow and snow makes me...MAD. I hate snow sometimes you freeze to death.

3/10/95: Saturday will be fun because I got a basketball game that my brother plays then I got a pancake feed to go to.

3/13/95: Sunday we...went to a play called the Secort Garden. It was OK but theier was a lot of singing. Then we went out to eat.

3/14/95: Tonight will be boring at Girl Scots. Just like the other times. Who knows what we are doing.

3/15/95: Tomorrow is the dance program and I know something that you don't know!

3/16/95: Tonight is going to be a bomer because both Grandmas can't come. But my Grandpa is coming and he is going to eat with us. I going to mak a cake for him.

3/27/95: Over break I had my Bests Friend Carolyn spent the night and we went to the mall then I had my Cousin spend the night and we went to the mall 2 time.

3/28/95: Last night I watched the Ocar Awards and that all I did. It was a boring night.

3/29/95: Today we are going to the planortraum for a wiard thing. I don't know what.

3/30/95: This Spring I am going to wait and wait to wear SHORTS!

3/31/95: Tonight I am having my Best Friend Carolyn over and we are going to walk this walk for MS.

Lori

MAY 30, 2016

It's been about six years since I've written in my journal.

Jim and I are closer than we've ever been. He works so hard to make me happy. When I'm happy, he's happy. I know, without question, Jim would move Heaven and Earth for me. I knew that before Jennifer died, but it is even more so after. We talk a lot now about how we are truly doing. He takes time to ask how I really am. He never accepts the "I'm fine" version. He looks out for me as I do him.

After Jennifer died, a lot of people were very concerned about me. They did a lot to make sure I was being taken care of, but from the start, I was concerned about who was taking care of him. I think sometimes men, especially "stoic" ones like Jim, often get overlooked in their grief.

Stoic may not be the right word; it sounds like someone without emotion. Jim's soul was just as crushed as mine, but he did not outwardly give in to his despair as I did. For me, it was not a choice; it was just what it was. I couldn't have been any different than what I was—a complete mess. If Jim hadn't held it together as he did, I don't know what would have become of us. He was wonderful just as he was, and is.

Jennifer's death changed Jim, as it did all of us. Because of it, he makes sure that his grandkids know how much he loves them. He's a wonderful grandfather.

Jim's devotion and never wavering commitment to speaking with MADD amazes me. It takes a toll on him to do so, in time, gas, and more than anything else, in emotion. But he never complains, and he never stops. Saving the lives of others is about as loving a tribute as a father could give. I think Jennifer would have been amazed by his ongoing, focused, and intensely passionate commitment to sharing her story. More than anything, she would be so proud of him. And his love for Jennifer shows in every presentation he gives.

JUNE 14, 2016

I "gave" each child a song that expressed my hopes and dreams for them. After a lot of contemplation, I would give them a CD of the song I had chosen. Jennifer was so reserved that I wanted to give her a song that would encourage her not to be afraid to stand out and take chances. "I Hope You Dance" was the perfect song for her. David's was "Simple Man" by Lynyrd Skynyrd, about valuing the important things in life.

I waited for a long time to find just the right song for Justin and only did so this month. I think it is one of the most beautiful songs I've ever heard called "Humble and Kind" by Tim McGraw. Justin told me he was deeply touched by it and that I could not have picked a better song.

JULY 26, 2016

I'm surprised that I don't feel angrier toward God. Other people I know feel enraged against Him because He "allowed" death to happen, but I don't think God is about death. I trust Him, so the rest of it doesn't matter.

From God's perspective, I think when we die, it is what I would feel like if someone I loved told me they were moving to Texas. I'd say, "Well, I'll miss you, but I'll be seeing you again." Death to God just isn't that big a deal. He knows the truth. He's been telling us all along—that anyone going there has just moved to Paradise.

OCTOBER 3, 2016

I used to find Jennifer's things everywhere throughout our house, and every time I did, it bothered me a lot.

Now, I don't find anything of hers anymore. I wish I did.

OCTOBER 10, 2016

Jennifer and Carolyn both liked photography. They went through a stage when they were teenagers where they'd do photo-shoots of each other in our yard, complete with several wardrobe changes. Sometimes these sessions morphed into the girls filming the "news." I think they would have made good news anchors. Both were beautiful, and many of their photos captured it.

Once, Jennifer managed to turn her camera around and take a couple of photos of herself. I came across them this morning and realized they were quite good. I think she should get credit for being the originator of selfies. I wish she could have lived to see smartphones.

NOVEMBER 16, 2016

From the start, I knew what I had to do. I had to find a way to be happy again. What choice did I have? Curl up and die? Jennifer wouldn't want that! That wouldn't have been fair to everyone else who was heartbroken too. I knew the key was finding a way to honor Jennifer and learning to enjoy life again. I didn't know if I had it in me. Wanting to do something and doing something are two very different things!

I knew where I wanted to be; I just had no idea how to get there, which was scary! I've always been good at knowing what I want and what I need to do to make it happen. If I wanted to get a college degree, I'd take classes. If I wanted a car, I'd save more money.

But how does a mother become happy after losing a child? I had no idea.

I still don't know. All I know is that fourteen years after Jennifer's death, I can say that I've found happiness again, or maybe, happiness has found me. I'm not sure which.

We aren't meant to live in sorrow. God doesn't want that for us. I think He places in every living thing a will to live. All along, I sensed a nudge from God to go on—to fight. And so, we did. Jim and I clawed our way back to happiness by some primitive survival instinct that only God could have made possible.

After Jennifer died, I was drowning. I didn't try to stop drowning; I just didn't let it kill me. Finding happiness is not something I thought a lot about. It was instinct. I didn't want to die. I knew we needed to heal. I didn't know how other than to trust God.

That's why so many people say it takes time. My progress was so gradual I wasn't aware it was happening.

For years people would tell me about stages of grief like I was supposed to go through them nice and orderly and check them off along the way. Lori, you're depressed—check! Denial—check! Anger—check!

Give me a break!

If I had stages, they weren't orderly. They were random and in no sequence. Half the time, they'd be at once. Then, they'd start all over.

Family and friends were frustrated that I wasn't living into their expectations of grief. They were frustrated out of love. I knew it, but I didn't have the energy to battle their expectations and my sorrow. Retreating was easier. So that's what I did.

I think that's why family gatherings were hard for so long.

NOVEMBER 22, 2016

A few months after Jennifer died, I remember thinking something was wrong with me. I went to the doctor and pointed to my lower abdomen and reproductive organs and said, "There's something wrong down here." He ran several tests, including a sonogram. The tests all came back negative.

Despite the results, I knew something was very wrong deep inside.

It's taken many years to be able to look back on that time and understand what my body was going through. The healthy, beautiful daughter I had given birth to was dead. My grief was not only killing me emotionally but physically. I thought there was no way I could go through such overwhelming grief without physically dying myself.

Looking back, I'm surprised I'm still alive. I really am. Jennifer's death was such a stressor to every fiber of my being, that I can't believe it didn't give me cancer or some other incurable disease.

JANUARY 15, 2017

Several years ago, if anyone told me that Jennifer's death would make me stronger, I would have scoffed. I felt so weak, so vulnerable, and so out of control for so long. And yet, now I realize they were right. I am a stronger person than I was when Jennifer was alive. Maybe it's because I did the impossible—I survived the death of a child.

Jennifer's death has made my marriage stronger too. And most importantly, it made my faith stronger. Before Jennifer died, I felt that I was mostly in control of my life. Losing her made me realize that wasn't the case. I had to learn to trust and rely on the only One who was.

For many years after Jennifer died, I wasn't completely present in anything or any place. I wasn't really living, nor was I dead. I was stuck, straddling the in-between of this world and Heaven. I wasn't really here, and I wasn't really there; only part of me was in each place.

Now, I feel, in the most literal sense, that part of me is in Heaven. Maybe that's because Jennifer is so much of who I am, and yet, I'm more fully present in my physical life here. I'm not mired in the line between them. I am in both.

MARCH 5, 2017

The problem with grief is that I didn't know how to get through it. It didn't matter how many other stories I heard of how other people handled their grief because everyone experiences it in their own ways. No one could make my grief go away. No one could make my life okay. No one could do the one thing that would fix everything, and that was to bring Jennifer back.

It helped that family and friends were there for me. They often thought of things I needed before I did. It helped that my church family never ceased caring and showing their love in tangible ways. But what I learned was that while people can be with you through the hard times, ultimately, everyone experiencing profound grief has to find their own path. For a long time, no one could say anything right. Well-meaning people would try, but nothing they could say or do would make me stop grieving.

It's strange, but what finally helped was when I realized that ultimately, other than with God, going through my grief was something that only I could do, and I had to do it alone.

SEPTEMBER 5, 2017

Since 2005 when we started the nonprofit organization Quilts for Angels, over 2,500 quilts have been donated to local hospitals to be used for those who lose their loved ones unexpectedly.

We have gotten many heartfelt messages and letters from nurses and parents describing the impact the quilts had on them. We know from firsthand experience that the quilts can help soften the blow of seeing a loved one dead. Providing for others is a small thing, but it's the best way I know how to give back.

The Quilts for Angels project has had the unexpected blessing of helping bring our family, friends, and our Kansas community together—making quilts, buying quilts, fundraising for quilts through motorcycle rides/events and fishing tournaments, and delivering them to the area's grateful hospital staff. I couldn't have done it without so many family and friends. Jennifer's close friends Heather, Marita, and Kelly worked tirelessly on these projects.

The office in our house is almost always stacked high with folded quilts waiting to be delivered. I hand stitch on each a label with an angel embroidered on it, and on most, I handwrite the words, "Donated in memory of Jennifer Dultmeier." Knowing where they are going is both heartbreaking and comforting—just as Jennifer's quilt is for us now—the one we keep in a special basket near the entrance of what was her bedroom.

SEPTEMBER 19, 2017

We recently had a family fall photo taken. Sitting on bales of hay, surrounded by massive pumpkins, were the smiling faces of our immediate family. There were twelve people in that photo: Jim and I, our sons, their wives, and their children. Everyone was there—everyone but one. There is nothing that can change that.

Every time I look at that wonderful photo of our beautiful family, full of love and life, what I notice first is the person missing. Jennifer should be there. She should be balancing a small child on her hip, with her older children standing by her side. Had she lived, it's how it would have been. I know it. Maybe next to her would have been the twins she always wanted. There is just no way to know the people missing from that photo and our lives. The impact never ends.

Jim

SEPTEMBER 21, 2017

Drinking and driving have taken a terrible toll on my family. In addition to Jennifer, Lori lost her grandparents and her nephew. My sister lost her husband. Her children lost their father.

It is still painful to watch people we love drink and drive as though they have little regard for what we've endured. They're flirting with death. I'm not anti-alcohol. I will drink a beer on the rare occasions when I know I don't have to drive, or at night when Lori and I get in the hot tub to gaze at the stars.

I remember the days when TV and magazine ads used to feature good-looking men and women, with cigarettes in hand, saying there was nothing better in life than a good smoke. Now, most people can't even stand the smell of cigarette smoke, thanks to an organized campaign against the glorification of smoking in advertising. I'm hoping that the same type of campaign that worked to help reduce tobacco use will do the same for alcohol and marijuana. But that won't happen as long as people keep arguing things like, "Marijuana should be allowed because it's not as bad for people as drinking." *Are you kidding me?* Driving impaired in any form ought to be made harder, not easier! And right now, we are making it easier for people to get addicted and stay addicted. *What are we thinking? How many more people have to die?*

Since Jennifer died, texting while driving has become a huge problem that scares me. A person who dies from texting, or being on drugs, is just as dead as one who dies from drinking and driving. All are bad. Something has to change.

DECEMBER 12, 2017

When I start to question whether anything I'm doing with MADD is making a difference, I think back to the day Lori and I were walking down the sidewalk, heading into our church. Coming at us were two teenage boys riding bicycles. I didn't think anything about it. Then one of them stopped and yelled out, "Hey, remember me?"

I said, "I'm sorry. I don't recognize you." By this time, he was walking toward me. Suddenly he threw his arms around me and gave me a bear hug. I was thinking, "Well, wait a minute, I don't even know who you are."

He told me his name, and that he had been in an Impact Class about a month before.

I looked closer at him and said, "I remember. You no longer are wearing that back brace." I'm surprised I hadn't realized who he was sooner. I never thought I'd forget his face—the one I had wanted to drive my fist through.

I had been waiting for an Impact Class to begin. The auditorium was packed. I saw a young man wearing a bulky back and chest brace. I went over to talk to him. He had been a passenger in an accident that had killed a fifteen-year-old girl. Even though he hadn't been driving, the young man in the back brace had been in the car, was under-age and had been drinking. He had been ordered by the judge to attend the class. He was sitting there, waiting for the presentation to begin, and laughing. He looked at me and said, "This class isn't going to change my life. I'm still going to drink."

I don't think I've ever been angrier with another human being than I was at that moment. I wanted to slam my fist through his smug face and wave at myself through the back of his head. I gritted my teeth and said to him, "You think this is a game?"

I had to force myself to remember where I was. I was there to do a class, and I wasn't supposed to judge anyone. I turned and walked away from him and gave my talk. When I was done, all the attendees were given a form to fill out. I looked over at the boy and saw that he hadn't left. He was just sitting there, even after everyone else left. I went over to him. He wouldn't look at me. He started shaking and then bawling. He was crying so hard I think the patrol officer thought I had hit him. I said, "It's not so funny now, is it?" He nodded his head in agreement.

A few weeks later, as we stood on the street, that same young man bear-hugged me. He said, "I don't drink, and I don't ever want to drink. I've grown up. Your talk helped me grow up. I'm back in school. I'm not going to live like I was." Then he hugged me again, hopped back on his bike, and rode off.

As we turned to walk into church, Lori wrapped her arm around my waist, and I put my arm over her shoulders. I knew then that the people who have told me over the years that good things can come from bad times were right. That kid was proof.

Lori

Some memories are my enemy now.

As a mom, I never thought about losing any of my kids. And because of it, I took their existence for granted. I know I did with Jennifer.

It's been a long time since Jennifer was a child, but one of those early memories haunts me the most. All these years later, it hurts to think of it. Over the years, I've tried to push it from my mind, but it's always there, fuel for guilt.

I had been really angry with Jennifer. I can't imagine that now. She was only about four years old at the time. She was such a meek little soul. *What could I have possibly been so mad at her about?* But I was mad, and I don't have any idea what it was about. She couldn't have done anything very bad.

I picked Jennifer up by her shoulders, and I sat her down really hard on a small bench in our kitchen. She sat there with this look of shame, sorrow, and fear. At that moment, she had been afraid of me. Then she wet her pants.

When she looked up at me with her big eyes full of tears, I saw something that made me feel even worse—shock and hurt that I had done something that made her afraid of me.

I thought, *My God! How could I have been so angry with this meek, little child? I just can't believe I did that.*

To this day, I can't believe I did that.

I think about that time at the most inopportune moments, and when I do, I start to cry. I can never take it back. It will haunt me for the rest of my life.

I can't think of that day without feeling the deepest sense of sick there is. The kind of sick that won't allow any recovery because I can't do anything to undo it. I can't even bear to open my eyes when I think of it.

I wish I could say that was my only regret with how I reacted in anger at any of my kids. But it's not. I have one instance with each of the boys that bothers me a great deal. But when I think of sitting Jennifer down on that bench, it just guts me.

I have told other friends about this, and they all have one or two things they beat themselves up about. One friend, trying to make me feel better, said, "Lori, none of us is a perfect parent. There isn't such a thing. Everyone who has ever been a parent has regrets. But good parents are the ones who realize right away what they've done wrong and learn to respond better the next time. An awful parent would have looked at Jennifer and screamed, 'Why'd you wet your pants?' Instead of doing that, you immediately recognized what you had done. And you've been beating yourself up ever since."

She's right. I have been. But when I ask myself now, "Did I take Jennifer for granted?" I'd have to say, "Yeah." I wanted a girl. And I had a girl. Most of my life was like that. If I wanted something badly enough, I got it.

After having Justin and getting pregnant with twins, I was just so proud of my body. It was like the super machine, the *Transformer.*

My body was normal, and then one day, I got pregnant, and nine months later, I went to the hospital. Within thirty minutes, I delivered not one but *two* healthy babies at seven and a half pounds each! And they were both so beautiful and so perfect, just like Justin had been. And suddenly, I was the mother of three little ones. I raised them. And then once they were nearly out of the house and headed out to college, I decided I'd finally go too. Everything was working out so perfectly. I was a Christian and knew that's why it must have all been working out. I had a wonderful husband who worked hard. I had a beautiful house. Everything was just wonderful because I worked so hard at it.

And then I got chopped off at the knees.

I had taken it all for granted. I was prideful. So now I ask myself, "Was I so prideful that God used Jennifer's death to teach me something I had overlooked? Like the fact that these kids weren't really mine? And that the blessings I was given, wasn't because of the things I had done. They weren't.'"

The Bible says he wants us to make our requests known to Him, but instead of asking God for things, I now thank Him. I begin all my prayers giving thanks for all the

243

things I have to be grateful for each day. When I do ask for something, I ask for wisdom in knowing how to talk to our boys about love, marriage, life, and death. I ask Him to bless their marriages. I want them to put God first in their lives.

Jim

APRIL 19, 2018

I've been a volunteer speaker for MADD for over eleven years. Four times a year, I make the one-hour drive to Kansas City to share Jennifer's story with an auditorium packed with DUI offenders. Lori often drives with me, but she can't bring herself to come in. She can't face the drivers, and she can't face the heartbreak of hearing me talk about Jennifer. Instead, she usually goes looking for a bargain on quilts to purchase for the Quilts for Angels project.

I'm on stage with two or three other parents, usually mothers, who have lost a child to impaired driving. Their stories are gut-wrenching. And once a month, I speak at our local courthouse for first-time offenders in our county.

For a long time, I spoke at a military base about an hour and a half from home as part of discharge training to help soldiers transition back into civilian life. I went once a month. The first time I spoke, there were about one hundred soldiers in the auditorium, some in uniform and some not. These combat-hardened men and women had seen a lot. After speaking for a few minutes, the first time, I realized the room was dead quiet. And then I saw why. They were crying. Many of them, I'm sure, were parents, and I know they couldn't imagine losing their kids. Just the thought was a nightmare to them. As they looked at me, I knew they were looking at someone they didn't ever want to be—a parent who had buried a child. They had seen enough death.

After every speech I give, I'm exhausted, emotionally, and physically, because I relive losing Jennifer. Every speech breaks my heart because I show a video I have of Jennifer at a time in her life when she was laughing and smiling. Most painful of all is seeing her on the video, where more than anything else, she was so very much alive.

My speech is animated. I don't sugarcoat anything. I tell the audience, "For some of you out there, this may have been the first time you've driven impaired. But my hunch is that isn't the case for most of you here today. Am I right? I would guess that most of you are probably like I was when I was a teenager. You think you're a pro at drinking and driving. Pros know what they're doing. Pros know how to handle themselves. Pros have done it many times, without issue. You've gotten home every time so far, haven't you? So, what's the problem?

"The problem, my friends, is that every time you get behind the wheel impaired—every time—you are playing Russian roulette with your life and the lives of others. Nine times out of ten, you'll get home okay. Nine times out of ten, you'll be safe. Your passengers are safe. The drivers who passed you are safe.

"But, one time is all it takes for someone to get hurt or someone to die. And if you continue to play this game, someday your 'one time' will come for you. And you don't have the right to play a game of chance with other people's lives.

"Each one of you here today is the lucky one. You've lived long enough to be caught. You've lived long enough to regret your mistakes. Jennifer never had that privilege."

After every speech, people are lined up to talk to me afterward, and nearly every one of them is in tears, thanking me for sharing Jennifer's story. They pass me notes to tell me that they're done drinking and driving because of what they have heard. I've occasionally run into someone afterward, often years later, who has said they recognize me from a meeting. People have told me that after hearing about Jennifer's death, they have never driven drunk again. Now, that's sorrow in action.

After hearing me speak, a young man said to me once, "I give you my word that I will never drink and drive again. I never want my mom or my dad to have to end up on a stage, speaking to strangers about my mistake. I owe them more than that."

I would give anything to show up at my next MADD DUI meeting, and be told, "Hey Jim, we don't have anyone here!" I dream of the day the MADD stage is empty, where there isn't even one parent who has lost their child to an impaired driver. Not one.

The most disheartening sight I see at almost every presentation is a packed house. The worst is when I look out and see people I know and love—even family. That's happened more than once. I want to ask them, *"What will it take? Wasn't Jennifer's death enough?"*

It's my prayer that someday Carolyn will join me on that stage, or if that is too hard, to have a video of her sharing her story. I'm not sure either of us could handle it, but if we could, it would be the most powerful testament I could imagine. It would save lives. And what better legacy could there be.

SEPTEMBER 10, 2018

I headed out fishing with my brother, Tom, this morning. As we stood in the parking lot, ready to launch the boat, we started talking to another man waiting to launch his boat. When I told him my name, he said, "Hmmm. That sounds familiar. I know that name. How do I know it?"

I didn't have a chance to respond when he said, "You aren't related to that young woman who was killed several years ago, are you?"

I just looked at the ground. Tom answered for me. "She was my niece." Tom nodded at me, "He's her dad."

The man's eyes grew wide. "I am so sorry! I worked at the funeral home and helped with her service. Of all the thousands of services we have done over the years, I have to tell you that funeral was the most heartbreaking experience I've ever been through. I've never forgotten it.

"Over the years, I can't tell you how many times I've thought about it and wondered how you all are doing."

Lori

SEPTEMBER 2, 2018

I am mad and will be until the day I die that I missed the fun of having adult years with Jennifer. So much of the time we had together was me raising her: first as an infant, then a little girl, and then came school. High school especially took so much of her time. We were finally at a place where we were spending time together, having adult conversations, and having a blast. Just as it was getting started, it was over. I hate that I won't have her with me as I grow old, as I am there in that way now for my mom.

I'm in a good emotional place now. I sense that I will be for a long time.

What I fear the most is losing my mom and outliving Jim. Neither will be there, nor will Jennifer. That is when I think I'm going to miss Jennifer the most.

Since the twins were born, I have spent nearly every Friday with my mom. We still do. I treasure every moment I have with my mom because I know she won't always be here.

Mom and I can talk about the big stuff and the small. I value her wise counsel. Although she never felt that she helped me as much as she wanted to through my grief, she was wrong. I could not have survived without her. I think of the time she took me over to see Stephanie. Mom said that day she had been so worried about me, and that my cry was so mournful that she thought I was going to die from grief. It was right then and there that she thought about her neighbor Stephanie, and how she had lost a twin daughter. She knew if anyone could help me, maybe Stephanie could. Mom was so wise that way.

For many years Mom has kept a special poem tucked into her Bible, written long ago called "The Weaver." It's about how God, from above, sees the big picture of life. But from where we are, all that is visible is the underside, with its messy knots and ties that seem to make no sense, but from above, the tapestry of life is beautiful.

Over the years, Mom has shared the poem often with me, and it has had a profound impact on my thinking about the challenges we face here on earth. Mom told me yesterday that even if she could, she would never wish any of those people back that she misses so terribly, like my dad and her two grandkids, Jennifer and Nathan. She said, "They've already been through death on earth and have experienced Heaven. I would never, for their sake, want them to come back."

That's my mom, always putting the interests of others above her own.

When I'm with Mom, neither of us has to pretend or be offended by what we say and do, like the times she asks me if she has any wayward chin hairs, and I help her pluck them.

Three months before Jennifer died, I was lounging by the pool in our backyard, lying on my stomach. Jennifer walked past, and she exclaimed, "Mom! The backs of your legs are so hairy!" And they were. I just shrugged. The backs of my upper thighs were not something that got a lot of my attention. It may have been no big deal to me, but not to Jennifer. She hurried into the house and came out a few minutes later with a razor and began shaving off the unwanted hairs.

Jennifer would have plucked my chin hairs. No doubt. My boys wouldn't have any part of doing that. I think I'll need to have a conversation with my granddaughters when they get older and tell them to feel free to pluck away.

I may be at a good place emotionally, but that doesn't mean I'm not pissed off about losing Jennifer. I am.

SEPTEMBER 29, 2018

Despite Jim considering leaving me for another woman, we were fortunate that if we had to lose a child, it came at a time when our relationship was strong.

All marriages ebb and flow. Ours was no different. Earlier in our lives together, had this happened, I'm not sure our marriage would have survived. We either weren't mature enough as individuals, or mature enough in our relationship with each other, or in our faith with God, to have withstood it.

Knowing Jim as well as I did helped me realize that the thing he had with his old girlfriend had nothing to do with me or the kids. It was about his inability to handle overwhelming grief.

Knowing him so well, and his love for me, and our family, made it possible for me to forgive his knee-jerk reaction to the pain. If our marriage had been any less secure, I don't think that would have been possible.

Jim

Many of my family and friends had no idea how to help me in the weeks, months, and years after Jennifer died, and there were times when I needed someone besides Lori to talk to. Some of that's on me. If I had picked up the phone and called any one of them, and said, "Please come, it's really bad for me right now," they would have been there in a heartbeat. But I never did. They all knew I was hurting, but they didn't know what to do for me. They had never lost a child or knew anyone close to them who had.

Over time, I got good at hiding how much I was hurting. People looked me right in the eye and asked, "How are you doing, Jim?" I'd look at them right back and say, "I'm doing well. When really, I was dying inside.

I wasn't deliberately trying to hide my pain. I didn't care if they thought I was weak; it's just that it took too much energy to tell them the truth. It was easier just to say I was fine. If anyone had looked closely, I think they would have said, "You're lying, lying, lying. You're not fine."

Now, when I talk to anyone who has lost a child, and they say they're doing okay, I say to them, "Bull. You can't fool me."

If it hadn't been for Lori, I wouldn't have survived. For the most part, I was honest with her about how I was feeling, but there were times when I was in bad shape. I didn't want to drag her down. So, I would say things like, "It was a good day," when honestly, I was shattered, barely functioning.

Throughout this ordeal, I've often felt the Lord's presence, taking care of me. And because of it, I thought that it was then up to me to take care of Lori. And I did too, as best I could until I lost it completely and wanted to run away with another woman. I thank God Lori was wise enough to get into my email. I thank God, she confronted me before anything worse happened. I thank God she had it in her to forgive me and to stay with me. It was all a reality check. The devil had me by the throat.

DECEMBER 5, 2018
Fifteen years after the accident, I went to bid a roof. I had just parked when an electrician getting into his van stopped to read the sticker on the back window: *I lost my*

only daughter to a drunk driver. I'm MADD. He looked at the name on the side of my truck: Dultmeier Roofing.

He nodded to the sticker, "Is that true?"

"Yes, unfortunately, it is."

"Did it happen several years ago, out on California Ave?"

I nodded.

"I was one of the first responders at the scene."

I felt the blood rush from my head. I've not been rendered speechless often, but I was then. It was a few seconds before I recovered.

We talked for quite a while. The responder's name was Chuck. His crew had just gotten into their fire truck after leaving a nearby house when they heard the radio call about the accident. He said they arrived less than two minutes after the call came in.

Chuck told me a lot about the accident I didn't know. At first, he was hesitant, but I told him I was ready to hear it.

"We found your daughter leaning with her back against a tree. Her legs were outstretched. The teenagers next door said it was how they found her. I think it's how she landed. She was unconscious. I tried to find a pulse but couldn't. I thought she was dead. The other two firefighters from our crew began working on her. I went to the car to try and help the driver. The car was upside down. The roof was crushed in with just barely enough room for me to slide through the back window. There was no room for anyone else from our crew to fit in there.

"During the extrication of the driver, I heard that your daughter was still alive. They were transporting her to the hospital. I was surprised they had been able to revive her. I was pretty certain she was gone by the time we reached her.

"I learned the next day that your daughter died at the hospital. I have a daughter who knew your daughter from high school. I've got to tell you, for a long time, I couldn't think of anything else. That could have been my daughter. "

The man shared even more.

"In all the years of doing my job, I've seen and experienced many things that I'll never be able to erase from my mind. Like a young teenage boy who hung himself after he had a fight with his seventh-grade girlfriend. His parents found him in their basement. We took him down. Then there was an intoxicated man who held a loaded gun to my head as we arrived to help his wife, who had called a suicide hotline. And then there were the hundreds of auto accidents. But your daughter's accident—and being the same age as my daughter—well, it was too much. That's the call that was the beginning of the end of my firefighting years. I knew then that I had to find something else to do. I just no longer had the stomach for it. It took a while, but I eventually left that profession."

There were tears in the man's eyes when he finished, and tears in mine. He said he ended up having to go to counseling after Jennifer's accident and all that happened. His wife was certain he was suffering PTSD from it. He later learned she was right.

Justin, Jennifer & David riding in
Grandpa Leon's 1931 Chevrolet in 1993

Lori's mom Doris & sister Melissa 1994

Jim's parents Leon & Mary 2020

Lori & Jennifer 1994

Lori & Jennifer 1987

Carolyn, Jennifer, David 1998

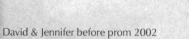

David & Jennifer before
prom, April 2002

David & Jennifer before prom 2002

Kelly (left) & Jennifer 2001*

Jennifer & David's 18th
birthday 2001

Jennifer 2000

Jennifer 2002

Jennifer & Justin 2000

Jennifer, Justin, David graduation 2002

Jennifer & Jim 1999

Jennifer & Justin 1997

*Photo courtesy of Wichers Photography. All other photos courtesy of The Dultmeier Family.

PART FIVE

ON MENDED WINGS

Mom, don't cry for me,
There's no other place I'd rather be.

—Poem by Lori Dultmeier, May 2005

Jennifer's Fifth Grade Class Journal

4/3/95: Over the weekend I did nothing. Sunday night I played Truth or Dare with the net door nabors. Theier cousin Drew had to lick the dirt.

4/4/95: On Hot day I like to play outside on the trapelene. Or go swimming in my pool.

4/5/95: Yesterday was not fun because my boyfriend broke up with me for a nother girl.

4/6/95: This weekend I am spending the night at Carolyn's house and then we are going to the mall for lunch and shopping. And a movie for her birthday. Katie Jamie, Jamen, and Jennifer are going. Ashley was but she can't go she is busy.

4/10/95: This weekend I went to a party. The mall, and saw Man of the House it was really stupid. I bought a big Tweety poster.

4/17/95: For Easter I had fun! We had a piñata and my cousin is in kindergran and he knoxed the head off of the rabbit. Then I hit it and all the candy came out.

4/18/95: Tonight is the skating party and I don't think I'm going. But after girl scouts I'm going to go shopping with my best friend CAROLYN!

4/19/95: Last night I went shopping.

4/20/95: I do like rain and puddles. I like to jump in them. I love rain!

4/21/95: Tonight I'm having MY BEST Friend over can you guess who?! This is the 2nd time in a row.

4/24/95: Saturday I went to the Carnival. There was this boy and girl there they frenched. Sunday I went to a move call Major Pain with Carolyn.

4/25/95: In this weather I wear shorts. I just wish I could go home and SWIM but 26 more day intell I can. But I get to have a swimming party this party!!

4/26/95: I wish that in buy day we could have Sweet Tarts, gum, cupcakes, passes for a day of no work for the whole class for 250 tickets.

4/27/95: Tonight on the math test I'm going to do all right, maybe good. I think I'm gong to miss 3 or 5.

4/28/95: This weekend I'm going to the Roylas game with my Uncle Kurt, my cousins Brooke and David my stupid brother.

5/1/95: Astronauts must follow each procedure carefully. Saturday I went to the Royals game. It was to start at 1:30 but it started at 3:00 because of the rain. I bought a ball for $6.00 and got 2 autograps. Sunday I went to Carolyns house. Went home at 8:00

5/2/95: Tonight I have a track meet. I hope we win. I am doing the hand off.

5/3/95: On Wednesday I go to curch. Yesterday my Grandpa had a hartattack. He keeps say I don't want to leave you guys. He was really scared.

5/5/95: This weekend I'm going to CAROLYNS House. I went and saw my Grandpa and he is doing better.

5/8/95: This weekend I went to Carolyns house. Then I spent the day with her and watch her sister get ready for the prom. ON Sunday I almost got bite by a Copperhead.

5/9/95: Yesterday I was going to vist my grandpa but no he went home SO we a going to let him get use to the house again. And let him rest. I made him a pot that says I love Grandpa. And it has flowers on it.

5/10/95: Tonight I get home then I take a shower then I go to chuch.

5/15/95: Over the weekend I did not do much. My neghors open theier Pool! We get to swim in it tonight!

5/16/95: This week I might have Carolyn over. Tonight for Girl Scots we are making dinner for them. It is going to be FUN!

5/18/95: Yesterday I came home and went upstairs and my room was painted a light yellow and then my mom and I put up cartoons and my new bedspreed.

5/19/95: One week of school left and I can't wait! Last night I went swimming and it was cold.

5/22/95: On the last buy-day, I going to spend, spend. In Tricia way shop till I drop.

5/23/95: Today I hope it goes allright. I wish we could go outside and get soke!

5/24/95: Friday when we sign yearbooks, I well have fun!

5/25/95: On the first day of summer I don't know what I'm going to do. Most likly go swimming!

5/26/95: The fifth grade was fun. I really like Mrs. Cress.

Lori

JANUARY 5, 2020

People ask me how long it takes to get over losing a child. There is no getting over it, not ever. There's only getting used to a new reality.

It's been eighteen years since Jennifer died. Thinking back over those years, I realize it took me the first five years to learn just how to live without Jennifer, another five years to accept our new normal, and five more years to learn to be happy without her.

In all, fifteen years of my life, but I would not tell that to anyone who had just lost a child. Because, for someone in that sort of pain, fifteen years would seem inconceivable, insurmountable, and impossible.

When I say I had to learn to be happy, it was just that, a learning process. It didn't automatically happen. I had to work at it and concentrate on it, just as diligently as if I were trying to strengthen the muscles in my body. Every day, I forced myself to find one thing to be happy about. I did this until it became second nature. Looking for happiness was something I never had to do before Jennifer died. Before then, it came naturally. It's true when people say that happiness is a choice. I could choose to dwell on the negative, but that would not benefit anyone or bring Jennifer back.

I recently saw my mom's neighbor getting out of her car. Stephanie has owned and operated a beauty salon in downtown Topeka for decades, and she looks just as beautiful now as the day I first met her. I went over and told her that I wanted her to know how the guidance she gave to me so many years ago helped me. She was surprised. She didn't recall even what she had said. I did. She had told me, step by step, what to do to get through each day: get up, shower, put on my make-up, and do the things I needed to do to get through that one day. Step by step. It's what I needed to hear. Then she told me to be grateful that I had nineteen years with Jennifer. It was a lot more than she ever had with her precious daughter.

"And Stephanie, I still have it."

"The music box?"

"Yes," I told her. "It's my favorite angel. I think of you, your daughter, and Jennifer, every time I play it."

JANUARY 9, 2020

Jennifer would be in her mid-thirties now, and I imagine her at that age. Her girl-friends all look like older versions of their teenage selves. I think the same would have been true for Jennifer. David, her twin, has changed a lot physically since he was nineteen. Both Jennifer's brothers have grown into very handsome men.

I've learned a lot in these last eighteen years, but none more than this: grief gets old after a while—really, really old. And yet, there is no way around it. It isn't something that can be willed away. For so long, I desperately wanted it to go away. But that's the funny thing about grief. Once it becomes a part of you, it will never fully go away because it becomes a part of who you are. It's melded into your DNA. Just as my hair is part of who I am, so is my grief. And in the same way I comb and style my hair each day, I manage my grief and try to make it look as good as possible.

Grief devoured several years of my life. It is complicated, multi-dimensional, and ultimately, more than anything else, grief is a thief of time.

FEBRUARY 9, 2020

I no longer mourn for Jennifer over what she missed out on—things like getting married and having children. I believe that whatever she is experiencing in Heaven is beyond my wildest dreams, and beyond anything she would have done here.

But I mourn for all of us who loved her. I mourn for what we missed out on doing with her.

It wasn't okay with me when she died, and it isn't okay with me now.

But I trust God enough to trust that He knows what He's doing.

APRIL 16, 2020

Not only is grief exhausting, it's boring. It gets so old, fast. And yet, there is no way around it. For so long, I desperately wanted it to go away, but I knew it wouldn't. The reality was, it was there, and it wasn't ever going to fully go away—not ever. But over the years, I've learned to live with it.

People ask me if there is really true joy in my life now. I tell them, "Yes, but it comes with a cloud."

My life is good now. My smiles are real, something that, for a long time, I wasn't sure would ever be true again.

But, hanging over everything is the reality that Jennifer is missing from our lives. And because of it, the order of nature had been disrupted; parents should never bury their children. They just shouldn't. Not ever.

APRIL 22, 2020
Jennifer's dear friend Kelly has offered to take over running the Quilts for Angels project when I am no longer able. I can't think of anyone who I would love more to do so.

APRIL 26, 2020
We all lost a piece of our hearts when Jennifer passed away much too soon. It has taken a long time to come to the place we are as a family now. I miss her in different ways as the years go by but just as much yesterday, as today, and as I will tomorrow. I hugged her to my body the day she was born and thankfully the morning before she died. Even though I will never understand why she died or be okay with her death, I have learned to count my blessings and not my burdens. Like the beautiful lyrics written by Horatio Spafford after four of his children tragically perished in a shipwreck, with God's unfaltering love and His promise—*It is well with my soul.*

JUNE 27, 2020
For many years after Jennifer died, I had an image of myself that kept coming to me, and sometimes it comes even now. In the beginning, I kept picturing myself like the caricature of Carol Burnett when she dressed as a maid, complete with hat and apron. I kept seeing myself as that haggard person and dragging a doll that looked just like Jennifer; it was a doll that was too heavy for me to do anything but drag behind me as I trudged through life. My shoulders were slumped.

Over time, my posture straightened, ever so slightly. Instead of dragging the doll, I began carrying it in my arms. She was heavy but manageable.

I envision myself now as that same maid-like person. Only now, my shoulders are straight and tall. My clothes aren't so shabby, although I still wear an apron. The Jennifer doll is now tucked away neatly in my little purse. She is completely out of sight to others. Strangers looking at me have no idea she is even there. Those that know me well probably suspect that she's still with me somewhere. They don't know the weight of the burden I still carry. They don't ask me, and I don't tell them.

When Jennifer died, the innocence I had known died with her—the innocence of life without sorrow.

Jennifer and I were very close. People commented on how she so often followed me wherever I went. But I was always her mother first, not her friend. If I got in her face and told her off, she understood where I was coming from. She said once she knew that I was tough on her because I loved her. I did.

I never contemplated suicide because I had so many other roles to fulfill. I was still a mom, wife, daughter, sister, aunt, and friend. I couldn't do that to any of them.

I'm at peace now, but I'm still not okay with Jennifer dying. It's an ongoing conversation I have with God: I don't like this; I'm not okay with this; I don't agree with this, but I have faith that You know what you're doing and that You're going to work this all out. It may not be until I'm gone, but I have faith that it will all work out. I just don't know how. No one does. I don't read about what happens when we die because it's all purely speculation. But I know it's going to be wonderful, whatever it is. It will all be okay.

When I think of myself, I feel sorry for the part of me that is Jennifer's mom.

When I look at old pictures of us all, before Jennifer died, I feel sorry for the people in the photos...even those of me...because I know what's coming.

I know, but they don't. God help them.

Jim

OCTOBER 30, 2020

I was lying in bed this morning, laughing. Lori rolled over and looked at me. 'What's so funny?"

The Barbie princess!" I snorted.

Lori let out a yelp, but not in pain. In laughter. An explosion of it.

All it took were three words: *The Barbie princess.*

Jennifer was six and dressed up for Halloween. Instead of wearing a homemade costume by Lori as she usually did, Jennifer had set her sights on a cheap, store-bought set with a pink dress, matching sparkly shoes, and a plastic Barbie mask—complete with a painted perfect Barbie smile. The mask had two cutout holes to see through and a little round hole to breathe.

We were headed to my parents' house so they could see the kids in their costumes. We had just completed trick-or-treating in Lori's parents' neighborhood. All three of the kids had already consumed *a lot* of candy. Lori opened the door to my old Ford Bronco to help the kids into the back seat. Jennifer put the mask back on and pulled the strap behind her Barbie-style ponytail to hold it in place.

"You're going to be hot in that," Lori said. "Why don't you wait until we get there to wear the mask?"

Jennifer's voice was muffled, but the answer was a resounding, "No."

Clearly, she wanted to stay in character for as long as possible. Lori shrugged, and the rest of us all piled in. We weren't even out of the driveway when Jennifer exclaimed, "I don't feel so well!"

Every head snapped to look at her, and before anyone could do anything, the Barbie princess threw up, right through the little hole, smiling brightly the whole time.

I rolled over in bed and grabbed Lori. I gave her the biggest bear hug that I had in forever as we drowned in laughter and remembering.

I'd forgotten how good it felt to hurt all over from laughter.

I had the feeling that somewhere, in that place where Heaven dwells, a young woman named Jennifer was laughing with us and looking far more beautiful in her wings of gold than any Barbie princess here on Earth ever had.

NOVEMBER 3, 2020

Earlier this year, two of my sisters opened up about Jennifer's death. Kathleen said, "We'd always been such a 'golden family' where bad things didn't happen, then Jennifer died. We had no idea how to handle it and especially how to relate to your and Lori's sorrow.

"Looking back, I'm so saddened by how hard it was for you both.

"I would look at you, Jim, and think, 'You're so strong and independent, you'll be fine. You don't need us. And Lori has her family. They always seemed to know what to do and how to help emotionally, so she'll be okay.' That was wrong of me. I think now of all the things we didn't do, the calls we didn't make just to see how you were doing. We should have checked in on you. We should have invited you over or brought you dinner. It was all our fault. We let you down. That's hard to live with."

Kathleen went on to tell me that when our sister Julie's husband died a few years later of cancer, it all hit home for her. "When Stewart died, you and Lori were the first ones to help. You were graceful and supportive. You could have been bitter in the ways we weren't all there for you. Instead, you and Lori were there, teaching us all how to help others."

Julie talked about how hard it's been coming to terms with losing her husband and the intensity of her grief.

I was glad she was willing to talk. While she still suffers, thankfully, she's learning to cope and is doing better. Her family and friends definitely stepped up. She said something that I thought was interesting. "It's strange, Jim, but whenever I really need it, God sends the most unexpected people into my life, people carrying torches of hope. I think that's what God does—He brings light to the darkness.

As we were saying goodbye, Julie looked at me and said, "For all of us, Jennifer's light shines on. She was so beautiful. No, she *is* so beautiful. She just isn't here with us."

NOVEMBER 5, 2020

Like our Heavenly Father's love is for all of us, my love for Jennifer is forever and unconditional. I've cursed at and cried out to God for taking her from us. Yet, I have come to realize that anyone who curses God for their sorrow of losing someone they love must also recognize and celebrate the Giver of life and love.

I have no doubt that Jesus was with us through our pain. I could feel His comfort. I know He hated it when we were hurting. But, He knows that our sorrow, though overwhelming, is fleeting. Jesus knows how it will all end. He knows that one day, our tears will be tears of joy and elation.

Despite how much it hurt losing her, I wouldn't exchange a moment of it for never having known the beautiful life that was, and is, Jennifer. Although my pain is still acute, my love for her is far greater.

Life is good for me now. It's taken a long time for me to be able to say that. Our happiness is real, and so is our laughter. But life will never be nearly as sweet as when Jennifer was here.

I continue to marvel at the words Lori spoke at the hospital, praying for God's will to be done, as the rest of us prayed for Jennifer to be healed. *Did some part of Lori know, at that moment, that we were going to lose Jennifer? Was that God speaking to us through Lori? Was he preparing us?*

I have wondered other things over the years:

Was it God's will that we would lose our only daughter?

Was it God's will that brought immeasurable heartache to everyone who knew Jennifer?

Was it God's will that our beautiful daughter would never live to walk down the aisle, have children of her own, or hold her twin brother's daughter in her arms?

Were all these things God's will? If so, why?

If God can stop it, why does He allow bad things to happen? Do our prayers matter? Does God even care? These are questions believers have been asking forever.

For a long time, I beat myself up, searching for these answers. I have heard a Bible verse for many years. It hasn't been until lately that I think I understand it, not only in my head but also in my heart. Isaiah 55:8-9 says, "For my thoughts are not your thoughts, and your ways are not my ways," says Yahweh. "For as the heavens are higher than the earth, so are my ways higher than your ways, and my thoughts than your thoughts."

There are things we aren't meant to know or understand, at least not while we are on this Earth.

As a father, I've tried to teach my kids the value of patience. It's a lesson I have to remind myself of often—some things will have to wait. Answers to my questions are one of those things.

There comes a time when there is nothing any of us can do but let a person go home to Heaven. Luck was not with Jennifer that night of the accident, but God was.

Shortly before we were taken to see Jennifer's body at the hospital, we were told that she had required massive blood infusions due to her severe internal bleeding. Because of this, only her corneas could be donated. We were sad about that as we would have liked others to have lived because of her. In thinking about that now, I'm happy that they could at least use her corneas. I hope they helped someone else see life as she did.

For a long time after she died, I could not forgive myself for the hurtful words I spoke to Jennifer just before she left for the evening. Now, by God's, I've been able to let them go because I know that God has forgiven me, and so has Jennifer. She was never one to hold a grudge. I like to think that she'd be saying to me, "Dad! There's nothing to forgive. Only something to celebrate—our love."

I know Jennifer would say the same to Carolyn. I hope she has forgiven herself.

A sword pierced my heart the moment we lost Jennifer, and it has remained embedded there ever since. A few months ago, I had a health scare that landed me in the hospital. My heart was beating erratically, and I needed a pacemaker. During the procedure, I wished the surgeon could have replaced the sword with the pacemaker, but when I woke, I knew the blade was still there. But it won't be forever. The source of my pain has an ending date, the day I die. On that day, my heart will be restored to its fullest.

I like to imagine the moment: Jesus handing that bloodied sword back to me—my blood and pain wiped clean. And Jennifer will be there with her big, beautiful grin.

I think Jennifer would be proud of her family. I know she would be proud of her brothers. Justin's been drug-free for over a decade. His strength and resolve to overcome the toughest of addictions were admirable and should give hope to others who think there is no way out. And David has gone on to become a wonderful husband, father, and businessman.

Both boys have taken over my business. I couldn't be prouder of them. Like all of us, they made some mistakes in their earlier years, but they have learned and grown stronger from them.

When our first grandson was born, I was terrified of opening my heart enough to love this new person. *What if I lose him too?*

But that's the thing about love; it comes whether we want it to or not. One look at that little boy, and it was over. Love was already there because life is love.

In time, I've learned not to be guided by fear and darkness, but rather to put my love for this little boy, and now, all our grandchildren, fully in God's hands. After all, God created each of them. No matter how much I love them, God loves them more. That's the way it is with a father. Whether they have one day or a hundred years, they will be cared for—on Earth or in Heaven.

Lori got it right when she said that remarkable prayer for Jennifer at the hospital so long ago. Hers is now my prayer, in everything—God's will be done.

Our U.S. currency motto, and Lori, got it right: "In God We Trust."

It's our best and only hope.

Our Heavenly Father, Thank you for giving us the strength to believe in You and to trust in You during even our hardest of times. Thank You for the wonderful years You blessed us with Jennifer. Thank You for my wife, our sons, and grandchildren. Be with them and all our family and friends as they journey through life. Let them make good decisions with their heart focused on You. Thank You for everything you have given us: our jobs, our home, and our health. Thank You for Your son, who gave his life for us, so that we can come to Your Heavenly home when our time on Earth is done. Thank You for the beauty of the Earth. Thank you for the strength to fight the evil one when he tries to derail us. Our Heavenly Father, be with all of our loved ones and friends as they miss Jennifer as we do. Bless Carolyn and her family as they continue to heal. Be with all those who hear Jennifer's story and let them never drive impaired or distracted. It will be the greatest gift to those who love them—and the greatest gift to the memory of our beautiful angel. In Jesus' name, I pray. Amen.

Lori

NOVEMBER 6, 2020

Jennifer died at 2:30 in the morning. By dawn, our home was full of family and friends. In the following hours, days, and months they brought food, flowers, cards, and more, but mostly, they brought loving hands for me to hold.

For months, I was catatonic and barely able to function. Those closest to me understood and didn't judge. They stepped in to do the things I was unable to do for myself. I will be in their debt forever. Jim handled his grief very differently; he was unable to stop moving. Outwardly, he presented a much healthier picture than I did, he talked a lot and even laughed, but his void was just as deep and dark as mine. He wanted so badly to find some way to fix his pain and all of ours. But that's not the way grief works. It can't be willed away.

People ask me the best way for them to help others facing devastating grief. My advice is simple: be there for them and hug them. For me, their hugs said far more than any words.

I appreciated most when people hugged me without saying a word, for I could then imagine what I thought they were trying to say, and what I most needed to hear.

I used to wonder how I could fill the massive void left by Jennifer. I knew that I didn't have the capacity on my own. I had prayed that God would do so for me.

I've recently realized that while that void will never be filled, God has answered my prayer. He's filled much of it with a loving extended family and friends. He's filled it in my relationships with Jim, my boys and their wives, and He's filled it with grandkids and their peals of laughter. He has done what I never believed possible—He has made the unbearable bearable.

When Tyson, our first grandchild, was born in 2004, I remember my first thought was, "How am I supposed to deal with this? I'm so mired in sorrow that I can't tie my shoes, and now I'm going to have a grandbaby? And I'm supposed to be happy?" The truth was, I didn't know if I could love anyone.

Hah! As soon as I held that little baby in my arms, I learned the folly of that thinking, for he instantly had my heart.

Very soon, it was clear what a great kick in the pants he was for us, for it was through him that we learned that life goes on. There is no greater proof of that than the arrival of a new baby in the family. He kicked me into gear and, in some sense, back to life.

Before his birth, I was dormant. Then Tyson came, and it was like, "Holy cow. This family is going on, no matter what."

Tyson's birth pushed all of us into the realization that we had to go on. Jim said to me after Tyson was born, "Lori, there will be more of these little people coming…ready or not." He was right. We now have seven grandkids: five girls and two boys, and another girl on the way. Thank God for the circle of life. It's more than a cliché—it is God's ultimate gift to each of us, his gift of life. That is love.

Since Jennifer died, five children have been named after her using either her first or middle name. Some of these kids are grandkids, and some by other family and friends. We heard that Jennifer's high school boyfriend and his wife named their daughter Renee after Jennifer's middle name. His wife must be a remarkable person. We are grateful to them and to everyone who honors Jennifer's memory in this way.

None of us knows how long we have on this earth. While my grief for Jennifer will never go away, and I miss her so much that there are times when I feel physically ill. I do know that for the living, no matter how much sorrow we feel, if we are open to it, there can be happiness again. It's all around us if we look hard enough.

So that's what I do. I look for the joy in the little things of life—in my marriage, in my relationships with family and friends, with my sons and their wives, and especially our grandchildren. Finding joy again, that's what Jennifer would have wanted for all of us.

When I close my eyes and think of Jennifer, I pray she can feel the love that we all carry for her in our hearts. And no matter how far or near she may be, I pray our love is enough to be felt. I pray wherever she is, she is dancing.

It's been over eighteen years since Jennifer died. In that time, I've learned a lot about life, love, loss, relationships, and God. And through it all, whether I was aware of it or not, two basic truths became clear and will continue to sustain me until I take my last breath.

God makes life possible—and loss bearable.

It's as simple, and as hard, as that.

Thoughts from Justin Dultmeier

2020

My parents have been through so much. Before Jennifer died, they were strong in their faith, and even so, after she died, darkness found them—not so much in a faith sense, but in a reality sense. For those loved ones left behind, death brings darkness. If you don't have the right people around you when you face something as terrible as losing a child, a sister, or someone you love with all your heart, you could be in the dark for the rest of your life. Mom and Dad had God in their lives and were surrounded by wonderful people, and even so, they were in the dark for several years.

Light has returned to my parents. They went from light to dark, and thankfully, back to light.

I've made a lot of bad mistakes in my life, especially in high school, when I flooded the gym floor. It was a stupid thing to do. The consequences were terrible for my family and me. Everyone knew about it, and so many people were looking down on me. I went from being in school every day to being kicked out and working three jobs to earn enough money to pay back the damage I had done.

My parents were devastated. I promised Mom I would find a way to graduate with my class. I had two teachers who were very understanding and took the time to come to my house and tutor me. I could not have fulfilled that promise to my mom without them.

The night Jennifer died, I woke to the sound of my mom screaming for me to wake up, that Jennifer had been in an accident. I can't explain it, but I knew that Jennifer was dead as soon as I heard the words. I just knew. On the way to the hospital, my mom was in the front passenger seat crying. My dad was driving 100 mph. I wanted to say, "Dad, we don't need to hurry. It's too late." Instead, I said nothing.

When the doctor came into the waiting room and said that he had done everything he could to save Jennifer, I couldn't breathe. I couldn't talk. I managed to go out to the hall and sank to the floor against the wall.

For a long time, people just walked past me, looking to find my parents to comfort. No one stopped. No one stopped to hug me, to hold me, or to tell me that everything would be okay. Instead, it was as though I was invisible.

It was a long, terrible night—the loneliest of my life.

It wasn't anyone's fault. Everyone was in shock and trying to cope as best they could. People knew my parents had just lost a daughter, but a brother mourning his sister didn't occur to them, at least not then. I'm glad they were there for my parents, but that night a new thought seared into me, "I'm alone in this." And no matter what, I couldn't get that thought out of my head for years.

I needed someone, anyone. I called my girlfriend's house. Her mother answered, sleepy and confused. I could barely talk. My words and voice didn't sound like me. I tried to tell her that my sister was in a bad accident, and I needed to talk to her daughter. I wanted her to come to the hospital. I wanted to tell her that Jennifer was gone. But my words were jumbled. She said she would tell her, and the call ended. Hours later, after learning what had happened, my girlfriend came to the house and told me that her mom felt terrible. She thought I was someone else just messing around, probably intoxicated, calling her daughter at three in the morning. Had she known, they would all have come immediately to the hospital.

In the next few days, I was just going through the motions. I wasn't really there at all. Someone would tell me what to do and where to go, and I did it. I was a zombie.

I felt completely alone. No one was to blame. It was the reality of the situation. I was at a hard age. I wasn't a kid anymore, but I wasn't really an adult either. Mom and Dad were struggling just to survive.

Two days after Jennifer died, my parents took me to see the casket they had picked out for Jennifer. Looking at it, I wanted to scream, "This isn't the way it should be! We aren't supposed to be here looking at her casket! We're supposed to be looking at the apartment we were going to rent together!" Jennifer and I hadn't told anyone yet, but we had been planning to get an apartment together. That's how close we were. She had become my best friend.

At the viewing, David and I walked to the front to see Jennifer's body. It was the first time either of us had seen her. I don't know what we said, but I know we stood there for a long time, talking to her.

After the funeral, Mom was sitting in the front row. I sat next to her. She turned to me and buried her face in my chest. I wrapped both arms around her. People walked up, trying to talk to her. "Mom can't talk right now," I said. I kept saying it over and over. At one point, my dad looked at me with my arms wrapped around her and nodded.

"I promise, Dad," I whispered, "I will take care of her. I will take care of Mom." Even while I was saying it, I was thinking, "How can I promise that when I don't think I can take care of myself?"

I saw the faintest hint of pride in my dad's eyes. I knew he was relieved that I was helping my mom. She was going to need all of us.

In the funeral home's limousine, driving from the service to the cemetery, it was loud and crowded in the car with the driver, both sets of my grandparents, my parents, David, and my girlfriend. People handle stress and grief so differently. I get that, but at the time, I didn't. I blurted at the top of my lungs, "Shut up! Will everyone just shut up?"

They did.

At the cemetery, David and I, and others, carried Jennifer's coffin from the hearse to the gravesite. One of the guys tried to lighten the moment with a casual remark about it being bad luck to walk on the graves of others. I almost exploded. I wanted to remember that moment of carrying Jennifer's body to her grave in silence. It was all I could do to keep from letting go and shouting, "I'm done! I'm not doing this!" In hindsight, I don't blame him at all. He loved Jennifer, and he was trying to cope as best he could in his sorrow. We all were.

Before Jennifer died, I'd been dabbling in drugs, but afterward, I dove in—full immersion. I was just numb and wanted to stay that way. In the months to come, I swallowed, smoked, snorted, and injected just about anything I could.

It took me a long time to realize that there was no pill I could take, no drugs I could shoot, and nothing I could drink to make it any better. Jennifer was still dead. The drugs and alcohol made me numb for a while, but the pain came when they wore off. So I'd start trying to get numb again. It was a vicious, dark, and terrible cycle.

Things went from bad to horrific fast. My parents tried to help, but I was on a one-way trip down. They'd get me in rehab; then I'd get myself kicked out or just leave.

Looking back, I realize two things played such a big part in my inability to deal with grief, and they wrapped themselves around each other so fully that there was no separating them. The first was that I really had no faith.

I had grown up in the church, but I hadn't truly believed any of it in my heart. I was like a balloon that was tethered to nothing. I had no direction and no purpose. I was just floating around, wherever the wind, or life, was taking me. I didn't know where I was going, and I didn't care.

The second was that Jennifer's death was the third in a string of devastating losses for me. The first was my best friend, Robert. He was killed one night when a cement truck ran a red light and struck the vehicle he was riding in. Another friend in the same car was seriously injured. Immediately after the accident, Robert was outside the car, talking to the police. Everyone thought he was fine. Suddenly he said that his chest hurt. He collapsed and died. An autopsy revealed that his aorta had partially pulled away from where it was attached.

I went to the hospital as soon as we heard about the accident. I was traumatized at the sight of my buddy's dead body. It was like looking at a mannequin. Where was my friend? Where was my vibrant, hilarious friend? I ran my hands through his light brown hair, willing him to wake up. His soft hair was the only part of him that still seemed like him. How could that cold, lifeless body be Robert?

After Robert died, I was lost. He was the one friend I could talk to about anything, and in the blink of an eye, he was gone. Jennifer began filling the void Robert left. Now that she was older, I found that she was someone I could really talk to without being judged. I'd come home, and we'd stay up half the night talking. I think she understood how much I missed Robert and how badly I needed a friend.

The second loss was a girl from school that I'd had a serious crush on for a long time. Although we never dated, thinking about her consumed much of my waking hours. I used to sit next to her on the bus to tech classes. I never had the guts to ask her out, let alone tell her how I felt.

She committed suicide when we were in high school. I wasn't responsible for her death, of course, but I felt that if I had done something, anything different, maybe that wouldn't have happened. After she died, I went over to her house, where her family and friends were gathering. Her parents had recently separated, but I saw them in the kitchen, embracing. It was an embrace of unspeakable sorrow and pain. I had seen the same grief in Robert's parents at the hospital the night he died. I remember thinking that no parent should ever have to go through that. Parents should never live longer than their kids.

So, well before Jennifer died, I had been coping poorly with grief. If I had had a strong faith, maybe my response would have been different. Without it, turning to drugs seemed like a pretty good option. I wanted a diversion, something to bring a little joy back to my life.

Then Jennifer died, and that was it. I was completely destroyed. I was done.

During the night in the hallway at the hospital, even though I hadn't taken any drugs, it was like I had ingested some sort of poison that altered the chemistry in my entire brain and body. I changed. I was screwed up. I didn't care about anything other than I wanted to be numb. I was afraid of getting close to anyone, afraid that I would just lose them too. I pushed everyone I knew and loved away, and I did so for a long, long time. Even though I had a girlfriend, I kept her at bay.

I was spiraling fast. You name it, I was taking it, but the worst was meth. It could make me feel so good like I could do anything or be anyone. Until it wore off, then it was terrible. I wrote a poem once when I was high on meth. I can now only remember one line, "Blue eyes turn to black." That's what happened to me. My life turned from light and filled with color to black. Darkness enveloped me. I would come down from a high and swear I'd never do it again. But I'd do it again. Drugs were easy for me to get until my first dealer committed suicide. Then, I had to find another source. I didn't have much money, so I learned that if I hung around the new dealer long enough and acted like a bouncer, he would figure out that no one would mess with him as long as "Big Justin" was there. My plan worked. He'd slip me whatever drugs I wanted.

I'd go home and take crystal meth any way that I could. I'd smoke it, sniff it, and even wrap it in bread and swallow it like a pill. I was a mess.

One day I was high and driving. It wasn't the first time. Thank God I didn't cause a wreck and hurt anyone. Looking back, I can't believe I ever drove impaired, not after what my parents had been through with Jennifer. But that was how messed up I was. It was like I couldn't connect the dots. I didn't care to connect them.

That morning I did something that I had never done; I took downers along with the uppers. I started to feel sick, real sick. Bright, excruciating pain pulsed through my body. Everything hurt. I couldn't see through the blinding pain, let alone drive. I pulled my truck over, stumbled out the door, and pressed the speed dial to my girl-friend. "Something's not right." I managed to tell her where I was.

The next thing I remember, things were very, very different. It was silent. Completely silent. And nothing hurt, not anywhere. I remember thinking that it felt really good.

I was looking down from above. I could see the field below, its tall grass blowing in the wind. The road and my truck were there. Someone touched my shoulder. A voice said, "It isn't your time." I turned around to see who had said it, but no one was there.

The next thing I knew, I was in the ditch, lying next to my truck. My heart thumped so hard that my entire body jolted. I could hear it pounding in my chest. My girlfriend was standing over me. She looked stricken.

It took a while, but eventually, she helped get me into her car. We left my truck. She took me to where we were living. I slept it off. And that same night, I did more meth.

Three days later, I was back roofing for my dad's company. He wasn't there. He had no idea I was high. I started hurting again all over. Every part of me was sick. I knew my heart and body couldn't take it anymore. For the first time, I was scared.

Shakily, I climbed down from the roof. The foreman frowned when he saw me and asked if I was all right.

"I can't handle this anymore."

"What are you on?"

"Meth."

He let out a long, slow sigh. "Wow."

"I think I'm dying. Again," I managed to say. "I overdosed the other day. I think I died. I mean, really died. I know my heart stopped. I can't explain it, but I came back. Someone told me it wasn't my time. I don't want my parents to have to bury another child." I was shaking and crying. "I can't do this anymore, but I don't know what to do."

He put his arm over my shoulder, "Get in my truck. I'm taking you to rehab right now."

"No. I don't want to do that again. I've tried, but it doesn't work."

"Then, the hospital."

"No. Not that either."

"Then, either you tell your parents, or I will."

That night I told my parents the truth that I needed help. I told them I wanted to go to rehab. I'm sure they were skeptical, knowing I likely would not stay long enough to get clean. But they took me to an in-treatment program. I lived up to everyone's expectations and got kicked out.

Then, I heard about a program strictly for men. It was out in the middle of nowhere—a thirty-day treatment plan. I knew I couldn't go home and stay clean, and Dad wouldn't let me work if I relapsed. I had nowhere else to go.

One of the leaders of the program was a burly man with a long, biker beard. He was a former drug dealer, and there was nothing I could pull on him. He'd seen it all. He let me sneak out and smoke cigarettes. I think he knew giving up hard drugs was enough. Cigarettes could come later.

He talked to me about life and told me stories of what he had done. I thought I had been bad until I heard about the things he had done. He understood where I was coming from, and the guilt I felt about the pain I had caused everyone I cared about.

He helped me understand that my grief and addiction were all lumped together. "Justin," he said to me one day, "you can't control tomorrow, but you can control what you're doing right now. Focus on that."

That old man, and the program, saved my life. I stopped it all, then and there—all the drugs. It about killed me, but I did it.

Somehow, my girlfriend had been willing to wait. I was going to be a father. Danae and I married. I thought I was doing the right thing, but I wasn't ready to be a husband, let alone the father to our newborn son. We managed to survive and would go on to have three children in all. They were great kids, but I was broken and still not coping well with much of anything.

We started going to a church where Danae was very involved. Despite her attempts, my faith was like a man hiding in the shadows. There were times when it made sense, and I would feel strong stirrings that God was urging me into the light to see him fully. But over time, I found it was easier to stay in the darkness.

We eventually divorced. I began spiraling again fast. I hid my hurt by pretending to be tough. What faith I had evaporated.

I mounted the mask of a wolf on my wall. Wolves are predators, and they feed on the weak. That's what I did. I wasn't about to let anyone, or anything, hurt me. I hurt a lot of people. I was acting in a way that would have made the devil himself proud.

I started running around with people who were making bad choices. I'm amazed now that I didn't either end up in jail, dead, or returning to drug use. Thankfully, I never did. "Gentlemen's Clubs" became some of my favorite hangouts.

It's strange, but I found that people seemed to be attracted to this new, confident me, even though I was tough and mean. I told myself that I didn't care who I hurt. In fact, I cared a lot. But I would never let anyone know it. Instead, I hid behind my new image of a tough guy. I played the part well. People were scared of me.

And then I met Emily. I was looking for someone who would accept my three kids and me. Emily had never been married, and she wanted a family. She must have seen something redeeming beyond my tough façade because remarkably, she agreed to marry me. Long ago, Jennifer told me to find someone who wants what is best for

278

me. Emily was that person. We had two more children of our own, and we managed to get by despite my inability to deal with deep feelings. Just like Danae, Emily was a good mom to all our kids. However, just like my first marriage, I wasn't the husband my wife deserved, or the father my kids needed. We fought a lot. I exposed the kids to things they should not have had to deal with. Eventually, I started stepping out of my marriage. My days at the Gentlemen's Club resumed.

Thankfully, despite all the other crap I put them through, Emily and my kids didn't have to deal with a dad on drugs, for the road of drugs only leads once place—a dead-end.

When I learned that my parents had asked a writer to help them write a book about how they, and our family, dealt with Jennifer's death, I was angry. I didn't want the world to learn any more bad things about me. Even though at the time, I'd been clean for over fourteen years, my life was still a mess. The last thing I needed was anyone knowing anything about me.

When I first met with the author, I was surly, scared, and unwilling to share much. She asked how I had dealt with Jennifer's death and about my faith, if I had any.

The truth was, I was still a very broken person. I wanted the whole project to stop. I appreciated my parents wanting to share what they went through because they thought it might help others facing the death and trauma of a loved one, and it may help people think twice about drinking and driving. But what will everyone think of me if they knew that long after Jennifer died, I continued to drive impaired?

I didn't want anyone finding out about that, or anything else. I'd had more pain than I could handle. I didn't want more pressure from friends, family, and strangers reading and learning about the stupid things I'd done. I'd already let my parents, grandparents, wife, ex-wife, and kids down enough. And now we were going to pile on more? No thanks.

Last year, David and I took over my dad's roofing business so that he could retire. I knew that day was coming for a long time. The business had been my life and my dream since I was a boy. I grew up on a construction site working side by side with Dad. I could lay shingles long before I could drive.

David has an excellent business sense, and with my onsite knowledge of roofing, everyone knew we'd make a great team. The problem was, I was lost emotionally and spiritually. I hadn't done drugs in nearly a decade and a half, but I was still running away from my grief and making bad choices.

Looking back, I think I was running from God. Deep down, I hated myself. I thought I was good for nothing. I couldn't understand why I was alive when Jennifer wasn't. I had made much worse decisions than Jennifer ever did. I felt I should have died instead of her!

That was the root of it. I hated myself, and I hated myself for surviving when my sister didn't.

For a long time, late at night, when I couldn't sleep, I had this recurring vision of me shoving all the painful thoughts I had over the years into a little jar. It was easier to stuff my feelings away than deal with them. I was so angry and scared about the prospect of the book coming out and people finding out about the things I'd done, that night after night, I would lie in bed thinking about cramming every stupid page of that book into the jar.

A couple of years passed. I hoped that maybe something had happened, and the book wasn't going to be published. Then my brother or one of my parents would mention something about it, and again I would lie awake those nights, and through clenched teeth, imagine cramming more paper into that jar.

A few months ago, the author gave me a rough draft of the story and asked for my input. There wasn't enough space in that jar for the pages I wanted to shove into it. I couldn't even bring myself to read it. Everyone was waiting for me to respond.

My heart pounded every time I thought of it.

My out-of-control life had reached its boiling point. I was having an affair with another woman. Emily found out. She wasn't going to tolerate me stepping out. Instead of facing my shortcomings, I took the easy way out and left her and the kids. No one was going to tell me what I could and could not do.

I moved into an apartment with almost nothing in it. I had disappointed everyone. Even my younger brother had had enough of me. David had always been mature beyond his years. He was very proud that I had overcome drugs, but when he found out that I had left my family, he was furious. He came to see me in the apartment and said that he could no longer work with someone he couldn't trust, and a man who cheats on his wife, he said, can't be trusted.

I felt like I'd been punched in the gut. When David closed the door behind him, I gasped for air. Everything in my life had crumbled away, like a great sandcastle after a punishing wave.

Alone in a stark apartment, I was as broken as I had been the day seventeen years earlier when I told the foreman that I had just overdosed and needed help. Like then, I was dying inside, but it was a different kind of death than what I experienced when I was on drugs. This was the death of my soul.

I looked around the apartment, cold and barren, and wondered, "How did I get here? What have I done?" I realized I had nothing. I had pushed out everything and everyone important in my life—my wife, my kids, and now my only remaining sibling. I had wanted to make my dad and mom proud of the company that we continued in their name. Instead, I would be responsible for destroying it.

Somewhere deep inside, hot fury started to churn, then erupted. With hands clenched for battle, I stormed around the apartment. I wanted to break something, anything. I yelled and swore so loud, my lungs burned. "Where are you, God?" I screamed. "Everyone says you're right here, but I don't see you! Where are you, Jennifer? I want to talk to you!"

I was so enraged. I could feel the blood surging in my temples. My head was pounding, and I wondered if I was having a stroke. I didn't care.

I started slamming my fists through everything in sight. I had brought an odd array of items from our home, including my old Bible and several glass vases filled with orchids that lined the kitchen counter. I trained my sight on the colorful vases, hating everything they and the flowers represented: happiness, light, and joy. One by one, I smashed them. As hard as I could, I threw them to the floor. It wasn't enough. I scooped up the broken pieces with my bare hands and crushed them. Blood seeped through the broken shards. I didn't even feel it.

On the counter were two bottles full of pills—one for sleeping and the other for pain—enough to turn off the lights once and for all.

I grabbed my water bottle and the pills, and just like I had the night Jennifer died, I slid down against the wall, this time it was the half-wall of the kitchen, not the long hallway of the hospital.

Seventeen years later, I felt just as alone.

I opened the cap of the bottles, shaking the pills. It would be so easy, so much easier than facing the loss of everything that meant anything to me.

I was crying hot, furious tears. The thought of my five kids flashed in my head. "Dad gave up," they would say. "After everything he had been through, he just gave up. It was easier." I closed my eyes at the image, hot tears burning the inside of my lids.

I flung the bottles, spilling the pills across the floor. I picked up my cell phone and dialed the number of my best friend, Wade. He answered on the first ring. I'm not exactly sure what I said to him, but he said he would come over. I told him, no, I would be okay. It was a lie. He must have known it was a lie. Because a short while later, Wade walked into my apartment, his eyes were wide with fear when he saw me still sitting on the floor, my hands still bleeding. He grabbed a wad of paper towels and sank to the floor with me.

Wade is married to my cousin Brooke, so we go way back. He had a rough childhood and faced more challenges in his youth than just about anyone I know. And yet, those experiences made him one of the strongest men I know. He has been a rock for me.

As we sat there on the floor with paper towels wrapped around my injured hands, Wade reminded me that some of the greatest heroes on earth are the ones that have faced the greatest obstacles. Heroes like his grandmother's brothers. During World War II, Wade's great-Uncle Bob was captured and imprisoned in a Japanese prisoner of war camp. It wasn't until shortly before he died that Bob ever told anyone what happened there, in the jaws of Hell, and later, when he was forced to endure the unimaginable on the Bataan Death March. His brother immediately enlisted in the Air Force after learning that Bob had been captured. Bill said, "I'm going to go help rescue my brother." And he did help, serving in the Pacific as a bomber.

For a long time, Wade and I have shared an interest in ancient Japanese customs. There is a Japanese saying that there are three faces or masks that we each wear. The first one is the mask we wear to show the world. The second mask is what we wear for close family and friends. The third mask is the one we never show anyone, and it is the truest reflection of ourselves. Wade is the only person in the world who has ever seen my third mask. He knows it all.

There are times when I think he knows me better than I know myself. We can go for days or weeks and not talk, and then we both pick up our phones at the same time to text one another.

As we sat on the floor, I told Wade that I was tired of being broken. He reminded me of *kintsugi*, the ancient Japanese technique of repairing damaged and broken pottery by using gold and plant material to fill in the cracks. The results are vessels far more beautiful and interesting than ones that have never been broken. And the gold veins reflect light in such a way that the vessel is illuminated when before, it was dark.

Wade also reminded me of the ancient *katana* sword used by the samurai. Its blade is one of the most beautifully crafted tools in the world and one of the most difficult to create. To make a *katana* in the ancient tradition, the purest of steel is heated and folded, hammered and forged, over and over and over, for weeks or even months. Forged and hammered, beaten and heated, beaten and heated, beaten and heated. Without the heat and pressure, the beauty of the object would never be formed. Without the heat and the pressure, the sword would never be strong.

Hours later, after he knew I was stable, Wade said, "If this ever happens again, I will come. I will take you out to the middle of a field if I have to, and I'll stay with you until it passes. I will buy two plane tickets and take you somewhere you want to go— anywhere where you won't hurt yourself." That is love. He would take a bullet for me and I for him.

We made a pact. No matter what, if either of us ever again is at the point where I just was, we would call each other. All we'd have to say was, "I'm going to turn the light off." No matter where we are or what we are doing, we will be there for each other.

Wade stayed for a long time and helped me clean up the mess. The next day I began working to repair the rest of the damage.

Two days later, I was as drained and lifeless as a balloon with all its air sucked out. The tirade had left me exhausted. I was still just as empty. The counter where the colorful vases had been was bare. My old Bible was the only thing remaining.

I wanted to spit at it. I felt despair and anger rise again in my throat.

"I'm done. I'm done! I'm done!" I cried. "I can't do this anymore. I'm tired of life and tired of everything! Everyone says that I should trust you, God. *Why should I?* God, if you're there, then prove it! Show me something!"

I grabbed the Bible, and with both hands, I slammed it straight to the floor as hard as I could, and then collapsed to my knees, sobbing.

The Bible landed open, sitting there as peacefully as if it were open at a pulpit, waiting to be read aloud. I scoffed and then stabbed my finger as hard as I could into the open page. My teeth clenched hard, wishing I could bore a hole all the way through the book to the floor. Instead, I looked at the words below my finger.

"But arise, and stand on your feet...," it said.

I blinked hard, looked at the sentence at the end of my finger, then at my knees.

I read it again. "But arise, and stand on your feet..."

The words sounded in my head, as clear and strong as the day so long ago when I heard a voice saying, "It's not your time."

The blood surging through my veins settled. Everything calmed, not as completely as the day when I was looking down from above, but it was quiet now too. This stillness seemed to come from deep within me. My anger and rage evaporated.

This was no coincidence. God was telling me, no, He was commanding me to stand up. Stand up. Stand up and be a man. Stand up and be a father to your children. Stand up and be a husband to your wife. Stand up and face your problems. Stand up and be a man of God.

I had just begged for a sign. Until that moment, everything in my life had been falling apart, and God said, "But arise, and stand on your feet." It was so obvious. He couldn't have gotten my attention more than if He had slapped me across the face.

I knew as I sat there on my knees, Jesus had opened the Bible to these words. Jesus was telling me to stand up. He had gotten my attention once before when He gently tapped me on the shoulder and told me it wasn't my time. But I hadn't been ready to hear Him then. I eventually convinced myself that it hadn't been God talking to me. It had to have been my imagination.

From the moment Jennifer died, I thought I had been alone.

There on my knees in the kitchen, I knew that Jesus had been there every step of the way. I just had never been in a place where I would allow my heart to open enough to believe it.

I recalled the story my mom told me once about a man who was drowning at sea. He called out to God, begging Him to save him. A man in a sailboat found him and threw him a life jacket. "Get on the boat," said the sailor. "I can't; I'm waiting for God to save me." The boat sailed away. A cruise ship came by, and the crew lowered its ladder. "Climb aboard." "I can't; I'm waiting on God to save me." The ship sailed away. Finally, a helicopter appeared overhead, and a man threw down a rope telling him to grab it. "I can't; I'm waiting for God to save me." The helicopter left, and the man in the sea drowned. When he got to Heaven, he asked God why He didn't save him. The Lord said, "I tried. Who do you think sent the sailboat, the cruise ship, and the helicopter?"

With my finger touching the words, "But arise," I knew I had been like the man at sea. I had refused help, turning my back on God and His saving grace. God had done more than tap me on the back and guide my finger toward some words in the Bible. He had surrounded me, time and time again, with family, friends, and strangers who had offered help, but I had been too blind to see. I thought I was alone, but I was never alone. God was there.

I reread the words, "But arise, and stand on your feet..." And so, I did. I stood up, got in my car, went to my wife, and asked for her forgiveness. While I was gone, she had been reading a draft of the book about our family after Jennifer's death that I had so feared. Reading it, she had a better understanding of the pain we had endured. She said it helped to open her heart toward understanding and forgiving my sins. It's funny the things that can be the most healing when you least expect it. I had been threatened by the prospect of anyone reading about our family and Jennifer's death, and now I see that it has helped in healing my marriage.

I thought back to all the times I had fought against this book; it was as if the jar had finally exploded into fragments of glass. I found that just like the pieces of the broken vases I had to clean up days earlier, I was forced to sit down and read about things I didn't want to hear. Things like: the time my mom collapsed in a janitor's closet, my dad feeling like he was a tree cut in half, Grandma saying she not only lost a granddaughter, but her daughter, and David having to learn to go on without his twin. And I had to deal with the unbearable reality of what Carolyn must have been dealing with all these years.

With every sentence I read, it was like I had picked up a broken piece of that jar, and would think, "Yeah, I never dealt with that." I'd read the next one and think, "Yeah, I never dealt with that either." The pain of feeling alone. My anger at God for allowing Jennifer to die. My deep fear for my parents and their ability to recover. Drowning my pain with drugs. My seeking answers in the arms of someone other than my wife. I now had to deal with all of it.

With each sentence, I could feel again how it had been a lot easier to hide the images away than to deal with them. I kept forcing myself to remember that real men don't keep running away from hard things—real men stand up and face them.

For years, Emily has asked if I would go to counseling with her. I repeatedly told her, "No way." Now, my answer was, "Absolutely." We did some research and found a four-day intensive retreat in another state. We needed time alone and away from the kids, to work on our marriage. We went, and it was life-changing.

I don't know many women as strong as Emily. She has seen the worst in me, things that a woman should never have to see in her husband. I had broken every vow I had made to her when we were married. I had promised to love, honor, cherish, and be true to her. And yet, by some miracle and God's grace, she has chosen to forgive me and to start anew. I had no right to even ask this of her. For a long time, I had blamed and held against her things that weren't her fault. In truth, I blamed her for my shortcomings. My insecurities came at her in the form of anger and resentment.

Emily and I are now going through a class at church. It is wonderful. It has opened many doors of understanding between us that before we had not known was possible.

Whoever says marriage is easy was reading the wrong chapter. Before, I would blame my wife if things weren't great between us. Now I remind myself, no matter what, that she is a child of God, and I need to treat her like He does, with love and kindness. When bad thoughts start finding their way into my head, I pray to be rid of them. I continue to be amazed—that they do!

I know I will have to remain vigilant because the battle between choosing good or evil is one that I will have to face every day of my life, as do we all.

Our marriage was built on fragile soil. Now, we are rebuilding it on a foundation of God. I am grateful beyond words that Emily has remained with me. She is a living testament to the power of redemption. She is a rock. I praise God for her. I know with certainty that I will never turn back to drugs and adultery. I see now that if I had left with the other woman, I would have found the same problems, with just a different face looking back at me. Leaving didn't solve the problem because the problem came with me. I was the problem.

I haven't been the dad or husband I should have been. I didn't realize it before now, but it's hard to be a good dad and husband when you've turned your back on the Creator of life.

I recently had the honor of being baptized for a second time, with David doing the baptizing. It was emotional beyond words. I had been baptized as a child but wanted to do it again after having rejected God and Jesus defiantly for so long. That David was willing to do it means everything. We've rekindled our work partnership, this time based on faith, and it is going great. I sense that he knows that in me, he has a partner he can trust and depend on. It's a commitment I plan to keep.

I made a promise to my dad at Jennifer's funeral to look after my mom. At the time, I had no idea how I could do that. It's taken a long, long time, but I finally figured out what I think my dad knew all along—the best way I could take care of my mom was to take care of myself.

For many years I hated myself. The funny thing was, though, if anyone had asked me, I would have told them I was happy. Before I "found God," I thought I was happy. But I was spiritually sick, like a cancer that grows undetected in a body until it's nearly too late.

I had dealt with my drug addiction long ago, but I had never really addressed my grief over losing Jennifer. First, I numbed it; then, I buried it. But it was always there, right behind every poor decision. I was tough to be around. I've always been a smart-ass. I grew up working on a construction site. I'd walk around all day looking up to some pretty rough men. They were doing things that I should not have looked up to.

Now, after all these years, God finally pierced my heart.

The Bible says in Colossians 4:6, "Let your speech always be with grace, seasoned with salt, that you may know how you ought to answer each one." Salt is a tenderizer. It softens. That tells me to be more forgiving. I need to work on that.

Now, when I find myself starting to get irritated with others, I imagine a circle that I'm inside. I can't fix anything outside of it. I can't fix anyone else. I can only fix me. And that is what I try to do.

The Bible also tells us that God can soften our hearts. He has mine. Throughout my life, I see now that God has given me so many signs of his existence. You can be the smartest person in the world and miss those signs if you're not ready to see them, or not open to seeing them. He finally had to nearly slap me upside of my head for me to see.

When a horse wears blinders, he can only see what is directly in front of him. That was how I was most of my life. Now, I've taken the blinders off.

I didn't know it, but God definitely had a plan for me.

I was a dead man walking. I don't know how I'm still alive. I shouldn't be, but I am. And I really don't know why I'm alive when Jennifer isn't. All I know is that, according to Jesus, who tapped me gently on the shoulder, it hasn't been my time—yet. That day will come. And when it does, I will be ready.

I begged God, "SHOW me something!" Then He showed me by literally opening the words of the Bible for me to read.

I tell people now, "You want an answer for anything? It's in the Bible. It's a life guide."

When my back was turned to God, the devil was good at encouraging me to hurt anyone I pleased. Then, when it all fell apart, he was right there, whispering, "You've done so much to hurt people. You're a piece of crap. You're worthless. Your wife doesn't respect you. No one does. The world would be better if you were six feet under."

Since I've turned to face God, straight on, my struggles just don't seem as difficult. I know that somehow, everything is going to be okay. It won't be perfect, but by hanging on to God, I know that I can get through anything.

For many years now, my mom always told me, "Give it to God, Justin." I had no idea what she was talking about. "Give what? How? Is He going to come down and fix "it"?

"No," my mom would say, "But He'll give you strength."

I used to roll my eyes at this. I didn't have enough faith to understand her words.

Now, I understand. It's not a physical thing—it's a faith thing.

I made some terrible mistakes for decades. Since my "arise and stand" moment, there have been many times when I've wept, knowing how badly I've hurt the people I love, including my parents. I can't undo any of it. But Jesus died on the cross for my sins long before I was even born, long before I even committed them.

I find it hard to believe I'm saying these words, after having fought against them for so long, but I've never been more excited about anything in my life as I am learning about Jesus, his life, and his message. I go to church excited. I used to dread going to church and rarely did so. Now, I cannot wait to go and learn. I'm amazed at the way I see God working in the lives of people around me.

I've learned more about the Bible passage that changed my life. It is from Acts 26:16, where Jesus says to Paul on the road to Damascus, " But arise, and stand on your feet, for I have appeared to you for this purpose: to appoint you a servant and a witness both of the things which you have seen, and of the things which I will reveal to you;..." Like Paul, I had been fighting Jesus.

Now, I realize if people don't have God in their lives, they are like I was, a balloon, floating aimlessly, and not belonging to anyone. When someone gives themselves to God, they're still like a balloon, but God is holding the string.

Christ has saved me in every way possible. It was only through Him that I could have been healed. I had tried fixing myself for a long time, and even though I had overcome the hell on earth that is drug addiction, I was still wounded. It took a long time for me to figure out that you can't put a Band-Aid on an artery. Me trying to heal without God in my life was just as futile.

I don't know if Jennifer had a hand in any of the things that have happened over all these years. I can't help but think that right now, she is rejoicing in Heaven at my transformation.

Ever since Jennifer died, I have avoided seeing Carolyn. It has been too painful, not because I blame her, because I don't, but because I know that when I see her, I will see Jennifer. From the time they were young, if I ever wanted to know where Jennifer was, I only had to find Carolyn. For years they were inseparable. I loved Carolyn. No, I love Carolyn, just like a sister. She was around so often; that was how I thought of her.

I wonder if Carolyn could use me in her life, especially now that I am something more than the broken man I was. I would like her in mine. More than anything, I want her to know that I'm here for her.

Once, a few months after Jennifer died, I went to Carolyn to hear what she could tell me about the accident. She answered my questions, but it was clear there was a lot about that night she could not recall. When I think back to that conversation, I'm sure that my asking her questions about that night, without ever really asking her about how she was doing, and not talking to her since, must have hurt her badly. I never meant that to happen.

About three years ago, Emily and I had just pulled into the parking lot of a large garage sale benefiting a charity. I was sitting in my car, and out of the window, I saw Carolyn walking toward the front of the car. I felt the blood drain from my head. My breathing stopped. I think my heart did too.

She was all grown up. In my mind, I always thought of Carolyn as a teenage girl.

When I saw her in that mirror, all I could think of was, "I'm seeing my sisters, both of them—Jennifer and Carolyn—all grown up." I felt like I was seeing both Jennifer and Carolyn at an age that I had never imagined either one. Carolyn was beautiful. I knew then that somewhere Jennifer was too.

I opened my mouth to speak, but no sound came out. I wanted to open the door and grab and hold her. Instead, I could not move. I was paralyzed.

Carolyn and Emily know each other, and I'm sure Carolyn saw Emily get out of the car. I know she must have known I was in the car also. I know she was probably deeply hurt that I didn't get out. Hurting Carolyn is the last thing I want.

I've recently tried to reach out to Carolyn. We haven't gotten together yet. When we do, I'm going to tell her that I hope and pray that she has forgiven herself. I know what it's like to go through life when you don't—and hating yourself. I don't want that for Carolyn. No one does. If she hasn't, Carolyn needs to forgive herself. Jennifer would want that. We all do.

Not only do I want her to forgive herself, but I also want her to find joy, true, deep-down joy. The kind of joy that can only be found when a person knows that no matter what, God above loves them, and knitted them in the womb so long ago.

I loved Jennifer fiercely. I still do. I always will. I haven't been out to her grave in many years. It's odd, but in all the years I've been clean, I haven't been able to go. Going there would mean I would have to deal with pain again. It's time, and it's time for me to take my kids there. I want them to know about her. I realize I won't be able to protect them from all the temptations out there, but I want them to know that anytime they are in trouble, or if they ever have been partying, that I want, no, I need them to call me. Day or night—no questions asked. Not one. I just want them to call me. I hope seeing Jennifer's grave will help them realize how important it is. I hope they understand that by calling, they will be showing that they love us enough to do that.

I am relieved now the book is coming out. If hearing about what I went through helps a person: one person who might otherwise commit suicide or one person who might realize that they too can get clean—then everything, everything that I've gone through will have been worth it.

In writing about my past, I don't want anyone to feel sorry for me. I feel sorry for what I've put so many people through, especially those closest to me! I've hurt a lot of people, and I can't undo that. I hope that I will be a better man in the future. That's all I can do. I can't change the harm I've done.

I'm just so glad that I'm alive again. And it feels so good. If it can happen to me, it can happen to anyone.

I hope I'm done with trying to fix everything myself. I hope I'm done with that chapter. But I know one thing, no matter what—when things are good, I pray. When things are bad, I pray.

And I know Jesus is listening.

Thoughts from David Dultmeier

2020

It's hard to put down on paper the memories of my life since losing a twin; I am a twin who lost his other half. I feel in a way that I'm writing this letter to Jennifer.

I will start with my faith in Christ and will end with Him. We were raised to know Jesus in a fallen world. We made mistakes and learned from them. But when we lost Jennifer, our faith was shaken to its foundation.

When I read my mom's journal of the intense periods of overwhelming crying fits and despair she experienced, it made me wonder if somehow because I didn't experience this, that I didn't mourn my sister enough. Yet, I know we each grieve so differently.

After the funeral, I remember telling my mom that I didn't know how to deal with my pain. She said, "This isn't like failing a test and knowing what you've got to do now, like studying harder to pass the next one. This isn't something you can pull from the past and know how to get through. You do what you have to do to get through it."

I knew she was right. So, I asked myself the simple question: "What would Jennifer want me to do?"

It was a simple, to-the-point question, but the answer was hard. How was I supposed to live for her? It came to me quickly. I needed to pull myself up by my bootstraps and carry on the best I could. That's what Jennifer would want. She would not want me crumbling to pieces or becoming bitter. She would have hated it if I used her death to stop pursuing my passions. She would have wanted me to go on. She would have wanted me to help my parents. I decided to stay home for a couple of months. When I felt they were going to be okay, I thought the best way for me to help them was to show them I was strong enough to return to a new life. I wanted the same for them. So, I headed back to school in Houston.

My life in Houston was something Jennifer knew very little about. That made my transition back easier in some ways, yet harder and lonelier in others, especially knowing that she would know nothing of it for the rest of my life. She'd never meet my future wife. She'd never know any of my children.

I'd only been in Houston a few months when she died. She hadn't had a chance to visit me or see my apartment. When I left home, we talked a lot on the phone. Before then, we had never been apart for more than a weekend.

If I had stayed at home, I would have seen her in every room, sitting on every piece of furniture, riding in every vehicle. But knowing that she would never know anything about my new life didn't feel right, not when you consider that all our lives we had known nearly everything about each other. We had never spent a birthday apart, not one. For much of our nineteen years, we shared the same friends and had many of the same experiences. We laughed a lot; she could never get through telling me a joke without laughing so hard and talking so fast that I never heard the punch line. I'd look at her with her head back laughing so hard she couldn't talk, and wonder, "What is so funny?"

We fought as siblings often do. When we were young, I teased her until she screamed in frustration, but through it all, we loved each other, and no matter what, I would always have been there for her, and she for me, just as we had been from the moment we were created. We were two parts, Jennifer and I—two parts of one whole.

The night of the wreck, I missed her call. I got home, but I didn't call her back. If I had returned her call, could I have changed the course of what happened? I've asked myself that a lot.

I know many people like me who have experienced bad things, and they do the same, wondering about the "What ifs...Should haves...Could haves..." Whenever I start down that destructive path, I remind myself that death is completely out of our control. None of us knows the big picture of God's work. We aren't meant to. All I can do is choose how to deal with what is.

Certain points in my life since Jennifer died, I could have used her death to be angry and bitter. I chose not to be that way. It took a lot of work with God's grace. Part of doing so was reminding myself that I have been forgiven for my wrongs. So, I need to forgive the wrongs of others. Life is too short and hard as it is to hold grudges.

Carolyn, Jennifer, and I spent a lot of time together when we were young. After the accident, I don't think Carolyn got a lot of comfort from her friends. People took sides. That was sad. After Jennifer died, I was driving impaired and caused a wreck. I was so lucky no one was hurt. Looking back, I'm ashamed of my actions. They are hard to understand, especially after what my family had been through. But it made me realize that what happened with Carolyn could easily have been me.

The night I had my wreck, I hadn't planned on driving after I had been drinking. But I did. It was a selfish and foolish decision. That's the problem with alcohol: most people don't plan to get drunk and then drive. But they start drinking, their mind gets altered, and they don't make clear decisions. I knew better, but I still walked out to my car and started the ignition.

Teenagers' brains are often not developed enough for them to think things through the way they should. They believe they are invincible. An older person who intentionally drives drunk or high is a different kind of stupid and mindless evil. God gave us a brain and the ability to choose right from wrong, and drinking and driving are wrong.

This book about our family is a story of hope, love, and forgiveness. That's it. Death has separated us from Jennifer, but in the scope of time, it is but a split second. I know we will connect with her again. In the meantime, my sister would want nothing but love and peace to all.

When I think about the Garden of Eden, I think, "That's how we were created to live." We weren't created to face death and destruction. No human can go through the death of someone they love, like we loved Jennifer, and not be affected. It just isn't possible. We aren't wired to handle it.

Our bodies are fragile. Jennifer's body wasn't designed for the violent impact of the accident. Those of us who loved her weren't designed to handle her death. It isn't in our DNA. Mom and Dad weren't programmed to bury their only daughter before she turned twenty. Justin and I weren't equipped to handle losing our only sister. My grandparents' hearts weren't strong enough to face the funeral of a granddaughter. And a teenage girl like Carolyn should never have to face the unspeakable guilt and anguish of living the rest of her life feeling responsible for the death of her best friend since childhood. None of us was designed to deal with any of it. We just weren't.

As much as I wished I had been there for my family the night Jennifer died, I'm glad I was spared the trauma of what they endured. Justin woke to the screams of my mom, telling him that Jennifer had been in an accident. I'm not sure I could have handled it. I think Justin especially suffered PTSD from the trauma of that night in ways I can't imagine.

I recently had the honor of baptizing Justin. In him, we have all witnessed a miraculous, new beginning. I pray that his journey of healing, strength, and renewal will continue. My parents must feel like they are living the Biblical story of the Prodigal Son; the one where the son who was lost found his way back to God and, thus, home.

Here Justin and I were, in the same situation, two brothers who lost a sister they loved. Two brothers with the same upbringing, in the same house and parents, and yet choose very different paths after Jennifer died.

Death creates its own sort of energy. It's an energy that needs to be released. I used that energy as a motivation to live for her and not let her death stop my life or slow it down.

By the grace of God, I found and married Becky, the love of my life. I know Jennifer and Becky would have been close friends. Becky and I now have a beautiful daughter, Ryleigh, and a wonderful son, Emmitt, and we have another daughter on the way! Being a father has allowed me to witness, deep within, a glimpse of God's love for us. It is immeasurable.

2 Corinthians 12:8-9 says, "...I begged the Lord three times that it might depart from me. He has said to me, 'My grace is sufficient for you, for my power is made perfect in weakness.'"

That passage speaks to me that in our hardships, God's grace can heal and return hope. I know it is true. He did it for me, and He did for our family. We survived losing Jennifer only because of God's grace.

When I arrived home and stepped out of the car the morning Jennifer died Mom, Dad, and Justin were all there. They grabbed me, and we held each other. That embrace, knowing we were all together in our despair, impacted me more than just about anything I have ever experienced before or since. We had lost Jennifer, but we were still a family.

Eighteen years later, our family has grown in ways that none of us in that embrace so long ago would have believed possible. We all still miss and love Jennifer, but I know we will see her again. And when we do, it will be in the Eden of Heaven, where our bodies aren't fragile—and neither is our love. With God, anything is possible.

Thoughts from Carolyn

Every person is different in how they handle grief, sorrow, and guilt. For me, talking about it makes it worse. No amount of words will change what happened.

Before I even opened my eyes in the hospital, I knew Jennifer was dead. I don't know how I knew, but I did. Looking back, I think it was because I had witnessed her being thrown from the car, even though it was a long time before I would consciously remember it.

I had suffered several fractures, including four on my pelvis. I was sent home in a wheelchair before they realized I had also suffered a traumatic brain injury.

I have a distant recollection of being at the visitation and the funeral. I remember feeling like I was dying inside. I wanted it to be me in that coffin instead of Jennifer. I recall struggling to speak. The words I wanted to say wouldn't come. I don't know if it was from the head injury or shock.

How was I supposed to live when Jennifer was dead?

It was a year before I started to remember what happened fully, and that's when the nightmares of the accident began.

In the years that followed, it was so hard on my family. Many of our friends were also people that knew and loved Jennifer. It was hard for everyone. Most people had no idea what to do or say. All of it was especially hard on my parents. They loved Jennifer, and yet, they were not really able to grieve her death, as they had to take care of me. When she died, they lost not only their daughter's life-long best friend but me as well. The person that I was before the accident was gone. Their daughter was now broken, emotionally and physically, and in need of constant care for a few months.

My family said that I spoke very little after the accident, and my silence lasted for a long time.

While the physical road to recovery was hard—I had to learn how to do so many things that I had always taken for granted, like walking—it was the mental anguish that was far worse.

Ever since the accident, I've worked hard never to repeat my mistakes of the past. I was just a young woman of eighteen who made a terrible mistake—that will haunt me for the rest of my life.

I would do anything to change the past. But no matter what I do, the reality doesn't change: Jennifer is still gone.

All I can do is try to be the very best person I can be and do whatever I can to help improve the lives of others. I hope it's enough for Jennifer.

From Author Nancy Sprowell Geise

Eighteen years have passed since the night Jennifer died. Carolyn and her family live every day with the pain of her death. Carolyn's mother, Beverly, is a retired nurse who has spent most of her life helping bring babies into this world, working at the same hospital where Jennifer died, before and after the accident. Before the wreck, Carolyn had been working at the hospital as a nurse's aide. She wanted a career caring for others.

Carolyn's parents, Carl and Beverly, still live in the same rural home where they raised their four kids, not far from the bus stop where Jennifer and Carolyn first met in the second grade. On a recent visit to their home, it was obvious that Jennifer was never far from their minds.

While at their home, Carl and Beverly said they'd like to show me something. They led me to the second floor of their farmhouse.

A soft glow from a small lamp on a dresser at the top of the stairs illuminated the hall. Next to the lamp was a beautifully framed photo of Jennifer. I later learned the photo was one Lori had given them after the accident. Next to the photo was a carved, wooden angel. Beside it were two framed poems/prayers. One was a Bible verse, Psalm 91:11 etched in glass about God charging his angels to protect them. Below was a golden pair of angel wings.

In the second frame were the words of the Serenity Prayer about accepting things that can't be changed.

Carved out of the lamp's base were three large angels that looked like they were from the Seraphim Angels collection. I asked if they knew that Jim had given angels just like that to Jennifer every year. They had no idea. Beverly's sister had gifted the lamp to them several years earlier, and when they saw it, they knew it had to be part of their memorial to Jennifer.

Though the memorial was simple, I could sense the heartache and sorrow behind all of it—of broken dreams, of countless tears shed, of hours of worry in the dark of night over a daughter they love, and the anguish for the loss of her best friend. A friend that was as close to being another daughter of their own as she could be.

I asked if I could turn off the lamp to better capture a photo of the memorial. They agreed, but then they had difficulty finding the switch. Beverly explained that they never turn it off.

It was obvious that their grief, like the memorial, was very private and profound.

Beverly told me that not a day goes by when she does not think of Jennifer. From driving by Jennifer's old house, to seeing her picture each morning when she leaves her bedroom, Beverly thinks of Jennifer. Before she retired, Beverly went into work every day and was greeted by the ER's signs. Each time, she was reminded of the terrible night when they got the call from the hospital that would change their lives forever.

While at their home, I learned that the night at the hospital when Jim and Lori stepped off the elevator after having just seen Jennifer's body for the first time and came face to face with Carl and Beverly, Jim thought they were on their way to see Carolyn. They weren't. They had just left her in the ER. They were on their way to see Jennifer. Until they saw Jim and Lori, they had no idea that she had died.

At that moment, Carl and Beverly faced what I believe is every parent's nightmare—a helpless inability to spare their child from unspeakable despair. They knew what was coming, but there was no way to stop it.

While Carl and Beverly could do nothing to change the past, they could make a difference moving forward.

"About four years after Jennifer died," Beverly explained to me, "we returned home one evening to find our son and several of his teenage friends outside, having a bonfire. It was obvious they had been drinking. We had no idea where they had gotten the alcohol, for it certainly wasn't from our home. My husband and I made each one of them give us their car keys. Then we told them, 'If you had planned to drive home, your plans just changed. Please call your parents and let them know that they can either come and get you or you'll be spending the night with us.' We put the keys in a shoebox and hid them under our bed. Several of the boys spent the night. The rest secured safe rides."

As I drove away from Carl and Beverly's home, I could not stop thinking about their decision to take away the car keys of those kids, and what a powerful example of how each of us can make a difference.

Like Jim speaking to drunk driving offenders, and Lori keeping the memory of Jennifer alive in bringing warmth and comfort to those grieving with Quilts for Angels, Carl and Beverly's actions were another example of sorrow in action—and of courage and love.

I could not think of a more beautiful legacy to Jennifer's memory.

When I crawled into bed late that night and reached to turn off my light, I paused, thinking of the lamp in Carl and Beverly's farm home. I knew that it was on, bringing light to the darkness of their home and lives. Its glow is a tender tribute to a beautiful girl named Jennifer whose life and death continue to touch so many. Like that lamp of love, the light of Jennifer's life will always remain lit.

Jennifer soared to Heaven the night she died, not on shattered wings, but wings made new and perfect. Left behind were those who loved her, forced to sift through the shards of their lives of heartache, guilt, and despair to gather enough pieces to love, laugh, and live again. And they have, each gliding through life on wings made stronger in the places they've been bonded, stitched together like the threads of a quilt made for an angel, no longer shattered—but tattered—yet, strong enough to fly.

Accident Site

Accident Site

Jennifer's Art

Jennifer's Art

IN MEMORY OF

Jennifer Renee Dultmeier

SEPTEMBER 23, 1983 - OCTOBER 26, 2002

1ˢᵀ PLACE SMITHVILLE

JULY 12, 2003

Fishing award honoring Jennifer

Jim's award honoring Jennifer

Lori with pet donkey 2020

Lori with quilts to be donated 2020

Quilts for Angels

Lori awarded for work with
Quilts for Angels 2020

Quilts for Angels

Lori with Jennifer's quilt 2020

Jennifer's quilt

Jim & Lori with their
grandchildren 2019*

Beverly & Carl's memorial
to Jennifer**

*Photo courtesy of Diana Farthing. **Photo courtesy of Nancy Geise.
All other photos courtesy of The Dultmeier Family.

POSTLUDE

TREASURES

*Mom, don't cry for me,
I'll love you and forever
live in your memory.*

—Poem by Lori Dultmeier, May 2005

—Jennifer Dultmeier (Sixth Grade)

My Own Story

I was brought into this world on 9-23-83, but I wasn't alone, I was a twin. My twin was a boy. My parents named me Jennifer Renee and my brother David August. I already had an older brother Justin Arthur.

My favorite hobbies are basketball, football, volleyball and soccer. I like to read books. And I love to listen to Mariah Carey.

We have 3 pets. Two are dogs, Tanner and Bo, and 1 cat, Sarah. We also have a tank of fish.

We live in the country. My favorite spot is in my room watching animals, birds and the sun go down. Sometimes when the sun goes down the sky turns all different colors. It is so beautiful.

—Jennifer Dultmeier (Sixth Grade)

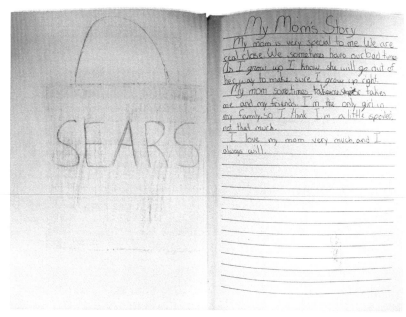

My Mom's Story

My mom is very special to me. We are real close. We sometimes have our bad times. As I grow up I know she will go out of her way to make sure I grow up right.

My mom sometimes takes me shopping, takes me and my friends. I'm the only girl in my family, so I think I'm a little spoiled, not that much.

I love my mom very much, and I always will.

—Jennifer Dultmeier (Sixth Grade)

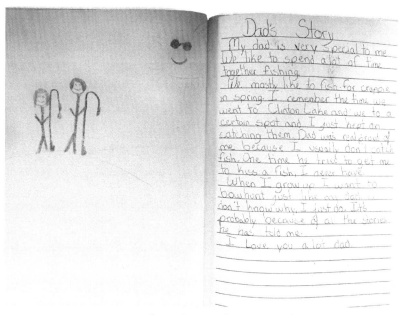

Dad's Story

My dad is very special to me. We like to spend a lot of time together fishing.

We mostly like to fish for crappie in spring. I remember the time we went to Clinton Lake and we to a certain spot and I just kept on catching them. Dad was real proud of me because I usually don't catch fish. One time he tried to get me to kiss a fish, I never have.

When I grow up I want to bow hunt just like my dad. I don't know why, I just do. It's probably because of all the stories he has told me.

I Love you a lot dad.

—Jennifer Dultmeier (Sixth Grade)

307

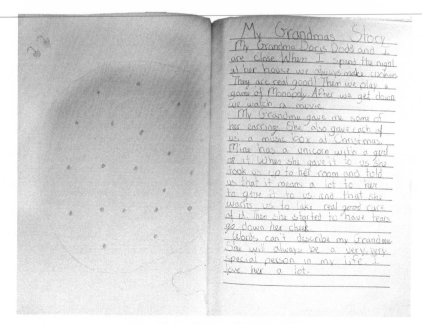

My Grandmas Story

My Grandma Doris Dodd and I are close. When I spend the night at her house we always make cookies. They are real good! Then we play a game of Monnopoly. After we get down we watch a movie.

My Grandma gave me some of her earrings. She also gave each of us a music box at Christmas. Mine has a unicorn with a girl on it. When she gave it to us she took us up to her room and told us that it means a lot to her to give it to us and that she wants us to take real good care of it. Then she started to have tears go down her cheek.

Words can't describe my Grandma. She will always be a very very special person in my life. I love her a lot.

—Jennifer Dultmeier (Sixth Grade)

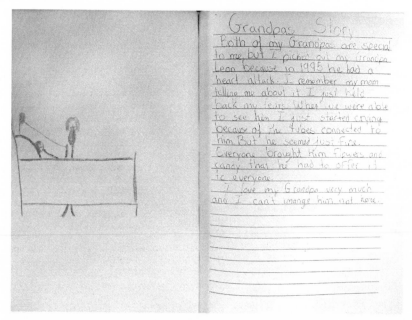

Grandpas Story

Both of my Grandpas are special to me, but I picked out my Grandpa Leon because in 1995 he had a heart attack. I remember my mom telling me about it I just held back my tears. When we were able to see him I just started crying because of the tubes connected to him But he seemed just fine. Everyone brought him flowers and candy that he had to offer it to everyone.

I love my Grandpa very much and I can't imange him not here.

—Jennifer Dultmeier (Sixth Grade)

Respect Yourself

By Jennifer Dultmeier

October 2, 2002
(Twenty-four days before she died)
ENGLISH 101,
WASHBURN UNIVERSITY, TOPEKA, KANSAS

I strongly believe that the quote, "Learn to respect yourself. He who seeks only applause from without has all his happiness in another's keeping," is true. This quote derives from the 18th century and was written by a British author named Goldsmith. There are several reasons why I feel this way. I am going to break this quote into pieces so that you get a better understanding of my opinion.

"Learn to respect yourself." You must be able to gain knowledge of yourself, know who you are and what you want. This is the first step toward honoring yourself and feeling you are a quality person. If you don't honor yourself, then how can other people possibly honor you? By knowing what you want on the inside makes you a stronger person and helps people to know the real you. People who don't respect and know themselves have no true identity. Their personality can change just from talking from one person to another. These people act like they will never fall, but in reality, this trait makes them even more susceptible to being knocked down. When they are disproved by someone, or are not given praise, they will often do anything to receive approval.

"He who seeks only applause from without..." is a person who strives for approval from everyone but themselves, is a troubled person. The only thing that keeps them going is the praise of others. These kinds of people can never show their true feelings, because there might be a slight chance that someone would look down on them. I have pity for these people because they will never truly be happy. It's as though these people wear a mask, and forever fear the thought of removing it. They are so insecure that they block anyone from discovering the person underneath, even themselves. I also feel many times that these people do not want to discover what's hidden beneath their mask because they feel that is the one thing they have to cling onto.

"...has all his happiness in another's keeping." This is describing someone who has to have the company of others to act happy, because without other people around to impress, they are not content. When they are not surrounded by praise, they are empty and lonely. These people cannot stand the thought of being secluded from their social life. They do not only seek applause from within, they live for applause from without.

In conclusion, this quote makes me sympathize with the souls of people who live in this manner. Everyone enjoys praise from others, but it is not the foundation of our being. The saddest part is that we all know people like this, and we see it every day. I will never fully understand the thought process of these people, but what I do understand is that I know who I am, and I respect myself.

Personal Notes

Dear Lori,

Tuesday will be your birthday, and you will be forty-one years old. I remember when you were born, it was cold and icy. The world was beautiful and sparkling with ice on all the trees when we went home. You were so beautiful and fat and precious. You grew into this curious-minded, energetic girl. You made me laugh and laugh, and even though you were so independent, you still needed me, greatly. I have always loved the way you approached life, so energetically and with such gusto. You can get things done, seemingly without much energy, like your Grandma Dodd.

When you had your babies, I could see you were a natural-born mother. You took to it with gusto, just like you did all other things. You are a good mother and wife; you created a warm, loving home. I always admired how you always prepared a good, sit-down dinner every night for Jim and the kids. You were like a mother lion with your kids; no one was going to hurt your kids. You protected them. Then came this thing with little Jennifer, and you couldn't protect her, none of us could, but God did.

I shared your grief so intensely; I tried to make it my own. I see now I can't do that, as much as I would like to do it for you, I can't. That's what mother's do, isn't it? But I can't do this. I realize now that we have to do this together but at the same time individually, with God. I was trying to grieve for you instead of with you, and this wasn't helping either one of us. My body was telling me this when it shook me up, and I said, "Hey, you're doing this wrong." I want to help you in any way I can, but I can't have you concerned about me in any way. God will show us the way, I don't know how He does it or how long it will take, but He'll get us there, I know it—nothing is impossible with God. He is able. We just have to listen and wait. I want the day to come when we can think about Jennifer, laugh about her life, from beginning to end, celebrate her, and talk about her with joy and not pain. It will come, just like it did after my mother died, and Grandpa and Grandma Dodd died. After a while, we could laugh and talk about them with joy.

Lori, I love you so much! This is going to be a rough, high mountain you climb. But know that God is your protector. The Bible promises that He will make your feet like deer's feet, which do not stumble. He will help you stand on steep mountains.

I know you have plenty to deal with just yourself, but guard and protect your husband, your children, and your marriage. This is a tall order, but strong women can do it. You are a strong woman, and Oh! God! How I love you! Love, Mom

To Lori from her friend Chris Perry, November 2002

My dearest Lori,

This second, this minute, this hour, this day, I am holding you in my heart ever so tight. Every day, every week, every month, and as the seasons change before us, and those months turn into years—my arms will be wrapped around you. My arms are wings filled with compassion, support, and oh so much love.

Never will I leave you, and always will I cherish you—Forever so thankful to have you as my friend.

Lori's note to Jennifer, November 1993

Jennifer,

You wrote this letter (below) after I told you kids that you weren't grateful. We were going to get pizza, and you were all arguing about not wanting pizza but something else. I thought you should all be happy just to be going out.

Telling you all you weren't being grateful wasn't probably that good of a thing to say, and obviously it upset you. Parents aren't perfect, either, though.

I love you with all my heart and soul. Love, Mom

Jennifer's letter to her mom, Lori, 1993 (age ten)

Dear Mom,

I am just writing this letter to tell you how much I love you. You take so much on, and we don't show you how much we love you. You really know how to take care of us. But we fight and call names but do we really show that we love you? We get in trouble, but we still love you. We will try not to get in trouble Love, Jennifer. P.S. I will love you even if I think I hate you.

Lori's note to herself (date unknown)

I hate looking at pictures of our family. I feel sorry for the people in the pictures. I don't know them anymore, not personally. It seems impossible not to have known what was coming. How can destruction not announce itself, like a tornado siren?

Jennifer's Handwritten Note to Herself (date unknown)

Listen to that voice in your head and do what that voice says and you will learn who you truly are.

In Loving Memory

Lori and Jim's Family Who Lost Their Lives in Alcohol Related Accidents

Jennifer Renee Dultmeier
September 23, 1983—October 26, 2002

Nathan Dodd
July 28, 1981—December 26, 2003
Lance Corporal, United States
Marine Corps

Lori's grandparents: **Dock F. Dodd**, February 22,1909—July 5, 1975,
Maud Dodd, August 26, 1909—July 5, 1975

I'll Cry for You Forever

Mom, don't cry for me,
I'm at home and I'm free.

Mom, don't cry for me,
No pain nor tears do I see.

Mom, don't cry for me,
There's no other place I'd rather be.

Mom, don't cry for me,
For it won't be long 'til we meet again in eternity.

Mom, don't cry for me,
Take care of our family.

Mom, don't cry for me,
Be patient and you'll see, just how good life again can be.

Mom, don't cry for me,
Dad needs you and the boys too. You've got so many things left to do.

I'll love you and forever live in your memory.
Mom, don't cry for me.

I'll cry for you forever,

'Midst the joy and pain of life.
I'll cry for you forever,

Although true happiness I'll strive.
I'll cry for you forever,

Wishing to hear your voice again.
I'll cry for you forever,

Knowing this battle, we'll never win.
I'll cry for you forever,

You were my soul's identity.
I'll cry for you forever,

Until I hold you again in eternity.
My precious, precious Jennifer, I'll cry for you forever.

—Poem written by Lori Dultmeier, May 2005

An Article Found in Jennifer's Keepsake Box

From Parent to Child

I gave you life, but cannot live it for you.

I can teach you things, but I cannot make you learn.

I can give you directions, but I cannot be there to lead you.

I can allow you freedom, but I cannot account for it.

I can take you to worship, but I cannot make you believe.

I can teach you right from wrong, but I cannot always decide for you.

I can buy you beautiful clothes, but I cannot make you beautiful inside.

I can offer you advice, but I cannot accept it for you.

I can teach you to share, but I cannot make you unselfish.

I can teach you respect, but I cannot force you to show honor.

I can advise you about friends, but I cannot choose them for you.

I can advise you about sex, but I cannot keep you pure.

I can tell you the facts of life, but I can't build your reputation.

I can tell you about drinking, but I can't say NO for you.

I can warn you about drugs, but I can't prevent you from using them.

I can tell you about lofty goals, but I can't achieve them for you.

I can teach you about kindness, but I can't force you to be gracious.

I can warn you about sins, but I cannot make your morals.

I can love you as a child, but I cannot place you in God's family.

I can pray for you, but I cannot make you walk with God.

I can teach you about Jesus, but I cannot make Jesus your Lord.

I can tell you how to live, but I cannot give you eternal life.

—Unknown author

Discussion Questions

1. In what ways did this story impact the way you think about life, death, and faith?

2. Why is it important that we have the freedom to find our own individual paths through grief?

3. What most surprised, impacted, or inspired you about Jim and Lori's journey through grief (and their faith journeys)?

4. In reading this story, what were the hardest parts for you? Why?

5. The lives of many were changed the moment they got a phone call about Jennifer's accident. Have you experienced any such life-defining event in your life, and how did it impact you?

6. Has this story changed the way you might respond to others experiencing grief?

7. When Jennifer was undergoing surgery, people were praying for her to be healed. Lori said, "No. We need to pray for God's will to be done." What are your thoughts about her words?

8. In what ways can you relate to the idea of the insignificance of regrets? Are there things you have done or said in the past that would be helpful for you to resolve now? If so, how?

9. Has this story made a difference in your thoughts about drinking and driving, driving distracted, or driving while on drugs?

10. What do you see as the best ways to help others understand the dangers of drinking and driving impaired/distracted and convince them not to do so?

11. Jim and Lori have channeled their grief into helping others. In what ways can you relate to this? What other examples do you know of healing through helping others?

12. How does forgiveness impact a person's ability to move forward?

13. Who in this story can you most relate to, and how?

14. What insights did you gain from reading Justin, David, and Carolyn's entries? What most surprised or inspired you?

15. Many marriages break apart after the loss of a child. What are some things that could be done to help couples avoid this?

16. Lori said that although she didn't agree with God allowing Jennifer to die, she trusts God enough to believe He knows what He's doing. In what ways can you relate to her sentiments?

17. What were the most powerful examples of faith or hope you found in this story?

18. Lori said, "Grief is a thief of time." Have you experienced this? If so, how?

19. Jim's sister Julie said she thinks that God brings light to the darkness. Have you ever experienced this? If so, how?

20. Several people in this story expressed being aware of God's physical presence. Have you ever experienced anything similar? In what ways?

21. When Justin dropped the Bible, fell to his knees, and randomly pointed his finger, it landed on the words telling him to stand on his feet. Was there a time when you felt God speaking to you just when you needed it most?

22. Jim said he wished he could call 1-800-GOD and ask him a few questions. If you could do the same, what would you ask?

23. In what ways are the trio of life, death, and faith expressed in the title *On Shattered Wings*?

Author Nancy Sprowell Geise Appreciation

I thank God and Jesus Christ for my life and the beautiful people woven throughout all of it. I am so grateful to Jim, Lori, Justin, and David Dultmeier for opening their hearts to me for this book.

A special thanks to my husband, Doran. Without him, none of my books would have been possible. I would like to thank my family for their on-going love and support, including my mom, Lucretia; my mother-in-law, Carolyn; our daughters and their husbands: Crystal/Andrew, Hallie/Gregory, and Natalie/Stefan; my brothers and their wives: Bob/Liz, Dave/Sue, Jim/Clare, and Tom/Jill; brothers/sisters-in-law's: Brandon/Molly, Evan/Wendy, and Alison/Randy and all my nieces, nephews, uncles, and cousins. And although they are gone now, my forever thanks and gratitude to my dad, Robert R. Sprowell, and my father-in-law, Dale L. Geise. The love and insight from these greatest of men are embedded into every word I write.

Thank you to all the teachers and support staff who helped me along the way, and especially to the two greatest English teachers a student could want: Mr. John Forssman and the late Grace Bauske who challenged me to write. Mr. Forssman, none of my books would be published today without your on-going insight and life coaching. Thank you.

Thank you to the family, friends, and acquaintances of the Dultmeier family for sharing your deepest thoughts and feelings. I know it wasn't always easy. Thank you especially: Doris Dodd; Brad and Sandra Dodd; Melissa Dodd Eskilson; Brooke and Wade Patterson; Leon and Mary Dultmeier; Becky Dultmeier; Emily Dultmeier; Tom Dultmeier; Kathleen Dultmeier; Austen Falk; Julie Douthett; Larry and Shelvie Cole; Cathy Cole-Gregory; Danae Diel; Chris Perry; Lon, Christine, and Alex Weaver; Lisa DonCarlos; Diana Farthing; Kelly and Nathan Hibbert; Jerri Blassingame; Heather Case Souther; Marita Ortiz; Stephanie Carter; and Carolyn and her parents, Beverly and Carl. Thank you, Chuck Hogan, (former firefighter/first responder); Karen Smart (formerly of MADD), and Lori Marshall, Programming Director Kansas State Office, MADD.

I have been blessed to have so many incredible professionals in the book publishing and marketing industry whose expertise and knowledge have helped make this book possible: Polly Letofsky (*My Word Publishing*); Bobby Haas (*Write On, Professional Editing*); Delta Donohue (*Proofing Pages LLC, Proof Editing*); Victoria Wolf (*Wolf

Design and Marketing); Nick Zellinger (*NZ Graphics)*; Donna Mazzitelli (*Writing with Donna* and *Merry Dissonance Press*); Amy Collins and Keri Barnum (*New Shelves* and *Free Advice Fridays*); and Josiah Engstrom for creating the powerful book trailer.

Thank you to my daughter Crystal Merrill for all of her on-going technical support for her technology challenged mother.

Thank you to the early readers: Doran Geise; Hallie Whitsell; Natalie Reiter; John and Sharon Forssman; Sally Robinson; Leisa Doran; Tina and Joe Bichler; Betsy McDermott; Anne Helke; Sara Hunt; Jane Penoyer; Jane Goding; Charlotte Bates; Molly Geise; Tom Sprowell; Lucretia Sprowell; Clare Sprowell; Janet Flax; and Connie Berman. Thanks to Cindy Frost and Donna Mazzitelli for their guidance in the early format concepts for this story.

There are many other professionals for whom I have gained so much in the book publishing industry over the years. I am grateful to each of them for sharing their knowledge and insight, including Richard Rieman (*Audiobook Revolution Productions*); John Kramer (*Open Horizons*); Joan Stewart (*The Publicity Hound*); Daniel Hall (*Daniel Hall Combined Enterprises*), Judith Briles (*Author U*); Susie Scott (*Susie Scott Media*); Anna Termine (*Foreign Language and Subsidiary Rights Advice*); Helen Sedwick (*Attorney/Author*); and Counsel for Creators.

To the fans of my other books—many of whom I've never had the honor of meeting, I thank you from the bottom of my heart for your encouraging letters, notes, and prayers. They mean more than any of you will ever know.

To the many people around the world who have opened your homes for me to stay and shared a meal with me while I was on tour, I am grateful and blessed by each of you! Thank you for inviting me to speak at your organizations, churches and synagogues, businesses, nonprofits, events, schools, and museums. You will never know how much each event has meant to me.

To the writers, radio, TV, and blog interviewers who have invited me to speak with your audiences, thank you. A special thanks to Ralph Hipp, (*WIBW*) Topeka, Kansas, for your continued support over the years, and Brooke Lennington (KSNT) for honoring Lori Dultmeier with the Jefferson Award for her work with Quilts for Angels.

Other Stories of Hope by Author Nancy Sprowell Geise

Auschwitz #34207—The Joe Rubinstein Story

The Eighth Sea

To contact author Nancy Sprowell Geise or to follow
events and happenings: www.nancygeise.com

If you would like to donate to the *Quilts for Angels* project in Memory of Jennifer
Dultmeier contact: https://www.facebook.com/QuiltsForAngels

National Suicide Prevention Lifeline: 800-273-8255

MADD's 24-hour helpline phone number
877-MADD-HELP or online at MADD.org

About the Authors

Jim and Lori Dultmeier met while in high school in Topeka, Kansas. They are the parents of Justin, Jennifer, and David.

Jim and Lori owned and operated a successful roofing business in Northeastern Kansas for over thirty years, helping thousands of customers. Jim and Lori are active members of their church and community. They love the outdoors, spending time with their large, extended families, and especially being with their grandchildren.

Lori and Jim have devoted their lives to keeping the memory of their daughter, Jennifer, alive. Lori is the founder of *Quilts for Angels*, a nonprofit that donates quilts to area hospitals to comfort those who have lost loved ones. Jim has spent over a decade speaking to thousands of people through the Victim Impact Panels of MADD (Mothers Against Drunk Driving) to encourage drivers not to drink and drive so that other parents will never face the immeasurable heartache of losing a child.

Author Nancy Sprowell Geise is the award-winning, bestselling author of two books: *Auschwitz #34207 The Joe Rubinstein Story* and *The Eighth Sea*. Nancy has been invited to speak around the world, including at the Library of Congress and the United States Holocaust Memorial Museum in Washington, D.C., and at the Auschwitz-Birkenau Memorial and Museum in Poland.

Nancy and her husband, Doran, met in high school in Ames, Iowa. They raised their three daughters in Austin, Texas, and Fort Collins, Colorado. Nancy and Doran currently reside in Topeka, Kansas. In her free time, Nancy enjoys playing pickleball, camping, and hiking.

Mom, don't cry for me,
I'm at home and I'm free.